Thinking About Shakespeare

Thinking About Shakespeare

Kay Stockholder,
revised and updated by Amy Scott

WILEY Blackwell

Registered Offices
John Wiley & Sons, Inc., 111 River Street, Hoboken, NJ 07030, USA
John Wiley & Sons Ltd, The Atrium, Southern Gate, Chichester, West Sussex, PO19 8SQ, UK

Editorial Office
The Atrium, Southern Gate, Chichester, West Sussex, PO19 8SQ, UK

For details of our global editorial offices, customer services, and more information about Wiley products visit us at www.wiley.com.

Wiley also publishes its books in a variety of electronic formats and by print-on-demand. Some content that appears in standard print versions of this book may not be available in other formats.

Library of Congress Cataloging-in-Publication Data
Names: Stockholder, Kay, 1928–1998, author. | Scott, Amy, 1979– editor.
Title: Thinking about Shakespeare / Kay Stockholder, revised and updated by Amy Scott.
Description: First edition. | Hoboken, NJ : Wiley, 2018. | Includes index. |
    Identifiers: LCCN 2018011956 (print) | LCCN 2018013585 (ebook) |
    ISBN 9781119059035 (pdf) | ISBN 9781119059042 (epub) |
    ISBN 9781119059004 (cloth) | ISBN 9781119059011 (pbk.)
Subjects: LCSH: Shakespeare, William, 1564–1616–Criticism and interpretation. |
    Shakespeare, William, 1564–1616–Philosophy. | Shakespeare, William, 1564–1616–Influence.
Classification: LCC PR2976 (ebook) | LCC PR2976 .S746 2018 (print) | DDC 822.3/3–dc23
LC record available at https://lccn.loc.gov/2018011956

Cover Image: © Romeo and Juliet, Act 3, Scene 5 [graphic]: Romeo, Juliet & Nurse painted by J.F. Rigaud R.A.; engraved by Jas. Stow. Image courtesy of the Folger Shakespeare Library licensed under CC:BY-SA
Cover Design: Wiley

Set in 10/12pt Warnock by SPi Global, Pondicherry, India

Printed in Singapore by C.O.S. Printers Pte Ltd

10 9 8 7 6 5 4 3 2 1

Contents

Acknowledgments

I am grateful to Norman Epstein, my mother's partner of many years, who in 2013 sent me the unpublished manuscript of *A Thinking Person's Guide to Shakespeare*. With that manuscript in hand I was fortunate to be able to share it with David Bevington, my esteemed colleague here at the University of Chicago. David knew of Kay Stockholder's previous work, and with great generosity volunteered to help steer this book towards publication. I would also like to thank Paul Yachnin for his careful reading of the text and for his scholarly introduction. And also Amy Scott who tended to updating the text so that it can gracefully enter the world of 2018. It gives me great pleasure to see this project come to completion; and I am sure that my mother would be thrilled. I am grateful to the many at Wiley-Blackwell who contributed their time and attention.

Jessica Stockholder (Kay's daughter)
2018

Foreword

Paul Yachnin

This book is about William Shakespeare. For some people, Shakespeare's name itself is enough to arouse anxiety. The name of the man who lived his life as a commercial playwright, theatrical promoter, and popular entertainer now seems to stand for a profound understanding of universal human truths, a language poeticized, shadowy, and obscure, and something called "greatness" (and sometimes something called "genius," which is worse). For many modems, Shakespeare is the ogre in the castle of highbrow Western culture.

This book, left completed by Kay Stockholder at her death, is an excellent introduction to Shakespeare because, while Kay loved the dramatist, she never idolized him, and she never feared him. You might say she lived with him for a lifetime, and of course there's nothing like long-term cohabitation to cure us of false idealizations and groundless fears. That's not to say that her familiarity with Shakespeare bred contempt. In all matters, Kay was a very affectionate person and a good friend to her intimates. I knew her well. She was keen to understand me in a deep way—she was a probing analyst of human frailty and complexity—but she also liked to see the good rather than the bad in those she held dear.

This book offers the fruits of a long love and penetrating study of Shakespeare's art. Along with its fearlessness, this book offers a series of detailed accounts of plays—from *A Midsummer Night's Dream* to *Hamlet* to *The Tempest*—within a broad understanding of Shakespeare as a particular person living in a particular social situation.

Kay also brings forward a bold theory about what is central to Shakespeare's dramatic art. By alternating between close-up analyses of imagery, language, character, source material, and dramatic and thematic structure on the one side and a wide-angle discussion of Shakespeare's life and work on the other, this book provides something like a whole picture of one of the most enduring figures in Western culture.

What exactly is the source of this book's overall understanding of Shakespeare? It's important to know that Kay was a psychoanalytic critic, a literary analyst who read Shakespeare's characters as embodiments of the patterns of feeling and behavior described by Freud and other psychoanalytic thinkers. Antony, the doomed Roman soldier and leader of *Antony and Cleopatra*, is caught between his fear of losing his individuality to an engulfing feminine or maternal principle (represented, of course, by Egypt's queen) or losing it to the hypermasculinity of Roman "civilization." The terrible irony is that, while Antony thinks of "Egypt" and "Rome" as external threats to his identity, which he must conquer on behalf of his own well-being, they are in fact integral to his selfhood. That means that when he at last defeats them, he also destroys himself.

This book develops psychoanalytic interpretations of Shakespeare's characters, from Bottom to Richard II to Hamlet to Iago and Othello—each interpretation alert to the particular dramatic context of the individual character's story. But the book's understanding of the psychic, sexual, and emotional lives of Shakespeare's characters is not limited to the dynamics of family life or the internal structure of the personality. Rather, the book combines the psychological with the social, integrating and indeed demonstrating the inseparability of the internal world of the person and the life of the person in society.

Here it is helpful to know that Kay was always involved in politics, an involvement that culminated with her becoming president of the British Columbia Civil Liberties Association in the years from her retirement from full-time teaching up to her death. The integrated socio-psychological understanding of characters like Antony (who, after all, is destroyed by a socially specific honor system as well as by an infantilizing relationship with Cleopatra) is thus of a piece with the integrity of Kay's own activities as a scholar and social activist.

The coherence of the psychological and the social gives the book its overarching theme—the relationship between personal liberty and the various forms of authority that impinge upon individuals and individual freedom. The book develops a rich account of the forms that authority can take in Shakespeare's playworlds and, by implication, in the real world where he and we are obliged to live. Authority, which is the offspring of human relations and by which people are measured, judged, and ruled, operates in the family (*Romeo and Juliet* is a good example of how it works between parents and children), in family-like relationships (like Lear's with his daughters), and in institutional structures such as the military (the context of the honour system that enables and then disables a character like Hotspur).

We find it also in the state, with its conflicting models of rule, and in the cosmos, where God and divine Providence function—ideally at any rate—as the final arbiters of human actions and intentions. Authority also circulates and gets inside people's heads and hearts in certain kinds of language—in the discourse of honor (as I've suggested), but also in the discourses of monarchical rule, parenthood, romantic love, divine Providence, and so on.

In Kay's view, all of these authoritative languages, along with the forms of authority they give expression to, are put in question in Shakespeare's plays, which restlessly probe the bases of power in Renaissance culture, whether the authority in question belongs to a king, a father, a warrior, a magus (like Prospero), or even God. It is not, Kay says, that Shakespeare, for all his skepticism, is ever able to dispense with authority altogether. Rather, it is that what authority has to say to us about how we must or should live is always open to question and argument.

Against the background of this questioning of authority, Shakespeare develops a wonderfully robust version of personhood. Hamlet, with his intense and detailed inner life, is exemplary here, and Kay points out that the Danish prince can even contribute substantially to the lives of real-life readers and theatre-goers. "For many young people," she says, "he functions as a literary liberator, because he seems so much like their secret selves—the person whom they feel themselves to be, unknown to their families and friends." The complex lives of figures such as Hamlet are very much at the centre of things in this book, and we are invited to encounter them as we would real people, to attend to their aspirations and sufferings, to understand them clearly and analytically but also to acknowledge them as our equals.

To see eye to eye with Shakespeare's characters is to begin to understand what they can teach us about our own lives, especially about the importance of an awareness of how individuals can achieve happiness only in relation to the structures of social authority. That, in an overarching way, is the story that the book tells about Shakespeare himself, whose plays represent his life-long dealings with the Elizabethan system of authority and the attendant scale of social prestige. Although he was a lowly player and playwright, Shakespeare desired a measure of status and success, and he might even have fantasized that his authority as an imaginative artist outweighed the pomp and power of kings and queens. Of course, the centuries have proved that particular fantasy true: Shakespeare's imagination has contributed far more to the shaping of individuals and societies than have all the earls and knights of the Elizabethan court (including Elizabeth herself). But the Shakespeare who emerges in this book is not the supremely confident artist who might bestride the whole history of humankind. Rather, he is a deeply unhappy man (and a great artist who can still speak to us). He was made that way by the split in his psyche between his serviceable loyalty to the system of authority and status and his illicit ambition for authority and prestige in his own right. In Kay's view, the acuity of both Shakespeare's representations of characters like Hamlet or Antony and his relentless questioning of the system of rule and rank is reflective of his own troubled relationship with the social order in which he lived.

* * *

I said that Kay left her book completed when she died. But those of us who valued her work and wanted to see it in print knew that it needed to be revised and updated. The manuscript had the good fortune to be placed in the care of an accomplished young scholar named Amy Scott. Amy's PhD thesis was a prize-winning study of how Shakespeare created an "ethical historiography." In it, she describes how Shakespeare's plays can help us attend critically, feelingly, and creatively to our connection with the dead. Amy brought her historical and literary learning and her philosophical understanding of the connections between the living and the dead to the tasks of editing and updating Kay's manuscript. But beyond those important tasks, there developed between the two—the deceased author and the living reviser—a remarkable meeting of minds, a searching harmony you will hear clearly in the Introduction and a relationship that provides a deep bass line throughout the book.

* * *

The book itself contains twelve chapters and an epilogue. Although the range of discussion is broad, including forays into thinkers like Freud or Machiavelli or sidelights on the history of the Tudor court or the Jews in England, each chapter is devoted to a single play, from the early *A Midsummer Night's Dream* to the late play, *The Tempest*. There are chapters on three comedies (including *The Tempest*), three History plays, six tragedies (all the major ones), and a chapter on the difficult-to-categorize *Troilus and Cressida*.

One very notable feature is that the discussion broadens and deepens as it progresses. Each chapter draws upon the previous ones, producing an overall account of Shakespeare that grows in complexity and fullness. While readers will learn a great deal if they open the book to, say, Chapter 10 (on *King Lear*), they will get even more benefit and pleasure by reading through from the beginning, and coming to the account of *Lear* with an understanding of how Shakespeare has used what Kay calls "a two-world principle" in the construction of *Dream* and *Merchant of Venice*, and how he reworks it in the great tragedy. Readers will appreciate how detailed discussions of particular plays are coupled with an emerging picture of Shakespeare's whole artistic undertaking. They will also appreciate the epilogue—a speculative socio-psychological biography of William Shakespeare, which is based on an adventurous reading of his last great character, Prospero, the Renaissance magician, magus, and virtual dramatist. This imaginative, intimate portrait of Shakespeare makes a fitting conclusion for a work of literary criticism that might also be described as a life-long correspondence between a great artist and his scholarly partner.

Introduction: True Minds

Amy Scott

> Let me not to the marriage of true minds
> Admit impediments. Love is not love
> Which alters when it alteration finds,
> Or bends with the remover to remove.
> O, no, it is an ever-fixèd mark
> That looks on tempests and is never shaken;
> It is the star to every wandering bark,
> Whose worth's unknown, although his height be taken.
> Love's not Time's fool, though rosy lips and cheeks
> Within his bending sickle's compass come;
> Love alters not with his brief hours and weeks,
> But bears it out even to the edge of doom.
> > If this be error and upon me proved,
> > I never writ, nor no man ever loved. (Sonnet 116)[1]

I first received Kay Stockholder's manuscript for this book as a kind of inheritance. I knew she had passed away after completing the manuscript, and I knew her children and her partner Norman Epstein wished it to be published. From the original author it had been, after some years, bequeathed to me, though I did not have the pleasure of knowing Kay personally. My task seemed monumental: I was to revise and edit the work of a woman I had never met in person. I felt the project invited in feelings, though, that were familiar to me in my own experience with mourning and inheriting. There is a sense of a great responsibility (which is also a great honor) to *do justice* to someone who can no longer speak for him/herself. There was always awareness that I should not put words in her mouth to which she might have objected. I have, therefore, tried to establish a connection with Kay, as if I were sitting in sincere and searching dialogue with her rather than trying to imitate her exactly.

I don't expect that I have written and edited exactly as she might have done, but I do hope that what I have added has formed a respectful and coherent conversation with the words she has left us. This, I believe, is what she herself did with Shakespeare during her long career. The manuscript read very much as an extended dialogue with a lifelong companion with whom she was intensely familiar. Her own often-poetic words bandy with Shakespeare's to produce a moving, insightful account of not just his plays but also some of his most enigmatic characters. Each chapter discusses one play, from some of his earliest to some of his latest, and over the course of the twelve chapters, all genres in the Shakespeare canon are represented.

Kay Stockholder was a critic whose work was heavily informed by psychoanalyses. She was therefore interested in what happens in our minds. What things do we acknowledge about ourselves in our thoughts and what things do we repress? How do those thoughts translate to feelings and actions in the world around us? In her 1987 book *Dream Works: Lovers and Families in Shakespeare's Plays*,[2] Stockholder writes that when artists create their works, in addition to drawing from "options made available by the contemporary culture and institutions," they will also be "guided by the emotional associations" of their inner life, their unconscious (ix). She goes on to say that in this way,

> all components of a work, from the grand structures of thought and plot to the finest detail of rhetorical nuance, can be read as a grid of associations. Character and plot become images writ large, and each component of this grid, and its relative prominence, acquires meaning in terms of the others. (ix)

Thinking About Shakespeare also approaches the plays in this way, as products of a grid of associations that produce overall meaning. The book's focus is indeed on the association between "thought and plot" – the characters' thoughts and the ways in which the action in the play derives from or shapes characters' inner lives. And those "emotional associations" mapped in the plays – how characters feel and what those feelings can tell us of how Shakespeare may have felt about his culture – convey the sense of a struggle to pursue intimate bonds and ideals despite how elusive they are.

The "Ever-Fixèd Mark": Sonnet 116 and Shakespeare's Bonds

Stockholder's work pairs well with the oft-quoted Sonnet 116 because *Thinking About Shakespeare* focuses on the efforts of individuals to find an object, purpose, or person to bind herself to, to remain constant to in the face of countless forces of "alteration" both within the self and also in the broader social and political world with which the self must inevitably contend. Love is one of those bonds that Stockholder pursues in Shakespeare's work so insightfully. But she follows many other kinds of unions: bonds that hold together friendships, political relationships, commercial agreements, and judicial order. While Sonnet 116 defends the idea that there is a version of love that is pure and authentic, instead of using the term "love" immediately, it calls a loving bond a "marriage of true minds" (1). To situate the engine of love in the *mind* is surely an unexpected maneuver. Juliet describes exactly where a loving union is traditionally imagined to originate, telling Friar Laurence "God joined my heart and Romeo's" (4.1.55). A few lines later, she describes the strength of her union with Romeo by calling her heart "true" (4.1.58). When he must leave Egypt for Rome, Antony seeks to soften the blow of their separation by telling Cleopatra "my full heart / Remains in use with you" (1.3.43–4). What place does the mind have in the formation and sustenance of love then? The Sonnet suggests a conception of love that is more complex than what we might view as a straightforward engagement of the heart.

In his 1505 mediation on love, *Gli Asolani*, the Venetian scholar and cardinal Pietro Bembo offers a definition of "true" love as one that requires both the senses and the mind. First, a virtuous and thus sincere lover uses the eyes and ears to appreciate the "beauty of mind no less than body" of the beloved (97).[3] Second, the lover's mind itself is a crucial part of the *keeping* of love. He explains that when the lover is far away from the beloved, "the same nature which provided these two senses [seeing and hearing] has likewise given us the faculty of thought, with which we may enjoy both kinds of beauty" (97).[4] Bembo's theory of love-at-a-distance highlights the importance of the imagination in the preservation of a loving connection. Imagination, the power of thought, offers the idea of presence in the reality of absence, the feeling of proximity in the context of distance. It acts in place of the eyes and ears. Antony and Cleopatra will turn to their imaginations to sustain their intimacy in the context of distance – spatial, but also crucially, emotional. Indeed, in Shakespeare's plays, lovers are often at a distance from each other even when they are in the same place. Thus, the spatial difference evoked in Sonnet 116, through the images of the ship on the sea, and the star, could indicate other forms of distance between the lover and beloved that the poem attempts to close.

Stockholder points out that unpredictable forces from within the self – changeable emotions and personal idiosyncrasies – and inescapable influences from without the self (social, political, and even supernatural/divine powers) can open up distances between people. Even when unions withstand the vicissitudes that Shakespeare's plotting brings about, it is not without significant challenges and changes. Although the ideal bond, the "true" marriage of two minds, is elusive and many bonds are destroyed entirely, the self-knowledge and imaginative powers unleashed in the process offer some compensation to the characters within the play and impart even greater rewards to audiences who watch Shakespeare's plays. Alteration, it seems, is impossible to avoid, but it is still possible for one person to maintain a meaningful connection with another in the midst of and in the aftermath of such changes. Sonnet 116's discussion of the nature of an "ever-fixèd" bond in the context of alteration and time's passage, of the possibility of a union between "true minds," offers a place to consider the twelve chapters and epilogue that comprise Stockholder's work.

Sonnet 116 particularly suits Stockholder's work because the speaker adheres to a belief that there are things we can know for certain and inalienable bonds that we can aspire to even while it contains an undeniable challenge: while the sonnet professes to describe what love is, it frames the discussion with a turn to negatives, words that express what love is not, words given particular emphasis with their line placement and prominence. The initial definition of love places the key negative phrase "[l]ove is not love…" at the end of the second line, forcing the reader's eye to move to line three to complete the definition. What remains most prominent to the reader's eye, then, is the complete collapse of a term in itself, the negation of love ("love is not love") before the remaining definition salvages it and informs us that love *is* something, even if we don't yet know what it is. Likewise, the final couplet affirms the poet's deep knowledge of love, his right to inform us what love is, but the last line is entirely negative if read or seen alone ("I never writ nor no man ever loved"). The poem's only positive assertion is that love is an "ever-fixèd mark" and a "star" that "is never shaken." The first definition is vague, a "mark" being a target of action but not a defined thing or place here. The second definition mystifies love further by using not just a metaphor but also one that implies distance. The speaker reveals that love is always available to guide our movements, but we cannot actually possess it. The implication is that love is a feeling, a force only of influence and direction, rather than an achievable state or available place.

Helen Vendler observes that "[t]he prevalence of negation" in Sonnet 116 indicates that the speaker of the poem is engaged in a "rebuttal" to an imagined previous statement from a lover who has admitted that he no longer loves the speaker.[5] In this imagined context, there is no "marriage of true minds," but a desperate attempt to argue for its possibility in the face of its dissolution. If we read as Vendler does, and I think there is ample evidence to do so, the sonnet is haunted by the transience of bonds. The sonnet is closely echoed in *King Lear*, when France tells Cordelia's other suitors, who want her solely for her share in Lear's kingdom rather than for her internal worth. "Love's not love," he says, "[w]hen it is mingled with regards that stands / Aloof from th' entire point" (1.1.242–4). Shakespeare and Stockholder ultimately show us that while an authentic bond may be "th' entire point," it is nearly impossible to achieve it fully and permanently or to express it if indeed it is truly felt. The inevitable longing and search for a definition and attainment of something "true," the values, ideals, and relationships that seem to make life meaningful are always "mingled" in some way, shaped by unpredictably shifting emotions and alliances.

We cannot ignore that, like Sonnet 116, Stockholder's work is concerned with the particular characteristics and permutations of *emotional* bonds, most prominently love. Yet, Stockholder also effectively charts how non-romantic interactions – of business, politics – seemingly distinct from romantic love, are imbued with its language. In turn, love relationships are shaped by and take on the language of commerce and politics. In his discussion of Shakespeare's dramatization of love, David Schwalkwyk explains that Shakespeare's plays are "concerned not just with the absences and inequities of desire but also with the pleasures of intimacy and demands of reciprocity" and that "the intimacy and reciprocity" are also crucial in other relationships, like those between "master and servant, that appear at first sight to be wholly unerotic."[6] Stockholder's work looks at those pleasures of intimacy and the demands of reciprocity in a number of different relationships and contexts across the twelve plays – comedies, histories, tragedies, one "problem" play (so-called because it doesn't quite fit any one genre), and one romance – that make up each of her twelve chapters. In the course of unpacking these diverse plays, she suggests that the kind of intimacy that will lead to a lasting bond and full reciprocity is shadowed by uncertainty in the real world but is an achievable target in imagination.

"The Edge of Doom"

What of the "real" world in Shakespeare, as Stockholder sees it, the world within time's "bending sickle's compass"? Bodies, and the emotions of those within those bodies, inevitably change over time. Sonnet 116 asserts that even those who transform physically through the passage of time will remain emotionally constant if their love is sincere. True love will be borne out to the "edge of doom," which is death or judgment day. It seems the only measure of "true" love or other kinds of ideals, like honor, can be made in their persistence over time to the point of the death of the body and its translation into something immortal and divine. Romeo and Juliet's love is perfect because they bear it out to their death, as do Antony and Cleopatra. In *1 Henry IV*, as Stockholder points out, Hotspur also adheres stubbornly to his notion of honor – referring to it even at the point of his death.

Sonnet 116's mention, however, of the "brief hours and weeks" introduces a note of ephemerality that the poem cannot quite banish, just as the characters in the plays pursue unchangeable ideals despite changeable emotions and aging bodies. As Stockholder points out across the chapters, the body itself, the inevitability that it will change over time, has a way of undermining or, at the very least, haunting the ideals represented by Romeo and Juliet or espoused by Hotspur. Inescapable materiality consistently challenges us. Juliet herself is sensible of the horrific sight of the bones in the tomb, bones that seem to compress unique persons into a gross and alarmingly infinite materiality. Hamlet, too, struggles with this evidence in the Gravediggers scene. Macbeth becomes aware of his mortality, and he senses that his accomplishments will be meaningless after his death; this leads him to forgo a possible lamentation about the death of Lady Macbeth. He is not sure what the point of such a eulogy would be. Lear and Prospero both feel the discomforts the physical body must endure as it ages. Romeo and Juliet's instant attraction is transformed into a perfect bond, as far as we can see it, not just because they may sincerely love each other but also because they are forced to choose death rather than reach it naturally and are thus never given the time to experience insidious alterations from within and without, like those experienced by Troilus and Cressida or Othello and Desdemona. As Phyllis Rackin observes, "[t]he absolute romantic involvement" explored in *Romeo and Juliet* would be "impossible if the hero were older or less impetuous, more involved in worldly affairs or less impractical" (19).[7] The constancy of our bonds may depend on when our "edge of doom" comes and how much time we are given to contemplate our own aging.

Stockholder also includes mature lovers in this book: Antony and Cleopatra. They have seemed to withstand the alterations wrought by time and are certainly able to "bear" their love to the "edge of doom." Cleopatra references her age – her tanned and wrinkled skin – but it is part of what makes her irresistible to Antony and to audiences. Though he seems to deny the effects of time on her when he says that "[a]ge cannot wither her," what he then praises as her "infinite variety" (2.2.245–6) can only be achieved over time, and the play makes a point of looking back at her past relationships to testify to her enduring charm. Likewise, Antony's Roman reservations about committing himself to her are not enough to draw him away from her over the course of many years. Their suicides come later in life than Romeo and Juliet's and seem to make their bond immortal, but the meaning of their deaths is always disturbed by the specter of her performativity. How much of Cleopatra's commitment to Antony unto death reflects their dedication to each other, and how much reflects her reluctance to be ridiculed by the Romans should she decide to live? Stockholder leaves this question delightfully open, as Shakespeare seems to, while at the same time conceding how powerful and natural is the connection between the two lovers.

The lovers that Stockholder discusses in this book are rendered natural – realistic – in that we can see their imperfections play out and we can see them either acknowledge or repress them. Unions that withstand tests, like Portia and Bassanio's bond in *The Merchant of Venice*, are nonetheless complicated and, for readers and audiences, changed by those tests. Unions that falter under tests, like Troilus and Cressida's and Othello and Desdemona's, are powerfully depicted because such connections dissolve due to a realistic combination of failure of trust within the lovers and pressures exerted by forces in the world around them. Though Stockholder notes that Desdomona's goodness makes her character seem unrealistic at times, that same goodness realistically inflames Othello's jealousy. Even the lovers who are influenced by the artificial love juice in *A Midsummer Night's Dream* experience entirely natural and realistic doubts and fears that predate their excursion into the forest while under its influence. Ferdinand and Miranda's perfect union in *The Tempest*, a true portrayal of instant romantic reciprocity that seems implausible in any "real" world, is framed by Prospero's enactment of the very tests of endurance that other lovers, in the tragedies and comedies, must endure, simulations of life's real challenges. Shakespeare's lovers, Stockholder reveals, are delightfully human, consistent only in their shifting emotions that give audiences a sense of the full range of human experience. They are capable of revealing to us the allure and the dangers of allowing oneself to enjoy the pleasures of intimacy.

In the history plays, Stockholder observes, bonds of loyalty between ruler and subject, fathers and sons, kings and kinsmen are also subject to alteration because kings like Richard II and Henry IV feel empowered by their notions of "divine right," the idea that kingship is conferred by God and that the king is God's representative on earth. This belief that they are superior to those around them inevitably leads kings to abuse their privilege, even as they become increasingly aware of their own mortality and audiences become aware of their personal flaws. Stockholder also refers to the notion that kings were thought to have "two bodies," a line of thinking described by Ernst Kantorowicz in his influential work *The King's Two Bodies: A Study in Medieval Political Theology*.[8] Kantorowicz writes that the body "natural" is the mortal body that is subject to time as all are, that alters and ages. The body "politic" is one that will not age. It is passed from one king to another and encompasses the commonwealth over which the king presides. This conception of power leads to an inevitably fractured experience of kingship, failures of rule, and inevitable shifts of loyalty among those kinsmen and subjects who have sworn to be loyal to the rightful king. Bonds are formed, dissolved, and reformed quickly in the history plays, leading to an impression that pure authority, derived from the "divine right" of kings or the body "politic," is an elusive ideal that the human body undermines. The king's kinsmen and subjects must also face the failure of principles that seem like "ever-fixèd mark[s]." Hotspur's links to the earthy realist Falstaff and his own failure to fully repress evidence that his own body is suffering shadow his seemingly unerring commitment to honor. Prince Hal transforms from a pleasure-seeking scoundrel to an ostensibly ideal king over the course of *1* and *2 Henry IV*, but, as Stockholder observes, his relationship with Falstaff complicates his intimacy with father and vice versa. We are never certain where Hal's loyalties lie.

The shifting alliances in plays like *1, 2 Henry IV* and *Troilus and Cressida*, as Stockholder sees them, also challenge the traditional notion, originally suggested by E.M.W. Tillyard, that Elizabethans saw the world as a carefully constructed hierarchy, a "general conception of order"[9] from the cosmos down to animals and plants. Stockholder notes that Ulysses' "universal wolf" speech from *Troilus and Cressida* is often used (indeed, Tillyard uses it), to demonstrate that Shakespeare subscribed to this ordered view of the world, that all creatures should remain in their place in the "chain of being." Stockholder, through her careful analysis of Ulysses' overall motivations in making the speech, points out the flaw in this line of thinking. The constant wrangling within the Greek and Trojan factions in *Troilus and Cressida* and among the families and factions in the history plays challenge the idea that there is a "fixed location" for each person. While we may wish to see ourselves as inhabiting a "proper" place in an orderly social world, Shakespeare shows us the difficulty of maintaining this illusion.

In tragedies like *King Lear* and *Hamlet*, this sense of order has been violated, and one of the "fixed-mark[s]" sought by titular characters is justice in the context of others' perceived transgression of natural law. This search too is heavily shadowed by the grim realities of the physical body's vulnerability and the characters' sense that some hold power over others without deserving it. "Natural law" itself is a term that Stockholder frequently uses, a term used to describe "essential justice,"[10] or eternal laws that do not change over time and apply to all. If men and women exercise their capacity for reason and follow natural law, they will choose virtue over vice, and if they do not, they will be punished. Both Lear and Hamlet struggle with the idea that those who have violated natural law have not been punished as they should. Ultimately, the imbalance of justice, a problem that tragedies never fully resolve, destroys bonds that cannot be fully recuperated.

In tragedies like *Hamlet*, *Macbeth*, and *King Lear*, characters cling to the notion that people can be known fully and dealt with because they fit cleanly into oppositional categories: natural or unnatural, masculine or feminine, good or evil. But as the messiness of the action unfolds, characters experience the collapse of these extremes as a kind of epistemological and ontological crisis, and tragedy ensues. The death of Hamlet's father and his ensuing disgust of his mother dislocate him from his sense of being within time and place, leading him to question why people act as they do. Macbeth regards the murder of Duncan as a horrific act, but the unnatural energies of the witches and Lady Macbeth envelop him and stir his own dark desires. Lear can dismiss his daughters as "unnatural" early in the play as a way of avoiding his own contribution to his suffering. All three protagonists see clear categories dissolve as the illusions they are, and they emerge into a world stripped of suppositions about who people should ideally be and how they should ideally behave. What is called "unnatural" may well be a part of human nature, and thus people are difficult to evaluate, to fully "know."

"Whose Worth's Unknown, Although His Height Be Taken"

As a metaphor for a person, Sonnet 116 turns to the image of the ship, the "wandering bark / Whose worth's unknown, although his height be taken." The speaker suggests that a ship's external features can be measured, but there is no way of knowing how much it carries within it, what value one can attach to its cargo. People's outward characteristics, the speaker implies, can be visibly assessed and measured like that ship, but their inner life cannot be known or assessed in the same way. That people can hide their thoughts and feelings from others or even from themselves makes establishing a "marriage of true minds" particularly challenging. Stockholder teases from Shakespeare's plays the insight that a person's "true" self may be unknowable or at least radically different from the socially visible or measurable persona they craft for others. Hamlet feels this difference acutely and struggles to reach the "true" self within those around him who seem so opaque. Cleopatra's hyperbolic, intense love could be sincere, but in its flair for drama, the play makes it difficult for audiences to truly "know" who she is and how she feels about Antony.

Shakespeare's overwhelming interest in the opacity of people leads to his association of the "real" world with the stage, the actions of "real" people with the performance of actors. This theme is most prominently unpacked in Stockholder's chapters on *A Midsummer Night's Dream* and *The Tempest* – those chapters that begin and end her work. As Stockholder says in her chapter on the former play, Shakespeare seems to ask "whether the imagination or the evidence of sense provides the truest version of experience." Indeed, desires that seem elusive in the real world can be satisfyingly addressed on the stage; even when desire is not fulfilled in the play, this failure can produce a satisfying theater-going experience if the audience can relate to, sympathize with, or ridicule such heartache. These are "real" feelings even if the fiction that has stirred them is not.

Stockholder gestures to the rich literary, dramatic, and historical source material Shakespeare uses to produce his drama. Shakespeare's additions to these sources lend his characters psychological depth and make the inherited stories uniquely his. Indeed, the literary heritage that leads to Shakespeare's portrayal of Troilus and Cressida is part of the characters' consciousness, a heritage of which the characters themselves seem sensible and with which Shakespeare then reminds us that they are also actors performing the roles in the theater. This echoing of past literary characters or past lives is also built in to characters who are also "real" historical figures. For *Antony and Cleopatra*, Shakespeare drew from Plutarch's account of Mark Antony in his *Lives of the Noble Grecians and Romans*,[11] and to depict the events of the history plays and the tragedies *Macbeth* and *King Lear*, Shakespeare turned to Raphael Holinshed's *Chronicles* among other works.[12] While these sources provide plot points, themes, and some speeches, they alone are not responsible for the intimacy that the audience is likely to sense between characters or feel for characters. The bonds that Shakespeare creates between his lovers and between the characters and the audience are the result of his poetry and stagecraft. These characters are "real" not just because they come from previous sources or they really existed; they produce "real" feelings of attachment or horror on the part of the audience.

Stockholder sees Prospero as Shakespeare's vehicle for making an argument for the power of theater. She writes that the late romances are "full of providential, magical, or quasi-magical powers" and implies that, whatever the complexities of his relation to Caliban, Prospero is aligned with Providence in his ability to use supernatural powers to ensure that the wrongs of the past are corrected. At the time of Shakespeare's writing, Divine Providence was believed to be God's just government of human affairs. If one believed the universe was governed by Providence, then the good would be rewarded and the bad would be punished as part of God's overarching plan. In many of his plays, Shakespeare is interested in how a belief in Providence will shape one's experience of events.[13] In *The Tempest*, Shakespeare certainly enfolds the traditional idea of Divine Providence, and the powers that it was understood to have, into Prospero's powers, but he also uses Prospero's powers to explore the powers of the imagination; in doing so, he lends weight to the idea that the feelings and reactions that the stage produces are more powerful than passing, ephemeral entertainment.

By linking the characters' pursuit of lasting bonds in the plays to the power of the stage to stir very real feelings, Stockholder indicates that the bonds within the play are not the only ones that matter to the playwright. When Prospero requests applause at the end of *The Tempest*, he indicates that the audience and playwright are bound together in a reciprocal relationship. The playwright must give pleasure – the pleasures that come from feeling intimate with finely drawn and well-acted characters – and the audience must appropriately respond to this offering with approval. Stockholder shows us that quite often and across all genres, bonds in Shakespeare meet with impediments and are subject to alterations. Only when the audience approves of, that is, feels for and with the characters on the stage, will an ephemeral performance become something more lasting. And this exchange of energies that signals the stirring of imagination and thought, is as close to a "marriage of true minds" as we are likely to get.

Notes

1 All references to Shakespeare's plays and sonnets use David Bevington's *The Complete Works of Shakespeare*. 4th ed. New York: Longman, 1997.
2 Toronto: University of Toronto Press.
3 Qtd. in Gordon Braden, *Petrarchan Love and the Continental Renaissance*. New Haven: Yale University Press, 1999.

4 Qtd. in *Petrarchan Love.*

5 *The Art of Shakespeare's Sonnets.* Boston: Harvard University Press, 1999. 488.

6 "Love and Service in *Twelfth Night* and the Sonnets." *Shakespeare Quarterly* 56.1 (2005): 76–100. 77.

7 *Shakespeare's Tragedies.* New York: Ungar, 1978.

8 For more on Shakespeare's incorporation of this idea, see François Ost, "Weak Kings and Perverted Symbolism: How Shakespeare Treats the Doctrine of the King's Two Bodies." *Pólemos* 9.1 (2015): 7–14.

9 *The Elizabethan World Picture.* New York: Vintage, 1943. 9.

10 R.S. White, *Natural Law in English Renaissance Literature.* Cambridge: Cambridge University Press, 1996. 1.

11 For more reading on Shakespeare's use of Plutarch, see H.W. Faulkner, *Shakespeare's Hyperontology:* Antony and Cleopatra. Rutherford: Associated University Presses, 1990; Roe, John. "'Character' in Plutarch and Shakespeare: Brutus, Julius Caesar, and Mark Antony." In *Shakespeare and the Classics.* Charles Martindale and A.B. Taylor Eds. Cambridge: Cambridge University Press, 2004. 173–87.

12 The sections of Holinshed used by Shakespeare can be read in Nicoll, Allardyce, and Josephine. Eds. *Holinshed's Chronicles as Used in Shakespeare's Plays.* London: Dent, 1943. For an overview of *Holinshed's Chronicles*, with a section on "Literary Appropriations," see Paulina Kewes, Ian W. Archer, and Felicity Heal. *The Oxford Handbook of* Holinshed's Chronicles. Oxford: Oxford University Press, 2013.

13 For more on Shakespeare and the idea of Providence, see Serena Jourdan, *The Sparrow and the Flea: The Sense of Providence in Shakespeare and Montaigne.* Salzburg, Austria: Institut für Anglistik und Amerikanistik, Universität Salzburg, 1983; David N. Beauregard, "Human Malevolence and Providence in *King Lear." Renascence* 60.3 (2008): 198-222; Alison Shell's chapter "Providence, Fate, and Predestination: From Tragedy to Tragicomedy" in *Shakespeare and Religion.* Arden Critical Companions. London: Methuen, 2010; Chapter 8 of Jeanette Dillon's *Shakespeare and the Staging of English History.* Oxford: Oxford University Press, 2012.

1

A Midsummer Night's Dream

High spirits, romance, and magic, as well as earthy humor, have made *A Midsummer Night's Dream* one of the most frequently performed of Shakespeare's plays. The essence of the play is so generous and embracing that even clumsy performances have the power to delight. Since the action is not dependent upon a particular historical moment, *Dream* lends itself to being staged in a variety of settings and periods. Indeed, the fairy world conveys such a sense of timelessness that it has been performed in settings all the way from ancient Athens to the outer-space world of the distant future. But for all the staging possibilities, there are really only two possible dramatic interpretations of the fairies. The fairies can be benign and gossamer presences, and their woodland world can be a thrilling but ultimately safe place to explore the joys of acting on and fulfilling desire, something like an amusement park ride. Or they can be truly frightening creatures, and the woodland can be an alien, dangerous space, where the supernatural threats to human well-being suggest that desire can be a dark force and emotional commitments in the play are impacted by its unpredictability.[1] In his influential work *Shakespeare Our Contemporary*, Jan Kott makes a darker reading of the play, writing that aside from *Troilus and Cressida*, nowhere else in the Shakespeare canon "is the eroticism expressed so brutally" (175).[2] Love, he observes, "falls down like a hawk" in its "suddenness" (175). Similarly, Louis Adrian Montrose acknowledges in the play traces of "sexual and familial violence [...] acts of bestiality and incest [...] sexual fears and urges" that emerge from "cycles of violent desire" (75).[3] These traces linger as bonds are made and re-made in the play, even when the lovers find their love reciprocated.[4] The vulnerability of relationships to desire's dark forces renders particularly absurd the laws and powers of Athenian "civilization," especially Athenian attempts to regulate romantic love.

Even if the "suddenness" of love might be violent, as Kott says, the play's comic structure and magical tone suggest there might well be something liberating about giving oneself entirely to the experience of desire. The fairies, however dark their power proves to be, also exemplify the risky and revivifying power of

Thinking About Shakespeare, First Edition. Kay Stockholder, revised and updated by Amy Scott.
© 2018 John Wiley & Sons Ltd. Published 2018 by John Wiley & Sons Ltd.

the imagination, its ability to create lasting bonds against all odds. The imagination is especially crucial when one is coping with the "real" world in which love and marriage, shaped by forces of social repression and passing feelings, do not always lead to a happy, harmonious ending.

Near the beginning of the play, Shakespeare focuses on different kinds of desire and love in the context of the wild woods of the fairy world. The king and queen of the fairies, Titania and Oberon, meet to discuss an unresolved conflict – Titania's refusal to give Oberon her "changeling boy." Aside from wanting the boy for a squire, Oberon offers no other reason for his deep desire to take custody of the child; his insistence, which seems like a whim, therefore, signals the play's larger interest in interrogating the differences between relationships forged by mere fancies and relationships of greater depth and breadth.

Oberon's seemingly unaccountable fancy seems designed simply to force Titania to relent more than express the value of the boy to him. When Oberon realizes Titania will not willingly give up the child, he says outside of her hearing "[t]hou shalt not from this grove / Till I torment thee for this injury" (2.1.146–7). As Montrose notes, "Oberon's preoccupation is to gain possession, not only of the boy but of the woman's desire and obedience" (71).[5] Oberon's desire is to contain Titania, keeping her within the confines of the "grove," so that he can exact some sort of punishment for her resistance. His characterization of Titania's refusal as an "injury" to him tells us something of his experience. Oberon's desire for the boy is not articulated as an emotional connection to either Titania or the boy, but he reveals himself as a vulnerable subject to Titania's physical punishment of him, perhaps pointing to a fear that Titania loves someone else more than she loves him. Montrose explains Oberon's tactics as a means of sundering "an intimate bond between women," which is "rooted in an experience of female fecundity (71) and prompts men to seek "mercantile compensation" since they can never share in that bond (72).[6] Conversely, Titania describes to Oberon her desire to keep the boy as part of an emotional bond, and she eloquently recalls her intimate friendship with the boy's mother:

> Set your heart at rest.
> The fairy land buys not the child of me.
> Her mother was a vot'ress of my order,
> And, in the spiced Indian air, by night
> Full often hath she gossip'd by my side,
> And sat with me on Neptune's yellow sands,
> Marking th' embarkèd traders on the flood,
> When we have laugh'd to see the sails conceive
> And grow big-bellied with the wanton wind;
> Which she, with pretty and with swimming gait
> Following—her womb then rich with my young squire—

Would imitate, and sail upon the land,
To fetch me trifles, and return again
As from a voyage, rich with merchandise.
But she, being mortal, of that boy did die;
And for her sake do I rear up her boy,
And for her sake I will not part with him. (2.1.121–37)

The speech is touching and complex. Each remembered activity suggests a companionate love despite the difference in their status.[7] Yet the passage also focuses on the idea of financial exchange and wealth in a way that would seem to degrade the sweet sentimentality of her words. Titania initially tells Oberon he cannot "buy" the boy, and further plays upon the idea of the votaress and her child as part of economic circulation with the prevalence of ship imagery in the memory. To what extent are the votaress and her son part of an authentic emotional bond with Titania? Mario DiGangi says that the votaress "functions as a kind of exotic commodity through which Titania justifies her possession of the boy" (82). In making this point, DiGangi focuses on Titania's image of the votaress as "rich with merchandise" when she carries "trifles" to Titania. The trifles, he says, indicate Titania's vanity and her willingness to exploit the votaress's service to indulge it. He calls the votaress Titania's "beloved domestic pet" (82) rather than a friend. While Titania certainly recalls the votaress as a ship laden with goods that are brought to her, the language of commerce is also in service of a tenderness that equals if not exceeds the financial terms of the relationship: if the votaress is like a ship, then the ships are like the votaress, with the votaress's pregnant belly mimicked in the ships' sails. Though Titania indeed likens her friend to a rich ship carrying "trifles," to this she adds a different idea of wealth when she terms her friend's womb "rich with my young squire." Titania sees her friend writ large in her surroundings, so enormously valuable is she to Titania. The passage cannot be affecting if we do not see that Titania *contrasts* the boy to mere trifles in order to suggest his intrinsic, emotional value to her. If the changeling boy is a kind of "mercantile compensation" to Oberon, Titania adopts the language of commodity to underline the boy's *emotional* value to her.

The memory begins with Titania telling Oberon, "set your heart at rest" on the matter, but it is clear Oberon's heart is not engaged, at least not with the boy, and that Titania says this because *her* heart has been touched by the votaress and her child. After her affecting decree that she will not "part with" the boy, Oberon simply asks "[h]ow long within this wood intend you stay?" (2.1.138). With what we are given, we can feel the strength of Titania's bond to the boy. Oberon feels not for the boy but feels only the "injury" Titania has done to him, and his wish to then "torment" Titania for withholding the boy paints a much darker picture of the nature of his desire and the qualities of his love.

The devastating effects of Oberon's whim on marital harmony are detailed in Titania's "wasteland" speech, which occurs immediately before

Oberon requests the changeling boy and in which the images of destruction go well beyond what seems called for by the dramatic action but which indicate the depth of Titania's emotional investment in both Oberon and the changeling boy. Addressing Oberon's claim that Titania loves Theseus, Titania says:

> These are the forgeries of jealousy;
> And never, since the middle summer's spring,
> Met we on hill, in dale, forest, or mead,
> By pavèd fountain or by rushy brook,
> Or in the beachèd margent of the sea,
> To dance our ringlets to the whistling wind,
> But with thy brawls thou hast disturbed our sport.
> Therefore the winds, piping to us in vain,
> As in revenge, have sucked up from the sea
> Contagious fogs which, falling in the land,
> Hath every pelting river made so proud
> That they have overborne their continents.
> The ox hath therefore stretched his yoke in vain,
> The ploughman lost his sweat, and the green corn
> Hath rotted ere his youth attained a beard;
> The fold stands empty in the drownèd field,
> And crows are fatted with the murrion flock;
> The nine-men's morris is filled up with mud,
> And the quaint mazes in the wanton green
> For lack of tread are undistinguishable.
> The human mortals want their winter here;
> No night is now with hymn or carol blessed.
> Therefore the moon, the governess of floods,
> Pale in her anger, washes all the air,
> That rheumatic diseases do abound.
> And thorough this distemperature we see
> The seasons alter: hoary-headed frosts
> Fall in the fresh lap of the crimson rose,
> And on old Hiems' thin and icy crown
> An odorous chaplet of sweet summer buds
> Is, as in mockery, set. The spring, the summer,
> The childing autumn, angry winter, change
> Their wonted liveries, and the mazèd world,
> By their increase now knows not which is which.
> And this same progeny of evils comes
> From our debate, from our dissension.
> We are the parents and original. (2.1.81–117)

Their quarrel assumes cosmic proportions. Titania tells us how the winds, angered by the fairies' failure to dance, have brought floods and sickness. Indeed, the fairies merge with the winds, becoming as much a cause of natural events as their victim. The dance, an image of joy and harmony, keeps the cosmos benign, and in its absence "contagious fogs" sweep in from the sea, bringing an evil rain that spreads disease and perverts the ordinary course of agricultural fertility: "the green corn hath rotted / Ere his youth attained a beard." By the using the image of a beardless youth, Shakespeare makes the decomposing corn a metaphor for the failure of manhood. This representation of masculine impotence carries over to images of thwarted or unproductive effort, that of the ox, straining its yoke in vain, and of the ploughman "losing" his sweat. The rejection of marital harmony leads to barrenness, not of a waste-land but to a land overgrown because it has not been husbanded by shared desire and a preserved bond. This infertility extends to the animal world too in the powerful image of the empty sheepfold filled with mud and pestered by crows fat with the flesh of dying livestock.

The infection eats away the foundations of the human bonds as well as the bond between humanity and the divine. The blessing of God upon the daily and seasonal round of humanity is lost: "The human mortals want their winter here; / No night is now with hymn or carol blessed." The raging disorder that stems from their disjunction alters the seasons themselves, and because the seasons are conventionally used to represent stages of human growth, the dis-order even becomes associated with an unnatural sexuality between the old and the young. This relationship, in which "hoary-headed frosts" fall into the "fresh lap of the crimson rose" and where the sweet buds of summer are wasted on winter's "icy crown" cannot lead to reproduction. All of this devastation, this "progeny of evils," derives from and expresses the division, or "ill-meeting," of the parent-like married fairies. Their divergent desires pull them in opposite directions, a movement away from each other that replaces the fertility that ordinarily results from the expression and fulfillment of an equally invested desire.

Titania's speech, in its enormous suggestive power, goes well beyond its immediate context, for on the face of things it has nothing to do with the Athens of the human characters. We haven't heard anything about a famine or an epidemic in Athens, so clearly we are not to take Titania's speech literally. Rather, it becomes a figurative expression of the more ordinary disorder that we find in the human city, where authority strives, against the grain of nature and without explanation, to suppress or redirect youthful desire. Egeus claims authority over Hermia, and Theseus, supporting Egeus' claim, advises Hermia to "fit" her "fancies" to her father's "will" (1.1.118), but, as the play makes clear, he gives no good reason for objecting to Lysander, who is as well-born as Demetrius, and who would make as good a husband for Hermia. Shakespeare also suggests that "fancies," which cannot be controlled entirely by reason in the way Theseus imagines, are most productive (and reproductive) when they are motivated by emotion that is reciprocated and explored. Egeus misuses his paternal authority merely in order to have "his will"; indeed, he excites the spirit of rebellion by interfering with the potentially happy, fertile, and altogether legitimate romantic love that his daughter feels for Lysander.

The play questions the nature and endurance of the bond forged by love from its opening announcement of the marriage between Theseus and Hippolyta, who, as king and queen of Athens are analogous to Oberon and Titania. We then are introduced to the young couples, and to the disturbed love of Oberon and Titania. But the love between Oberon and Titania indicates that it is not only misused authority that causes problems in affairs of the heart and prevents the formation of harmonious and fertile couples. Their relation suggests that one source of romantic dissension is the uncomfortably close link between giving oneself over freely to a shared love, and, at the same time, submitting oneself to another's power, a theme perhaps carried over to the somewhat problematic depiction of the relationship between Theseus and Hippolyta. Many critics find the parallels between the two couples emphasized by the fact that they were probably played by the same actors (they never appear on the stage at the same time). Since Theseus and Hippolyta's marriage frames the dramatic action, one might assume that it is happy, but many readers and playgoers have been disturbed by Theseus when he says:

> Hippolyta, I wooed thee with my sword
> And won thy love doing thee injuries;
> But I will wed thee in another key,
> With pomp, with triumph, and with revelling. (1.1.16–19)

The new key in which their love is to be rendered seems to have little to do with affection or tenderness, and the former Amazon's answering silence gives no assurance that, to anticipate the image Hermia uses later, her heart consents to Theseus' sovereignty.[8] One may stage the scene with gestures that make her silence signify her loving submission, but one may as easily stage her silence as sullen resignation. Some performances make up for this silence by having her take his arm in an affectionate way, but others have her draw away from him, and, by implication, distance herself from his joyous anticipation of wedding.[9] Furthermore, throughout the play they compete with and argue with each other, although in doing so they seem relatively equal despite the unequal beginning. But it isn't likely that he intended them as exemplary of gender equality, especially since the play's resolution depends on her submission to him in marriage, on Titania's willing surrender to Oberon, and even on Hermia's yielding to Lysander's authority.

Hippolyta and Theseus' romantic bond is further entangled with Titania and Oberon's conflict when the latter begin to argue about the changeling boy.

Initially, the disagreement between the two fairies has nothing to do with the boy. Indeed, Titania explains that she has rejected their shared bed and resisted terming herself Oberon's "lady" because she cannot forget that Oberon has left fairyland to meet Hippolyta, whom Titania terms Oberon's "mistress" and "warrior love" (2.1.71). In turn, Oberon chides Titania for her love for Theseus, a love so intense, Oberon alleges, that she has encouraged Theseus to "break his faith" with other women (2.1.79). The effect of these accusations, which Titania dismisses as "forgeries of jealousy" (2.1.81) on Oberon's part, is to undermine the bonds between both the fairy and human couples and to more widely challenge the idea that fulfilled desire can lead to the kind of married love that the comedies move toward – a challenge that is further articulated in troubling or tragic terms in *Troilus and Cressida* and *Othello*.

The dilemma inherent in the idea of romantic love appears most clearly in the representation of the two young couples. On the one hand, loving marriage is represented as an essential core of a well-ordered natural, civic, and cosmic life, but the love that plays so crucial a part on the cosmic stage is romantic love – a love that must develop spontaneously and that cannot be controlled by reason or dictated by authority. It is not a love that can be expected to develop between two people who are chosen for each other by their parents. It is the kind of love that we would recognize, one that depends on both members of the couple being erotically and spiritually drawn to each other with equal passion. Hermia objects to being told that she must see Demetrius through her father's eyes, for romantic love must spring from the body and soul's depths and be untouched by social calculation. Thus, the idea of others choosing whom one will marry, the fabrication of a bond by figures of social authority, conflicts with the romantic ideal. Patricia Parker brilliantly explores the idea of "joining" in the play, a term literalized by the joiner Snug, one of the mechanicals. For Parker, the play associates the joining of two people in marriage to joining as a trade – "the artisanal, material, or artifactual" (88) – in order to underscore "the dependence of place and distinction not on the 'natural' but on the artificial or made" (87).[10] This dependence, she reasons, highlights the "unsettling possibility that degree, hierarchy, and place were themselves less products of nature than forged or fabricated constructions" (87). We can see, too, that Egeus' attempt to control Hermia's marriage is a maneuver of social fabrication, one that exposes how unnatural "joining" in marriage can be. Egeus and Theseus fail to acknowledge that a romantic, unregulated attachment, strangely enough, is crucial to a well-ordered society. As Titania and Oberon's conflict has shown us, mutual desire leads to a shared bed and a shared bed leads to natural fertility. The rejection of the bed, the absence of reciprocated desire, leads to fruitless efforts to husband the land, to barrenness.

These difficulties, of desiring and joining, might be insurmountable enough, but the play reveals a further problem with a worldview that gives romantic love such spiritual power. The play makes clear what all of us know: falling in love is not in our control. We may like, admire, respect, and have affection for a potential marriage partner, and yet have no sexual or romantic passion for him or her, and we may fall hopelessly in love with someone who is, perhaps even in our own judgment, unsuitable. In Shakespeare's depictions of lovers, one tends to find that the spiritual health of the young person is indicated by the appropriateness, including social appropriateness, of his or her choice of partner. The plays subtly inculcate the idea that a virtuous person will find him or herself spontaneously loving another, not because of social propriety, but in accord with it.

This strange marriage of desire and social order is part of Shakespeare's effort to accommodate an individualistic conception of romantic love to a well-ordered world. The more explicit problem is that love is changeable. Romantic passion bathes the beloved in a golden aura, making her or him seem the glowing center of all of life's meaningfulness. But time passes, the glow fades, and as though waking from a dream we wonder what we loved, and how we could judge so poorly, as Titania does when she wakens to find herself with the ass-headed Bottom.

Parker argues that the play shows us instances of "reversal" or "exchange" in the fairy world to suggest that theater is capable of disrupting the usual order of things and exposing the artifice that structures human experience. The unexpected promotion of the lowly mechanical Nick Bottom, transformed into an ass by Puck, to the place of lover to the fairy queen exemplifies one of the play's comic reversals.[11] Bruce Boehrer notes that Bottom supplants not only Oberon but also the changeling boy as Titania's love object; he suggests that these substitutions require a "simultaneous reconfiguration of the social affinities that underlie the act of loving" as well as the "biological articulation of the act itself" and the "terms by which love receives its expression" (108).[12] When Shakespeare allows for the reconfiguration of relationships in the fairy world, it is mirrored in the experience of the human lovers. The ending that would seem to restore heterosexual, marital accord in both worlds cannot fully reverse these reconfigurations.[13]

Once romantic love becomes the standard for marital harmony, nothing can make us so happy as mutual love, nothing can be so painful as unrequited love, and nothing can be so devastating as love withdrawn. Not only is the anguish and humiliation of unrequited love portrayed in the confused anguish of the four lovers wandering in the dark forest, but so are the hatred, jealousy, betrayal, and humiliation that occur in its name. How can it be that something so important as romantic love, the generative core in these plays not only of personal, but also of civic, public, and spiritual happiness, should be so wayward, changeable, irrational, and unpredictable? And, given that we know it can be all those things, how can something so unstable lead to secure joinings that promote personal and social harmony? A marriage based on force is distasteful and untenable, but a marriage based on a perfectly mutual love seems elusive if not impossible. Shakespeare allows the specter of both extremes to infiltrate the play, perhaps in an effort to show us that "true" (that is, realistic) love exists somewhere in the middle.

Dream makes it clear that the mutability of love comes not only as the consequence of fairy magic, for even without the benefit of Puck's magic flower Demetrius has changed his love from Helena to Hermia before the play began, and he leaves the stage still influenced by the love-juice. Shakespeare links the magic fairy world to the portrayal of the real civic world, and he emphasizes the symbolic meaning of the fairies' magic: it stands for the unaccountable mutability of human emotion and, more positively, the kinds of desire that imagination, another form of "fancy," can fulfill. The woodland world, to which the humans resort for a cure for their ills, differs from the real world in that there is a controlling presence that can manage that mutability. Though Oberon has only partial control of the wayward Puck, ultimately he has enough power to set things right, first in his own world by punishing Titania for her rebellion, in the process changing the way she sees things, and then in the human world, the happiness of which is thus shown to depend upon the dream-like fairies, just as Titania claimed it did.

The play adds a more psychological dimension to the problems of human inconstancy in love when Hermia describes an unsettling dream after falling asleep beside Lysander in the woods, a dream that anticipates Lysander's rejection of her once the love-juice is mistakenly given to him. "Methought," she says, "a serpent ate my heart away, / And you sat smiling at his cruel prey" (2.2.155–6). In one sense the dream reflects reality in that it is simultaneous with Lysander's betrayal. However, another dimension appears in the particular content, which expresses the fears of a young girl about to leave her maiden life and her camaraderie with Helena to embark on her maturity. The phallic serpent and the coldly smiling Lysander represent her fear of male sexual desire, which seems antithetical to abiding love. These fears were suggested earlier when, as they settled down to sleep in the woods, Hermia required Lysander to "lie further off, in human modesty" (2.2.63). In her subsequent dream, the image of the heart, which is the symbolic seat of love, being consumed is also a fitting metaphor for jealousy. In *Othello*, Iago famously calls jealousy the "green eyed monster which doth mock the meat it feeds on" (3.3.179–80). Hermia's dream of a snake, a version of Iago's monster perhaps, eating her heart is a particularly compelling metaphor for jealousy or doubt because she experiences it as a force simultaneously externalized and internalized, a predator from the outside of the self that invades and then consumes the self from within. The image gives us a sense of the frightening vulnerability required to fall in love and give oneself over entirely to another person – the potential for performances to play Hippolyta as resistant to submitting to Theseus in marriage and, the manipulations and cruelty to which Oberon subjects Titania expose that vulnerability. One can desire union with another in love and marriage, but in the "two images of Hermia's dream, the eating snake and the smiling lover," Shakespeare poses "larger questions of fidelity and possession between men and women" (14).[14] The message of love that emerges from both worlds depicted in the play is that "to be intimate is to risk oneself with another" (16). Shakespeare gives us, in this moment, a sense of the gravity of that choice, that assumption of risk.[15]

Because the figures of authority in the city are intermeshed with, and to some extent cause, romantic problems for the lovers, the city cannot be the site of their resolution. As in many of his other comedies, Shakespeare has recourse to a contrasting venue, or world, a pastoral "green" or "golden" world to which the characters from the city must resort. This natural and/or supernatural alternative world not only enables the lovers to resolve their problems, but also enables them to renew the social harmony of the city from which they fled. The process of renewal involves plunging the characters with great intensity into a nightmare experience of some of the darkest sides of human nature. Helena abases herself in her unrequited pain and willingly betrays her best friend for the bitter-sweet pleasures of being rejected by Demetrius; the childhood friendship between the two women turns to bitter envy and distrust; and rivalry in love brings out murderous hatred in the men, both for each other and for the women. The play highlights the illusory nature of rational control, the irrationality of human emotion. Helena believes that Hermia's distress is a "confederacy" to make fun of Helena, a "false sport," (3.2.194); she marvels that Hermia would "rend asunder" the "ancient love" (3.2.215) between the two women with a cruel taunt. While that ancient love is not truly threatened, because Hermia is honest in her distress and Lysander's betrayal will be corrected, Shakespeare forces Helena and the audience to consider the ungovernable impulses and emotions that can so easily compromise bonds of love that seem to have held true over time. Helena's quick judgment of Hermia, that her sorrow is an act designed simply to torture her, a cruel whim, in fact unmasks Helena's own fundamental suspicion of her friend, a darker emotion that may have lurked in and feasted on her heart since the moment that "ancient love" was born. This sundering of a female friendship parallels Oberon's belittling of the bond between Titania and her votaress. Bruce Boehrer finds that the play is "fascinated by same-sex attachments and communities" that compete with "various visions of heteroerotic marital fulfillment" (102). Mutual love between a man and a woman may be possible, but what happens to other important relationships when lovers give only each other their all?

Lysander's rejection of Hermia also demonstrates the darker side of love, revealing a vindictiveness that isn't entirely explained by the love-juice's effects. Under the influence of Puck's magic, Lysander leaves the sleeping Hermia wishing that she never come near him again, he says:

For as a surfeit of the sweetest things
The deepest loathing to the stomach brings,
Or as the heresies that men do leave
Are hated most of those they did deceive,
So thou, my surfeit and my heresy,
Of all be hated, but the most of me! (2.2.143–8)

The characters bring with them from the real world all the turbulent emotions that comprise human experience. These unpredictable feelings threaten the transformation of romantic desire to married love and make an emergent desire superior to an "ancient" love. These emotions are stirred when the fairies reveal the vulnerability of the desiring body to forces beyond its control. The forces that inhere in the fairy world intensify and foreground these problems in the process of providing a solution that revitalizes both the characters' lives and their city. Our foreknowledge of the happy end, together with the limited exploration of the way the characters experience their own plight, allow these scenes, apart from those involving the mechanicals, to be the funniest in the play. But the laughter is satisfying in direct proportion to the potential gravity, a gravity that will appear more clearly when we come upon this pattern again, not only in comedies, but also in later plays, particularly *King Lear* and *The Tempest*, where this process will take on overtones of spiritual therapy.

The dangerous imaginings, which torment the foolish mortals but which also renew the human community, connect this play to the tragedies and the late romances. All these plays are concerned with the imagination and its relation to what is ordinarily taken as reality. This theme first appears in *Dream* in the scene with the mechanicals, the humor of which depends upon their being unable to distinguish between reality and a stage presentation. Like people who send letters to characters in soap operas, they cannot distinguish between reality and its representation. The literal-minded Bottom, who wants to play all the roles in *Pyramus and Thisbe*, accepts as completely real his dream-like experience as a dream, but we know it is as real as anything else in the play.

Toward the conclusion of Act 4, when the human couples awaken after Demetrius's love for Helena and Lysander's for Hermia have been restored, they all say they have been dreaming, but they are puzzled because each one's account of the night confirms the others'. Theseus disbelieves them too, but Hippolyta wonders that so dream-like an experience should pass the reality test of mutual coherence. Of course, we, having witnessed both, know that their "dream" experience is as real as their ordinary lives. Though we know the play as a whole is a representation, we are driven to confirm the reality of a portion of it against disbelieving characters who exist within it. In this way, the demarcation between stage and audience is called into question. This dividing line is further attenuated when the mechanicals stage their play. The device of an inner play has an inherent double effect; on the one hand, it necessarily calls attention to the artifice of the play that we watch, while on the other hand, in making the outer or frame play real in relation to the inner play, it challenges the distinction between reality and its theatrical or imaginative representation.

Hermia's dream is a "real" dream in the play in that it is truly experienced when she sleeps. Yet her reaction to it shows us how powerful dreams are, and thus how powerful all the experiences characterized as dreams in the play are. Real dreams and real experiences that *seem* like dreams show us the powerful effect of imagination on the body itself, the ability of a passing fancy to affect one's physiological and emotional response and to thereby outlast its moment of performance. Her own dream is so vivid, Hermia believes it is real even as she wakes, begging Lysander "to pluck the crawling serpent from [her] breast" (2.2.152). Not realizing that Lysander has left, she informs him she is "quak[ing] with fear" (3.1.154). Once she realizes Lysander is gone, she says "I swoon almost with fear" (3.1.160). The ideas conjured and the emotions stirred by the dream have transferred into Hermia's waking world in the way that dreams commonly do, eliding the gap between mind and body, imagination and reality. Shakespeare plays with the idea further when the mechanicals perform a play for Theseus and Hippolyta to celebrate their marriage, and Theseus reflects on what makes imagination so powerful.

The play of *Pyramus and Thisbe* as performed by the mechanicals adds to the deliberate confusion of levels of reality, for the comedy we have seen to its happy conclusion not only explores deeply contradictory impulses and perceptions, but it also touches upon situations that in the real world cause intense pain. The inner play enacts a tragedy that ensues from the same situation that initiated the comedy, that is, a father's interference in romantic love. However, the comedy of its maladroit performance overwhelms the tragedy of its matter, which is similar to that we will encounter in *Romeo and Juliet*, a play that Shakespeare wrote within a year of this one. One might say that the inner play points toward the more subtle ways in which the outer play generates its bright laughter from the dark recesses of the human heart. In doing so, this less "real" inner play reminds the audience of the ways in which the seemingly more real outer play can misrepresent life. To put this in another way, the human lovers laugh at the mechanicals' rendering of the tragedy of Pyramus and Thisbe, in which a potentially tragic version of the lovers' own story is rendered funny by inept acting. The courtly audience laughs at the mechanicals, but we are invited to laugh at *them*, since their somewhat smug amusement highlights their blindness to Pyramus and Thisbe's mirroring of their romantic adventure.

This tonal doubleness appears as well at the very end of the play. On the one hand, the sense of real danger to vulnerable humanity appears as Puck sweeps the threshold to protect the sleeping denizens of "this hallowed house" (5.1.383) from evil spirits and as Oberon invokes a spell to render their offspring healthy. On the other hand, Puck's last words seem to disperse this sense of danger when he tells the audience that if they are offended they should think that they have been dreaming. Puck, of course, demurs from reflecting on how, over the course of the play, dreaming has acquired far-reaching and profound significance.

Finally, the same issue is raised in the discussion between Theseus and Hippolyta about whether the audience can compensate from their imaginations for the deficiencies of the actors. Again, this questions whether the imagination or the evidence of sense provides the truest version of experience. All of these currents coalesce in Theseus' speech when he equates the poet, who "gives to airy nothing / A local habitation and a name" (5.1.16–17), to the lover and the madman.[16] Madmen will appear in later plays, but in this one lovers have been shown to have a dream experience that is as real as the rest of the play, and certainly as real as the authority that would have upheld Egeus' tyranny. Since that is so, it would follow that the airy nothings for which the poet provides a local habitation and a name, that is, this play that we have been watching, is as real as anything else in the world of Athens or early modern England or indeed twenty-first century Canada.[17] In fact, while the play represents a passing fancy, a work of imagination, the emotional effects of the play are something real, something that can claim a kind of lasting power even if the play itself is impermanent and even if the emotions roused are not precisely as the author/actors intend, as in the case of Pyramus and Thisbe. Just as Hermia wakes from her dream still emotionally and physically "feeling" the dream, the audience of Shakespeare's play can leave the theater still feeling the effects; the "local habitation" given to "airy nothing" may well be the bodies and minds in the audience, stirred to life by the performance.

In these elaborate ways, Shakespeare plays with the boundary between reality and the products of the imagination. He seems to be making something like an argument that the products of the imagination, whether manifested as dreams or as plays like the ones he writes, can claim a reality that rivals, or supplements, our ordinary reality. The products of imagination may be able to satiate an audience's real desire to feel affected by events and people in a work of art, but how far do those effects carry? The play's fairyland, according to Hugh Grady, is an "ideal space" that makes it possible "to represent and contemplate determinate human wants and needs and their impediments, and to imagine alternatives to the world as it currently exists" (283).[18] The issues raised here about the relation of stage reality to ordinary reality will find further expression in *The Tempest*, but in the imaginative world of *A Midsummer Night's Dream*, at least, we can explore and experience "human wants and needs" without assuming any of their risks.

Notes

1 For a discussion of the various interpretations of the forest, see Laurel Moffatt, "The Woods as Heterotopia in *A Midsummer Night's Dream*." *Studia Neophilological* 76.2 (2004): 182–187.

2 London: Methuen, 1964.

3 "Shaping Fantasies: Figurations of Gender and Power in Elizabethan Culture." *Representations* 2 (1983): 61–94. Norman N. Holland writes that "cruelty pervades" the play. He says that "all proclaim love, but they also threaten violence or humiliation" ("Hermia's Dream." In *Representing Shakespeare: New Psychoanalytic Essays*. Eds. Murray M. Schwartz and Coppelia Kahn. Baltimore: The John Hopkins University Press, 1980. 1–20).

4 Montrose argues that the play calls attention to and reproduces male "anxiety about the power of the female" in the context of Elizabeth's rule ("Shaping Fantasies," 66). The play represents "fantasies about the shaping of the family, the polity, and the theatre" in response to Elizabeth's self-expressed autonomy from male partnership.

5 "Shaping Fantasies."

6 "Shaping Fantasies."

7 Titania's relationship to the votaress and the changeling boy are not straightforwardly mutual, according to Mario DiGangi. He argues that the "status difference between Titania and her nameless votaress cuts across any attempt to categorize their relationship definitively in terms of an egalitarian friendship" (*Sexual Types: Embodiment, Agency, and Dramatic Character from Shakespeare to Shirley*. Philadelphia: University of Pennsylvania Press, 2011. 81).

8 Laurence Nee says that here Theseus "presents love as the violent compulsion to satisfy bodily lust" ("Pagan Statesmanship and Christian Translation: Governing Love in *A Midsummer Night's Dream*." In *Souls With Longing: Representations of Love and Honor in Shakespeare*. Eds. Bernard J. Dobski and Dustin A. Gish. Lanham: Lexington Books, 2011. 87–116. 88). For more on Theseus and his "various heterosexist abuse" (108), see James W. Stone, "Indian and Amazon: The Oriental Feminine in *A Midsummer Night's Dream*." In *The English Renaissance, Orientalism and the Idea of Asia*. Eds. Debra Johanyak and Walter S.H. Lim. New York: Palgrave Macmillan, 2010. 97–114.

9 See Philip C. McGuire, *Speechless Dialect: Shakespeare's Open Silences*. Berkeley: University of California Press, 1985.

10 Patricia Parker, *Shakespeare from the Margins: Language, Culture, Context*. Chicago: University of Chicago Press, 1996.

11 One theory is that the play was staged to celebrate a courtly wedding. Annabel Patterson suggests, however, that another theory "assumes the play is motivated less by the social needs of the Elizabethan court" ("Bottom's Up: Festive Theory in *A Midsummer Night's Dream*." In A Midsummer Night's Dream*: Critical Essays*. Ed. Dorothea Kehler. New York: Garland, 1998. 165–178. 167) and instead explores the "festive impulse in human social structures" (174) that is "deeper and more generous than the courtly reveling" (175). Bottom represents, she says, Shakespeare's "inquiry into the way in which the lower social orders, as well as the lower bodily strata, function," and this inquiry suggests that "the service they perform and the energies they contain are usually undervalued, even to abuse" (174). For an interpretation of Bottom's various names in role prefixes, see Lina Perkins Wilder, "Changeling Bottom: Speech prefixes, acting, and character in *A Midsummer Night's Dream*." *Shakespeare* 4.1 (2008): 41–58.

12 Bruce Boehrer "Economies of Desire." *Shakespeare Studies* 32 (2004): 99–117.

13 Gabriel Rieger suggests that Oberon wants Titania to fall in the love with Bottom, thereby cuckolding himself, because it is part of his effort to humiliate her, contributing to the theme of "erotic dominance and submission which underpin the domestic, social, and political economies" of the play (" 'I woo'd thee...':The Erotic Economies of *A Midsummer Night's Dream*." *The Upstart Crow* 28 (2009): 70–81. 70).

14 Norman N. Holland, "Hermia's Dream." In *Representing Shakespeare: New Psychoanalytic Essays*. Eds. Murray M. Schwartz and Coppelia Kahn. Baltimore: The John Hopkins University Press, 1980. 1–20.

15 For more on the latent symbolism of Hermia's dream, see Matthew A. Fike, *A Jungian Study of Shakespeare: The Visionary Mode*. London: Palgrave Macmillan, 2009. 19–23.

16 In "A Kingdom of Shadows," Louis A. Montrose write that Theseus is Queen Elizabeth's "princely surrogate" who attempts to "understand and to contain – the energies and motives, the diverse, unstable and potentially seditious apprehensions of the ruled" (232). Ultimately, he argues that the play "internalises and distances the relationship of the public and professional theatre to the pressures and constraints of noble and royal patronage" (*A Midsummer Night's Dream*: *Critical Essays*. Ed. Dorothea Kehler. New York: Garland, 1998. 217–240).

17 Fike writes that according to Jung, the imagination "operates apart from reason" and will "enable one to gain conscious access" to the unconscious place "where art originates" (28).

18 "Shakespeare and the Impure Aesthetics: The Case of *A Midsummer Night's Dream*." *Shakespeare Quarterly* 59.3 (2008): 274–302.

2

Romeo and Juliet

Romeo and Juliet is a play so frequently performed, so well known, and read in so many versions that the names and stories of the central characters have become bywords, signifying romantic love even to those who have never witnessed or read the play.[1] Allan Bloom writes of its message as "somehow expressing the essence of love, what it ought to be, a permanent possibility, a fulfillment of every renascent hope and a thing to be admired" (5).[2] This being so, it is easy for readers and audiences today to take the play for granted. However, we should not lose sight of how unusual it was for its time, or to forget that part of our cultural understanding of love derives from this play. Nor should we forget that Shakespeare's depiction of perfect romantic love is ultimately one that surges toward death and tragedy. It is useful to remember Lloyd Davis's suggestion that the play's insistence on the connection of love to death, initiated in the Prologue, helps to "unveil a dark skepticism about desire, despite bursts of romantic idealism"(58).[3] If it is to exist at all, the romantic ideal must be shaped against a backdrop of darker forces.

Coppélia Kahn says that the play is about "a pair of adolescents trying to grow up" (5),[4] but critics are quick to point out that growing up would have inevitably changed the quality of their love. Marianne Novy points out, "anyone who has lived longer than Romeo and Juliet [...] has made more compromises than they have" (109),[5] and Bloom humorously writes if Romeo and Juliet had been allowed to grow old, such an ending would be a lesser tragedy: "their settling down together, watching their beauties disappear slowly with age while they became bored with each other" (8). Bloom's humor reveals that death is the key to their ability to embody a union of equal desire and perfect reciprocity, the key to the impact that their love has had on our culture; it is crucial that they never have the chance to "grow up."[6] Shakespeare intimates that the only reason Romeo and Juliet's love survives in its perfection in the play world and in our culture is that the lovers are not permitted to experience the alterations – both mundane and dramatic – wrought inevitably by the passage of time.

Thinking About Shakespeare, First Edition. Kay Stockholder, revised and updated by Amy Scott.
© 2018 John Wiley & Sons Ltd. Published 2018 by John Wiley & Sons Ltd.

Because the world in which Romeo and Juliet live cannot accommodate their love, the sense of isolation from common life that generally accompanies the experience of love is intensified and exaggerated, and gives the play its dominant tone. Stanley Wells describes this isolation as an "enclosed and private world" that cordons off the lovers from activity around them (156).[7] Novy says that in this isolation, Romeo and Juliet can attain "a mutuality in which both are active and genders are not polarized," but adds that "in the external world, masculinity is identified with violence and femininity with weakness" (100). The radical separation between the lovers and their world appears from the play's first scene, in which first the servants of the two houses quarrel, then the relatives, and finally the parents of the two houses join the fray under the hot Verona sun.[8] It is no accident that all of the aggressive jests made by the servants are based on sexual puns. Bloom calls such characters the "backyard of the barnyard" (20), and notes that they "talk most explicitly and unromantically about sex" (19).[9] Samson and Gregory, Capulet servants, boast that they will keep a better position on the sidewalk than the Montagues and "take the wall," (1.1.12), by which they mean the Capulets will take an inside position and force the Montagues into the gutter. After Gregory implies that Samson is being weak by keeping to a safe position, Samson's verbal play descends into coarse sexual violence. "[W]omen, being the weaker vessels, are ever thrust to the wall" he says, "[t]herefore, I will push Montague's men from the wall and thrust his maids to the wall" (1.1.15–18). He then jokes that he will either "cut off" the heads "of the maids" or take their "maidenheads" (23, 25–6). In the Verona that Samson and Gregory give voice to, people associate sex with violent misogyny and think of it when they are in the grips of a deep hatred. Romeo's separateness from this world is suggested by his absence from this first scene, by the mention of his name only after the fight has dissipated, and the description of him as one who seeks dark and lonely places, avoiding the sun that has drenched the scene we have just seen. The love that separates Romeo from everything in his world is not yet the mutual love that he will experience with Juliet; it is rather the dubious pleasures of nursing the sweet melancholy of unrequited love, which is one of the conventions – though no less real for that – of the courtly love tradition. For Romeo, Rosalind is the unattainable goddess of chastity, invulnerable to Cupid's darts, and Romeo's love of being in love is the preliminary stage for falling in love. But this love has no place in the world of Verona, which is characterized by family hatred that is indistinguishable from a crass, violent desire for sexual dominance.[10]

Juliet is also introduced as set apart from her family from the moment she takes the stage. Her mother's practical desire for her to marry, and the Nurse's earthy, verbose, and occasionally suggestive conversation align them with the atmosphere of the first scene and contrast with Juliet's demure and quiet figure. Shakespeare emphasizes this stillness and restraint. She begs her Nurse to stop talking in Act 1, Scene 3, when the discussion of Juliet's need to marry is derailed by the Nurse's lengthy story from Juliet's childhood. After Juliet's terse response to her mother's broaching of the subject of marriage – "[i]t [marriage] is an honour that I dream not of" (67) – Juliet falls silent while the conversation circles around her. That sense of her stillness carries over into the scene in which Juliet and Romeo meet at the ball. Time seems to stop as the timeless moment of their falling in love is marked by the sonnet their dialogue creates:

> *Romeo* [to Juliet]
> If I profane with my unworthiest hand
> This holy shrine, the gentle sin is this:
> My lips, two blushing pilgrims, ready stand
> To smooth that rough touch with a tender kiss.
>
> *Juliet*
> Good pilgrim, you do wrong your hand too much,
> Which mannerly devotion shows in this;
> For saints have hands that pilgrims' hands do touch,
> And palm to palm is holy palmers' kiss.
>
> *Romeo*
> Have not saints lips, and holy palmers too?
>
> *Juliet*
> Ay, pilgrim, lips that they must use in prayer.
>
> *Romeo*
> O, then, dear saint, let lips do what hands do.
> They pray; grant thou, lest faith turn to despair.
>
> *Juliet*
> Saints do not move, though grant for prayers' sake.
> Then move not while my prayer's effect I take. [He kisses her.]
> (1.5.94–107)

Here the imagery of pilgrims, saints, and shrines recalls the religion of love that was a prominent feature of the medieval and early Renaissance conception of romantic love, voiced pre-eminently by the Italian poet, Petrarch. These images in which Juliet and Romeo articulate their physical desire give it an aura of sanctity, emphasize its otherworldliness, and anticipate the end in which the city is transformed by their tragic love. Their desire, as the sonnet makes clear, also brings them together as equal forces. Novy observes that here they "share the initiative" (102).[11] Romeo frames his kiss as an attempt to improve upon the touch of his rough hands, but the audience knows Romeo's touch reveals nothing of the violence that Samson has described in the first scene, in his horrific fantasy of "thrusting" maids against the wall and cutting off their heads. Juliet knows this too. Her response to Romeo's "rough touch" is framed as chastisement ("you do wrong your hands too much"), but this is reassurance, balancing his self-denigration with praise, affirming his worth and approving his "mannerly devotion." Her portion of the sonnet has the effect of bringing the two closer to union, indicating her willingness to *receive* his touch. In the immediate context, the playful use of religious imagery suggests the charming mixture of young shyness and desire. The perfect melding of two souls, the sense of the lovers' deep suitability for one another, is also expressed by the sonnet form in which the formal distance between them is conveyed by the separate quatrains each speaks. That the two quatrains compose the octet of a sonnet bespeaks their underlying connection, a connection that becomes more manifest as they alternate in speaking the lines that compose the sextet, which closes with their kiss.

Juliet says that she, like a saint, should not move to initiate a kiss. Romeo approves that sentiment, prolongs the religious metaphor, and encourages her to stay still while he moves to her. Her passive role here is deceptive in its stillness. Though she does not begin the kiss physically, her sweetly seductive play with the conceit of the immovable saint gives Romeo the opportunity and permission to touch her, an address for which he implicitly rather than overtly asks. In the end, Novy notes, Juliet "insists on her sharing of his humanity" by giving up on the "sainthood" that her part in the sonnet has assumed and returning the kiss in mutual action.[12] Though he says that the lovers ultimately "make it convincing" (83), Charney calls this moment one of "extreme stylistic artifice," containing "far-fetched, ingenious conceits" (83).[13] He picks up on the play's peculiar ability to show a union that is simultaneously impossible, its sonnet-achieving poetry impossible to replicate in spontaneous conversation, *and* emotionally resonant.

The divide between the still, timeless world of the romantic lovers and the ordinary, bustling world is conveyed not only by the content of the sonnet but also by the timing of the action. Just before the lovers meet, Tybalt rages when he realizes Romeo is at the Capulet ball. This sequence at one and the same time emphasizes the beauty of their love by contrasting it with Tybalt's hatred and suggests the dangers that surround it. The otherworldliness of love is also suggested when the evening that had barely started before the lovers' meeting is about to end by the time that the sonnet concludes with their kiss. Normal dramatic time gives way to the lovers' psychological time and lifts their love to a timeless realm.

Moreover, the secrecy of their marriage in Friar Lawrence's cell contrasts with the bustle and business of the scenes set in the Capulet house. The same secrecy separates their love as well from the comedy that early in the play heightens the contrast between the lovers and the world they occupy. Just as in *A Midsummer Night's Dream*, Shakespeare allows serious tones to give substance to his comic matter, so here he uses comic business to highlight the tragic action. The exchange between the servants that begins the play, the bustling matter-of-fact earthiness of the Nurse, and the witty exchanges between Romeo and the light-hearted and anti-romantic Mercutio all depict the ordinary world and its attitude toward love. In an extended speech about Queen Mab (1.4.53–94), the fancy-free Mercutio mocks Romeo for his lover's dream, and satirically evokes the fairy safety of *Dream,* thus making a poignant contrast to the dangerous streets of Verona. This contrast is heightened when Romeo goes, with a foreboding of death, from his bantering meeting with Mercutio to his tryst with Juliet.

Were it not for the family feud, the lovers would make the necessary compromises with the ordinary and comic world, but the feud associates their love from the first to the last with the darkness of night and the moon, rather than the business of life under the sun. The secrecy of their marriage and the separation of Romeo's inner from his outer world makes Romeo hesitate to fight Tybalt, and so precipitates both Mercutio's and Tybalt's deaths. With Mercutio's death, all the comedy drains from the play. The same secrecy isolates Juliet from her family and from the earthy common sense of the Nurse, whose old person's slowness irritates Juliet, but also dramatically counterbalances the rush of events toward the tomb. Juliet's isolation becomes absolute when the Nurse, her last confidante and link to the ordinary world, advises Juliet to forget the absent Romeo and marry the handsome Paris as her father desires. Here, the extremity of the Nurse's earthy practicality, its fundamental failure to understand desire that flows into enduring romantic love, removes her so far from Juliet's romantic realm that the link between them breaks. As Juliet drinks the Friar's potion, she is left alone to confront her terror of awakening in the grisly tomb. This isolation of the lovers and their pursuit of a timeless, constant bond carries their love toward the final isolation and timelessness of the bonds of death.[14]

The inevitable realization that, as Rackin phrases it, "[d]eath seems to be a necessary condition of absolute romantic love," (19)[15] can be felt in other ways, for it pervades the play's language and action, and it constitutes the sense of a Fate that is so powerful that it overwhelms any sense of individual will. However, if one looks carefully at the Prologue, one sees that fate in the play has particular associations that relate it to the family feud.

> Two households, both alike in dignity,
> In fair Verona, where we lay our scene,
> From ancient grudge break to new mutiny,
> Where civil blood makes civil hands unclean.
> From forth the fatal loins of these two foes
> A pair of star-crossed lovers take their life;
> Whose misadventureed piteous overthrows
> Doth with their death bury their parents' strife.

> The fearful passage of their death-marked love,
> And the continuance of their parents' rage,
> Which, but their children's end, nought could remove,
> Is now the two hours' traffic of our stage;
> The which if you with patient ears attend,
> What here shall miss, our toil shall strive to mend.

Notice the emphasis placed in the first line on the equal dignity of both houses. Just as in *Dream*, Shakespeare emphasizes that by all accepted criteria the lovers are socially suitable for each other, and, therefore, that their love does not reflect some inner poverty of judgment or taste. Rather, the feud destroys the civic order that could, if intact, transform romantic desire into married love and procreation. Notice the play on the world "civil," which has the meaning of civilized, but also of belonging to the city. The shades of meaning that inhere in the word emphasize that the blood of uncivil citizens turns the city, the birthplace of civilization, into the site of uncleanliness and mayhem. This emphasis on the feuding families depicts Verona as a kind of throwback to a feudal order, organized around kin groups. Part of the enterprise of the Tudor dynasty was to break the hold of these ancient families and to impose a centralized power, the monarchy, over them. The prince, then, embodies this centralizing power, and the city's disorder is a consequence of their putting family loyalty above civic duty. This is not to say that the play is a conscious political allegory, but rather that an Elizabethan audience would be expected to decry such disobedience, and the play as a whole upholds the values and vision upon which a centralized authority depends. It is much more likely that Shakespeare would expect his audience to condemn the unruly families than it is that he would expect them to condemn their children.

The next line of the Prologue particularly emphasizes that in this uncivil civic condition the loins of this family, the source of fertility, are perverted; they give birth to death. The word "fatal" carries the sense of death-dealing, but also of the source of Fate. The Fate that draws the lovers to the tomb issues from the loins of their parents, and by extension, from the feud that divides them.[16] In a sense, their love is born from their parents' hatred, and their lives are a sacrifice to it.[17] They enter the Capulet monument, which is full of the bones of long dead and warring ancestors, as a sacrifice and kind of scapegoat. Once Romeo and Juliet's fathers are told the full story of their children's deaths, their hatred quickly melts. As a gesture, Montague promises that he will create a funeral effigy, a statue upon a tomb, in gold so that "whiles Verona by that name is known, / There shall be no figure at such rate be set / As that of true and faithful Juliet" (5.3.300–2). Responding in kind, Capulet promises that the statue of Romeo will "by his lady's lie" (303–4). The golden statues suggest the transformation to come. Gold is the metal of transformation, the object of the alchemical quest. For some the quest was for the formula that would turn actual metals into literal gold, but others quested for the elixir of life that would turn the base metal of the flesh into the gold of the spirit. The golden statues are radiant with the symbolism of spiritual transformation that derives from the various love traditions discussed earlier. But gold is nonetheless cold and inanimate; the lives of Romeo and Juliet are cut short, and the city, no longer torn with the strife of the feuding families, can only inherit the benefits of the transforming power of their love.

Shakespeare casts a romantic spell; so strong and pervasive is the imagery of death, the beauty of the isolated lovers, and the sense of inevitability that characterizes all tragedy that one can lose the sense of the tragic in a kind of poetic swoon. The magic of this romantic love is suggested throughout by the richly poetic language that distinguishes the lovers from the other characters.[18] Much of it takes the form of prolepsis, or foreshadowing, that occurs at frequent intervals as the lovers intuit the destruction that awaits them. For example, as Benvolio breaks up the battle of wits between Mercutio and Romeo to remind Romeo that they will be late for the Capulet ball, Romeo says:

> I fear, too early: for my mind misgives
> Some consequence yet hanging in the stars
> Shall bitterly begin his fearful date
> With this night's revels, and expire the term
> Of a despisèd life closed in my breast
> By some vile forfeit of untimely death.
> But He that hath the steerage of my course
> Direct my suit! On, lusty gentlemen. (1.4.106–13)

On the level of the speaker, this passage portrays a person of intuitive depth. On the level of the text, it reminds the audience of the fate that awaits the lovers in a way that both emphasizes the inevitability of the tragedy, and, through Romeo's reference to the stars, connects that inevitability to the warring families mentioned in the Prologue. When Juliet sends the Nurse to find the name of her mysterious lover, she reflects, "[i]f he be marrièd, / My grave is like to be my wedding bed" (1.5.135–6). The tense relationship between the individual and the world that she inhabits and that composes her is suggested by her being both right and wrong. Her grave will be her wedding bed, not because Romeo is married, but rather because he isn't. We see her consciousness moving closer to that of the audience in her response to the news of Romeo's identity: "[p]rodigious birth of love it is to me / That I must love a loathèd enemy" (1.5.141–2). At this moment she does not think of death, but the intimate relationship between love and hate, already established in the Prologue, links this line to the earlier image of her grave as her wedding bed. Moreover, something that is born can die, and thus her association of love with the natural human life cycle suggests its ultimate powerlessness against mortality. This image, along with the imagery of the pilgrim lips that kiss in the lovers' sonnet, is fulfilled when the dying Romeo says, "[a]nd, lips, O you / The doors of breath, seal with a righteous kiss / A dateless bargain to engrossing death!" (5.3.113–15). After they consummate their marriage and Romeo climbs back down her balcony, leaving her as a condemned man for the murder of Tybalt, Juliet feels that approach of "engrossing death." "O God," she says, "I have an ill-divining soul! / Methinks I see thee now, thou art so low, / As one dead in the bottom of a tomb" (3.5.54–6). The pilgrimage has been toward death from the very beginning, led by forces that echo in the travelers' souls but are well beyond their horizon of consciousness.

The sense of inevitability produced by the rich poetic texture gains added intensity from the many references to and instances of haste.[19] These begin with Benvolio's worry about being late for the ball, and they continue as Capulet hurries his servants as they carry food across the stage, and Juliet hastens to send the Nurse with her plan to meet at the Friar's cell. The sense of haste reaches a crescendo after Tybalt's death when Capulet, who at the play's beginning acted like the model of an affectionate and, for the time, modern father who respected his daughter's desires, suddenly transforms into a tyrant like Egeus and cannot abide to wait an extra day to see his daughter married to Paris. Though as an individual he is ignorant of Juliet's secret marriage, he acts as though he has been taken over by the haste that seems to emanate from the jaws of the tomb that imagistically has been awaiting the lovers from the opening Prologue.

The rushed pace of this action is tied to the symbolism of time and pace in the play. Images of gun and cannon powder in the play suggest not only an accelerated pace to the journey between birth and death but also the strong but brief nature of deep love. Here, as in *Dream*, Shakespeare wonders if love can remain untouched by alterations. As Romeo anticipates his marriage in an exchange with Friar Laurence, he brushes aside "love-devouring death" with the belief that "one short minute" (2.6.7, 5) with Juliet will outweigh all sorrow. Friar Laurence then advises Romeo to "love moderately" because "violent delights have violent ends / And in their triumph die, like fire and powder, / Which as they kiss consume" (2.6.9–14). The Friar believes that moderate love leads to "long love" (14). Romeo, a typically anxious bridegroom, welcomes the perception of accelerated time because he cannot wait to marry Juliet and consummate the marriage. In this frame of mind, he also believes that true, deep love will somehow triumph over time and flout death because a "short minute" with Juliet is so powerfully delightful. Yet Friar Laurence's grim advice challenges Romeo's excitement by reminding him and the audience that love at first sight, like gunpowder, makes for a spectacular, but brief, explosion. The union created by this spark of desire will, once consummated, be burned away. If Romeo and Juliet weren't fated to die because of their ancestors' grudge, would their love persist beyond the moment of infatuation? This question offers a darker, less romantic subtext to the lovers' rushed journey from their love's birth to their death. The intense hatred between the families that limits the lovers' time together may well be the necessary spark to ignite Romeo and Juliet's love. In a broader sense, Shakespeare reminds us that inside us all, darker emotions are the secret companions to the lighter ones, and the amount of time we have to indulge in love, often determined by the amount of restriction on it imposed by the world around us, may well dictate how we perceive and experience that love. Delights may be, after all, inherently violent in nature.

And yet, the entire play demonstrates that it is precisely because we cannot always control the circumstances that give rise to and shape our love that we cannot entirely control the depth and intensity of our love. The Friar's advice to "love moderately," then, represents his failure to understand that a person's will is incapable of fully governing emotion, the same misunderstanding that marks Egeus and Theseus's view of "fancy" in *Dream*. Because Romeo and Juliet are swept up together in a love that is destined to be consumed, the play is enduringly romantic. The romantic power of this rendering of a love that is destined to be consummated in death is all the more powerful for the absence of the kind of counterplot by which Shakespeare characteristically casts multiple, and therefore distancing, lights on the central action. There is nothing in the play's formal structure to impede the rush of events toward death. However, Shakespeare does build into his play an imagistic countercurrent. Some of the language seduces one into regarding death as the loss of oneself in the dark embrace of a mysterious lover, but some of the language and action functions to remind the audience that death is horrible. As Juliet contemplates drinking the poison, she thinks of awaking in the tomb and imagines the sight of "the bones" of her ancestors "packed" in the vault, and her imagination wanders to Tybalt, whom she imagines "festering in his shroud" (4.3.40–2).

Moreover, imagery of poverty and disease pervade Romeo's description of the poor apothecary from whom he buys the poison (5.1), and Friar Laurence's messenger explains that his possible contamination by the plague is responsible for the failure of the crucial message from the Friar to reach Romeo (5.2). All these images of and references to disease and decay remind the audience that death is inescapable and omnipresent. Death, even romantic suicide, comes with a grim reminder of the ultimate susceptibility of the human body to decay.

This play differs from Shakespeare's later tragedies in that the tragic forces are all external to the lovers. It isn't that the central characters are perfect, but their flaws and imperfections are those natural to young people in love, and they would not be a source of tragedy in a well-ordered world. Some commentators try to make it into a conventional tragedy by emphasizing Romeo's folly in entering the fight with Tybalt and his temporary fall into self-pity after he has been exiled. This effort to make *Romeo and Juliet* conform to the pattern of the later tragedies ignores the poetic force of the love motif. Compared to the later tragedies, which draw their sense of inevitability form the characteristics of the protagonists, this play seems more sentimental, less mammoth and awful. It is, perhaps, a smaller kind of achievement, but it is perfect of its kind.

Notes

1 In *Shakespeare and Modern Culture*, Marjorie Garber explores how the play has become "cultural shorthand for romantic love" (New York: Pantheon Books, 2008. 35).

2 *Shakespeare on Love and Friendship*. Chicago: University of Chicago Press, 1993.

3 ("'Death-Marked Love': Desire and Presence in *Romeo and Juliet*." *Shakespeare Survey* 49 (1996): 57–67. 58. Stanley Wells suggests that the play is "an elegy for wedded love, a condition in which sex, while it is important, is subsumed in celebration for a spiritual as well as physical unity" (*Shakespeare, Sex and Love*. Oxford: Oxford University Press, 2010. 167). Dympna C. Callaghan points out that at the time of Shakespeare's writing of the play, "the ideologies and institutions of desire – romantic love and the family, which are now for us completely naturalized – were being negotiated" (59). Callaghan's feminist reading is important because it suggests that the play participates in the creation of "multiple and contradictory discourses" of desire that serve as a "dislocation and relocation of authority" (86). She reminds us that there is a cultural and historical context for a seemingly "timeless" depiction of love (in *The Weyward Sisters: Shakespeare and Feminist Politics*. Eds. Dympna Callaghan, Lorraine Helms, and Jyotsna G. Singh. Oxford: Wiley Blackwell, 1994.

4 "Coming of Age in Verona." *Modern Language Studies* 8.1 (1977–8): 5–22.

5 *Love's Argument: Gender Relations in Shakespeare*. Chapel Hill: University of North Carolina Press.

6 For more on the link between love and death in Romeo and Juliet, see Clayton G. Mackenzie, "Love, Sex, and Death in Romeo and Juliet." *English Studies* 88.1 (2007): 22–42; Norman Rabkin, *Shakespeare and the Common Understanding*. New York: Free Press, 1967.

7 Wells makes this description in relation to the play's sonnet-producing dialogue in Act 1, Scene 5, suggesting that their mutual poetry writing sets them off from the "surrounding bustle of the dance" (156).

8 Maurice Charney calls this dialogue a "farcical conflict," which contributes to the play's comic beginning (*Shakespeare on Love and Lust*. New York: Columbia University Press, 81).

9 *Shakespeare on Love and Friendship*.

10 Romeo's experience of love is also contrasted by Mercutio's "cynical attitude to women and love," which Wells calls "brutal" and "gross" (157, 159). In *Shakespeare on Love and Friendship*, Allan Bloom writes that Mercutio is "one of Shakespeare's most obscene characters" (18), who reveals his "powerful intelligence" (18) with a "foul mouth" (19).

11 *Love's Argument.*

12 *Love's Argument.*

13 *Shakespeare on Love and Lust.*

14 See Clayton G. MacKenzie. "Love, Sex and Death in Romeo and Juliet." *English Studies* 88.1 (2007): 22–42, and Ronald Knowles. "Carnival and Death in *Romeo and Juliet*: A Bakhtinian Reading." *Shakespeare and Carnival: After Bakhtin*. Ed. Ronald Knowles. London: Macmillan, 1998. p. 36–60.

15 *Shakespeare's Tragedies.*

16 Douglas D. Waters calls the play a "tragedy of fate" in "Fate and Fortune in *Romeo and Juliet*." *Upstart Crow* 12 (1992): 74–90.

17 Paul A. Kottman argues that the lovers are in a process of self-realization that alienates them entirely from their community ("Defying the Stars: Tragic Love as the Struggle for Freedom in *Romeo and Juliet*." *Shakespeare Quarterly* 63.1 (2012): 1–38).

18 Rackin advises that "[o]ne useful approach to this play is, in fact, to regard it as a poem – a great, lyrical, metaphorical definition of romantic love" (*Shakespeare's Tragedies*). Charney says that *Romeo and Juliet* shares with *A Midsummer Night's Dream* an "intense lyricism" (*Shakespeare on Love and Lust*, 81).

19 Rackin writes that the play seems to "rush before our eyes in a whirlwind of events over which the lovers have no control" (*Shakespeare's Tragedies*, 18). Lloyd Davis calls the play's pace a "breakneck speed" that "sees the ordained end bear relentlessly on the lovers," who are "caught between a determining past and future" ("Death-Marked Love," 57).

3

The Merchant of Venice

The Merchant of Venice, like *A Midsummer Night's Dream*, presents romantic love in a comic vein, but in the process of doing so hints at aspects of the social realities within which romantic love is embedded in ways that the other comedies do not. This chapter concentrates on the significance of the contrast between Venice as a commercial world, represented by Shylock, and Belmont as an idealized Neoplatonic world, represented by Portia, as well as by her dead father. More than any other play by Shakespeare, *The Merchant of Venice* makes visible the deep psychic, emotional, and social consequences of the new importance of money in Shakespeare's world. As in so many of Shakespeare's plays, we find an intermixture of comic and serious modes, but unlike the serious matter in *A Midsummer Night's Dream*, the serious matter here has sufficient force to constitute a threat to the play's comedy. This threat plays out through the motif of the "bond," which, as a supposedly clear and uncontestable contract between the moneylender and the borrower, is the source of overt tension between Shylock and the Christians. A bond can also be read as an intangible, unpredictable force of desire or amity that connects one person to another emotionally. The Christians of the play imagine that emotional bonds, like the love between Portia and Bassanio or Antonio and Bassanio, cannot be contaminated by the material concerns that define financial transactions. But as Katherine Eisaman Maus points out, the emotional bonds forged between people in this play "can be conflated" with commercial connections even as characters continually feel compelled "to distinguish between them" (60).[1] Moreover, the play highlights the contingent and changeable nature of even financial bonds. Graham Holderness writes that "the wealth of trade" is "chronically exposed, open to the arbitrary onslaughts of wind and tide, reef and rock" (60).[2] Antonio's ships, lost at sea but recovered inexplicably at the end of the play, foreground this unavoidable uncertainty.

Emotional connections likewise seem as if they are continually exposed to threats even as characters profess their love to be unalterable. As Leonard Tennenhouse observes, relationships in the play are "based solely on forms of

Thinking About Shakespeare, First Edition. Kay Stockholder, revised and updated by Amy Scott.
© 2018 John Wiley & Sons Ltd. Published 2018 by John Wiley & Sons Ltd.

dependence and trust" and are "constantly subject to the threat of betrayal" (58).[3] The song sung when Bassanio contemplates which casket to choose in order to win Portia ruminates on the source and duration of love. In the first verse, it asks "where is fancy bred, / Or in the heart, or in the head? / How begot, how nourishèd?" (3.2.63–5). It seems to add some urgency to the question, begging "[r]eply, reply" (66). The song's second verse responds, as if from a second speaker, that fancy dies in its infancy, "[i]n the cradle where it lies" (69); and the verse ends by tolling the bell for fancy's demise. The song implies with the two initial questions ("how begot?" and "how nourishèd?") that fancy can be "born," or start, one way, but prolonging it requires adding something more to fancy. In fact, the second speaker replies resoundingly that it isn't prolonged at all, that fancy cannot last. Catherine Belsey points out that the play reminds us "desire can be satisfied only at the level of the imaginary" because once we achieve what we want, we no longer want it (43).[4] In opposition to fancy, the idea of faith is represented in the play as something constant that operates in and outlasts the destabilizing effects of uncertainty and betrayal. The play will explore the many incarnations of a faithful bond – religious, romantic, married, and monetary – its strengths and its limits.

The money that shapes and unsettles the emotional bonds between friends and between lovers creates a tension that strains the comic fabric of the play. Perhaps the most "untidy" and controversial element of the play is the depiction of Shylock, one that has modern audiences wondering what Shakespeare's intentions might have been, and one that has scholars cringing, searching for ways to "rehabilitate" his words and actions, that is, make him seem less a villain and more a victim.[5] This is the first topic that must be confronted in discussing this play, because whether or not it was a laughing matter for the Elizabethans, it is not for us. Marjorie Garber emphasizes the sweeping effect of Shylock's characterization on modern audiences: "the play worries us. Worries us individually and collectively. Worries us as readers, as performers, as teachers, as scholars, as students. Worries us as members of the modern world" (128).[6] There are, of course, many different views on this issue. The play can be interpreted as blatantly and thoughtlessly anti-Semitic, given how Antonio and the other Christians in the play rail against Shylock, dehumanizing and mocking him, and given Shylock's own cruelty and apparent avariciousness. Derek Cohen argues that the play, for him, is "profoundly and crudely anti-Semitic" (104).[7] Likewise, in Shakespeare: The Invention of the Human, Harold Bloom describes the play as a "profoundly anti-Semitic work" (171).[8] He finds in the depiction of Shylock "a savagery" that the complexities of the play cannot "alleviate" (189). Performances of Shylock can, in playing into the stereotypical elements of the character, emphasize his qualities as comically absurd or dark and vicious – Shylock has been laughed at and feared over the centuries. Charles Macklin's performance as Shylock in 1741 made the character "unyieldingly malignant" (96), so terrifying that one theatergoer alleged that King George II could not sleep after seeing a performance (96).[9]

Yet there are alternatives to these interpretations and performances of Shylock.[10] Many performances emphasize or even add moments that sympathetically highlight the tragic losses Shylock endures. Most notable of these is Edmund Kean's 1814 portrayal of Shylock as a "tragic figure" (65),[11] and Henry Irving's nuanced 1879 performance that emphasized the "dignity" of the character and his victimization by the Christians (128–9).[12] A 1970 production with Laurence Olivier as Shylock famously added a "final offstage chanting of the *Kaddish* or memorial prayer" (303) to lend the character further dignity and his circumstances deeper tragedy.[13] What is clear, in light of these vastly different interpretations is that the play itself offers fodder for many, often conflicting interpretations. Marianne Novy argues quite rightly that "the play frames him [Shylock] so that the attitude audience members can take toward him may vary widely at different moments" (17).[14] For Novy, the play's anti-Semitic elements "call attention to anti-Semitism rather than justifying it" (19).[15] Martin D. Yaffe goes even further, writing that the play always attends to "the moral issue" (45) and declaring:

> I find no evidence to indicate that Shakespeare himself endorses the prejudices articulated by his characters who are unfriendly to the Jews and much to indicate that he understands those prejudices fully for what they are, namely, as dubious and damaging opinions, and so encourages his reader to do likewise. (23)[16]

Yaffe describes "Shakespeare's own openness to the theologic-political situation of the modern Jew" and as part of his "quest for tolerance" (23).[17] Kenneth Gross takes an even wider view, suggesting that Shylock's character illuminates the "enigma" not just at the heart of Christianity but also at the heart of the human, a core that he calls the "most shadowy of things" (19).[18]

Though we cannot determine Shakespeare's intentions with Shylock, we can consider the overall effect of his presence in the play, especially in relation to the Christians with whom he is supposed to contrast. They might seem to represent virtues like charity, mercy, and selflessness, but readers have found evidence that the act of giving in the play is not without undercurrents of tension. Antonio likes to differentiate himself from Shylock, but his gestures of generosity are potentially as manipulative and avaricious as Shylock's are imagined to be.[19] Indeed, even the witty, beautiful, and lovable Portia, the comic heroine of the play, can be read as ruthless in her resounding defeat of Shylock in court and her savvy manipulation of Antonio and Bassanio. Harry Berger Jr. points out that while Shylock does indeed seem the villain early in the play, "complicity gets redistributed throughout the play" and he "shares the discourse of villainy with the Christians who conspired to bring him down" (19).[20] He calls Portia's giving of the ring to Bassanio a "devious power play," and contends that she "gives gifts that can be transformed into debts" (31).[21]

This chapter will tease out some of the subtleties of characterization that make the play's message so challenging to pin down.

If we can see blame for the tensions between characters in the play dispersed among all characters, Janet Adelman's position that the play as a whole "persistently troubles the distinction between Christian and Jew" (4) is particularly resonant.[22] At the time Shakespeare wrote the play, there were hardly any Jews in England, for they had been banished in 1290 during the reign of Edward I, three centuries before Shakespeare lived, and were not allowed into England until the mid-seventeenth century when, under the Commonwealth, Cromwell invited them back.

Jews had been expelled from England in 1290, but at the time of Shakespeare's writing of the play, London was home to many *conversos* – Jews who converted to Christianity. In addition to the *conversos*, there were probably a few remaining Jews who kept their religion a secret. About two years previous to Shakespeare's writing of the play, a Portuguese Jew, Ruy Lopes, who had converted to Christianity, and who had served Queen Elizabeth as a doctor, was put to death after having been accused of participating in a plot to poison her. His death caused a scandal, with some people arguing that he was innocent and had been used as a scapegoat by those who were guilty. If one sees the play as in some way a response to that incident, the nature of that response depends upon how one regards the figure of Shylock. But, in general, for Shakespeare and for most of his contemporaries, the word "Jew" carried a stereotyped image that derived from long-standing prejudices, an image that was neither checked nor exacerbated by knowledge of actual living Jews. Generally, Jews were part of a larger category of strangers or foreigners, all of whom were held in some suspicion by the xenophobic English. Specifically, the Jew was associated with money, an association that grew out of the fact that during the preceding centuries, the Jews, who were forbidden to own land in many countries, were much sought after in the courts of the wealthy as advisers on financial and other issues. In times of stress between the rich and the poor, this position rendered the rich Jews easy scapegoats for the elite groups that employed them, while poor Jews were associated with the marketplace and money. Many did become moneylenders, but despite the official disapproval of the Church, so did many Christians, including members of the clergy.

The *conversos* were unsettling to Christians because it was impossible to know whether they had really converted to Christianity – were they still practicing Judaism, and was their conversion a mere guise? In *Shakespeare and the Jews*, Shapiro argues that the *conversos* did not cause the anxiety about Christian identity, but rather intensified an already burgeoning anxiety or served as an object for its energies. For Shapiro, the question of whether Shakespeare is "anti- or philosemitic" is "ill-suited for gauging what transpired" for Jews in Shakespeare's time (11)[23] in this context because at the time of the play's writing, there were "unprecedented changes in how collective identity was constituted" (6). The English, he explains, imagined Jews were committing ritual circumcision and murders of Christians, and he reads the "pound of flesh" that Shylock wishes to extract from Antonio as Shakespeare's incorporation of this cultural anxiety. The problems caused by the increasingly fuzzy boundaries of identity can be read as intrinsic to Christianity itself, as Janet Adelman observes, because Christianity, with its roots in Judaism, "represents a kind of originary turning away from Judaism" that "can never be wholly complete" (65).[24] For her, Shylock embodies the idea of the *converso* in the play, as the "living contradiction within" Christianity (11), its "internal alien" (12).[25]

While we cannot banish the anti-Semitic content of the play, the difficulty in asserting a definitive reading of Shylock and the play as a whole inherently challenges the stereotypical elements and contributes to Shylock's undeniably powerful presence. René Girard's sensible advice is that "we do not have to choose between a favourable and unfavourable image of Shylock" (247); instead, we must acknowledge that the play is "not unlike a perpetually revolving object that, through some mysterious means, would always present itself to each viewer under aspects best suited to his own perspective" (249).[26] The task must be not to simply reaffirm one's perspective but to challenge it. My own view is that Shylock's character is based on anti-Semitic clichés, that they served Shakespeare's purposes because in the popular mind they were associated with the avaricious craving for money, but that Shakespeare's psychological penetration leads him to undermine the suppositions that uphold a clear demarcation between Christian and Jew, Belmont and Venice, Antonio and Shylock, faith and fancy, love and money. The complexities of the play may not "alleviate" the anti-Semitism as Bloom might wish, but they do require us to do more thinking – they stir us in ways that are uncomfortable but crucial. Identity, religious or otherwise, might well remain a mystery, but Shakespeare's Shylock forces us to acknowledge this mystery; no identity is free from contradiction or complexity, however much we claim to know and value someone.

Shylock's character is associated with the force of the desire for financial wealth. Money was the focus of a central contradiction at the heart of the Elizabethan social fabric. On the one hand, it was increasingly necessary to buy the luxuries that served as the signs of traditional wealth and honor, while on the other it was a sign of aristocratic honor to scorn the base desire for material gain or in any way to appear money grubbing. Shylock embodies both sides of this conundrum; he is at once necessary and hated, and hated the more because he is necessary.

There are two other factors to consider in thinking about how Shakespeare might have expected his audience to react to Shylock. The first is that it was commonly known that not only Jews lent money at interest; indeed, since there were no Jews in England and moneylending was practiced, it was practiced by non-Jews, and the interest rates were beyond the 10% that defined usury. Now, people being who they are, they could know that and still enjoy hating Jews without giving the matter much thought. The second factor in gauging the light in which Shakespeare's audience would see this figure is that he would count on his audience having seen Christopher Marlowe's play *The Jew Of Malta*, in which the central figure, Barabas, is considerably more a stage villain than is Shylock. Barabas is not a moneylender; he is a merchant, acquiring wealth by buying cheap and selling dear, as do all merchants, by definition. Interestingly, his ways of making money are like those of Antonio, rather than those of Shylock. Nonetheless, his involvement in the world of money places him in opposition to the aristocratic Christian rulers, who confiscate Barabas's wealth in order to pay tribute that they owe the Turks.

Though at the play's beginning we see Barabas thus victimized, in the course of the play he kills so many people, including his own daughter, and becomes so thoroughly the stage Machiavel that the original wrong done him is easily forgotten. However, for all the evil of the figure, Barabas is so clever as he plots to get rid of his enemies that one's sympathies can be aroused by his sheer ingenuity and delight in his own evil devices. This tendency gains further strength as the play unfolds because Barabas, though more openly ruthless, has the same motivations as the other characters who profess the Christian values by which they condemn Barabas. Marlowe, Lisa Hopkins notes, "makes it abundantly clear that Jews do not by any means have a monopoly on wickedness" (33).[27] Likewise, Andrew Duxfield suggests that religion is used in the play "to cloak the ambitious motivations of individuals" (100).[28] All this is both subtle and hard to know even at our distance, so one is quite uncertain about how Elizabethan playgoers would have taken the relation between Barabas and the Maltese governor, just as one is unsure about how they would take the relation between Shylock and Antonio.[29] But one thing is certain: Shylock is portrayed with much greater complexity and intensity of feeling than is Barabas, a fact which might weigh on the side of seeing Shakespeare's play as an advance on the conventional view.[30]

* * *

The Merchant of Venice is constructed on a two-world principle. As we saw, *Dream* contrasts the disordered city to a forest world that is defined by forces sufficiently powerful to control and correct the disorder. *Romeo and Juliet* also has, in a sense, two worlds, that of the disordered city and the private world of the lovers. But the lovers have no escape from the disordered city, and therefore are left to the dark loneliness of their own love. In *Merchant*, the two-world principle is present in the aristocratic order of Belmont, associated with the transcendent values of a well-ordered polity, which is contrasted to the commercial world of Venice and its dedication to values that are associated with material gain. The structure of the action relates this conflict to the issues of love and marriage that center around Portia and the fairy-tale-like casket motif. As Holderness observes, though, "the two locations are not discrete societies but aspects of the same one: both are Venice, although in the one, merchants trade and Jews practice usury, while in the other, cultivated gentry enjoy the sophisticated leisure of their stable landed estates" (65).[31] In these different settings, Shakespeare toys with the idea of a lasting bond in ways that suggest all characters, whether in Belmont or Venice, are grappling with an "internal alien" with which they cannot quite come to terms.

In Belmont, Portia's dead father is framed as a benign, magical figure. From beyond the grave, he can ensure that his daughter will not only marry an appropriate man, but also a man whom she, as Nerissa says, "shall rightly love" (1.2.32). His will controls her marriage choice, just as Egeus and Capulet sought control over their daughters' marriage choices through, in another sense of the term, their wills. But in this fairy-tale world, the father is not portrayed as tyrannical and unreasonable, but rather as spiritually elevated. Accordingly Portia, as though aware of her father's more than natural powers, submits, somewhat unwillingly, to her father's will: "so is the will of a living daughter curbed by the will of a dead father" (1.2.23–25). The text, however, also makes it clear that though the marriage is to be a romantic one, it is not without material concerns.[32] These appear when Nerissa rebukes Portia for indulging her melancholy by reminding her of the abundance of her wealth, saying to her that she, too, would be weary of the world if her miseries were "in the same abundance as your good fortunes" (1.2.3–4). If one puts aside the fairy-tale aura, one can see Portia's father as like the head of a great family who was made all the more anxious by having only a daughter through whom to control the disposition of his wealth and the fate of his family.

With Portia's happy union with Bassanio attached to the casket device, the play reveals that married faith is multifaceted and layered. It results from a combination of an emotional bond and a financial contract and is achieved both by individual choice and by chance (or fate). We cannot positively assert where Bassanio's love is "begot" – is it Portia's wealth or her personal qualities that create his desire and his ability to make the right choice? Thus, the seemingly sincere joy the lovers feel when Bassanio picks the correct casket flows seamlessly into the language of value, currency, and contracts. Bassanio claims he won't believe his success until "confirmed, signed, ratified" by Portia (3.2.148), and in turn Portia wishes herself "a thousand times more fair" and "ten thousand times more rich" to be higher in Bassanio's "account" (3.2.154–5). The language of contract and value culminates with Portia's gift of the ring to Bassanio. She makes the terms of the contract explicit: "when you part from, lose, or give away, / let it presage the ruin of your love / And be my vantage to exclaim on you" (3.2.172–4). If Bassanio fails to maintain his faith, an emotional bond that is materialized in the ring, Portia has set out her recourse, her "vantage," enfolding Bassanio in a contract. What quickly follows is Gratiano expressing desire to marry Portia's maid Nerissa, a declaration he makes in "good faith" (3.2.210). Because a material contract encompasses but cannot regulate emotion, it is an inadequate measure of faith even if the contract is upheld in its strictest terms. Yet the emotion of love on its own seems a frighteningly unsecure guarantor of faith. The conflation of love with a contract highlights both the power and limits of both kinds of bonds.

Shakespeare emphasizes the limits of the feeling of love and its contractual counterpart when Gratiano and Salarino are surprised that Lorenzo is late for his departure with Jessica. Salarino observes cynically that "ten times faster Venus' pigeons fly / To seal love's bonds new made than they are wont / To keep obligèd faith unforfeited" (2.6.6–8). Sealing of the "bond" is eagerly sought, but "keeping" it that way it is another matter entirely. Love transforms, through the act of marriage, into something that is "obliged," with demands and pressures that Salarino expresses through the language of commerce. Shakespeare intimates that indulging a fancy is easy, but preserving good faith is difficult. Shylock is ridiculed by the Christians for keeping strictly to the terms of his bond with Antonio, especially since he cannot explain why he feels compelled to exact his due beyond its undeniable legality. But viewed in another light, his strict "faith" in that agreement, his stubborn vow to maintain that "obligèd faith," is what is valued when an *emotional* bond is made between two people. His version of faithfulness, despised by the Christians in the commercial setting, is precisely what the Christians value and test as they establish their marital relationships in Belmont.

The Christians create the façade that the bonds made in Belmont differ from the bonds made in Venice. The play, however, reveals the problems that arise when distinctions are made between the two places by subtly linking Belmont's traditional wealth to the despised money on which Venice depends. The material base of the play appears in sharper relief if one considers Bassanio's social position. That nothing overt is said about it suggests an impulse to obscure crass concerns, but some details allow us to flesh out the picture. Bassanio appears as an impoverished aristocrat when he says to Antonio, "I have disabled mine estate / By something showing a more swelling port / Than my faint means would grant continuance" (1.1.123–25). It is no wonder that Launcelot Gobbo prefers to work for the improvident Bassanio rather than the money-hoarding Shylock, but when shorn of the romantic glow, Bassanio does not appear so admirable. One can either think of him as the wastrel son of an impoverished aristocratic family, or as an improvident younger son who has lived beyond his means. In either case, in this social context the affection, or love, between Bassanio and Antonio is based on a trade-off whereby Antonio, in return for his money, gains "admiration and love" from the association with Bassanio. Bassanio "borrows" money from Antonio but gains wealth (in both senses) from Portia. In neither case does the material motive cancel the emotional one, but it makes them interdependent in a way that "disturbs" the romantic ideal.

Later Shylock will be the object of mockery as he conflates his runaway daughter Jessica with the money and jewels she has stolen to finance her defection from Shylock's house to become Lorenzo's wife and convert to Christianity. Shakespeare describes Shylock's reaction to this loss through Solanio's disdainful re-telling of it, claiming that Shylock, in "a passion so confused" wanders the streets of Venice saying "'My daughter! O, my ducats! O, my daughter! / Fled with a Christian! O, my Christian ducats!'" (2.8.15–16). He will be a more heinous version of the tyrannical father than Egeus or Capulet, but Portia's father's arrangement for her marriage conceals a similar conflation of daughters to ducats or marriage to money. This conflation appears in the detail of the casket device, wherein the leaden casket is associated with Portia, and the golden casket with the image of "carrion Death" (2.7.63).[33] That configuration on the face of it makes a radical separation between love and marriage and material considerations, but the underlying fusion of love and money appears in the association of Portia with the "golden fleece" (1.1.170). On the one hand, that image presages Portia's function as representative of spiritual gold, but the denied material desires appear when we consider that Portia is a material golden fleece for Bassanio, who seeks her partly in order to repay the debts he has already incurred in his quest for a rich wife. Bassanio's admiration for Portia, as he expresses it to Antonio, treads uneasily on the overlap between her spiritual and financial wealth. His first description of Portia is that she is "richly left" (1.1.161), and while he situates her worth in her beauty and nobility, his assessment of these qualities are that they are *valuable*. Portia's virtues are framed as a kind of currency with which Bassanio hopes to be rewarded. He admits that if he can present himself favorably, he will achieve "thrift" and be "fortunate" (1.1.175–6). Bassanio's words have double meanings. To ensure thrift is to be successful *and* be profitable, and to be fortunate is to be lucky *and* to possess wealth. It would indeed be Bassaio's good "fortune" in all senses of the words, if he can win Portia. Antonio picks up on the financial meaning of "fortune" when he reminds Bassanio immediately after this that his "fortunes are at sea" (1.1.177). The gold and the silver caskets are rejected because both are overtly associated with the coin that debases these otherwise symbolically significant metals, but Bassanio needs Antonio's money to win Portia, and Portia then needs money to bail out Antonio. The hidden link between Portia's wealth and Antonio's commerce emerges at the end of the play when, without explaining how she knows, she informs him that his ships have come in.

The conflict here between the noble and the commercial, the emotional and financial, is related to the social struggle in Shakespeare's time between traditional landed wealth and the newer wealth that accumulated from the circulation of money from one dirty hand to another. Bassanio's aristocratic blood is supposed to be revealed when he rejects "gaudy gold," which is the "seeming truth which cunning times put on / To entrap the wisest," and silver, which he dismisses as the "pale and common drudge / 'Tween man and man"

(3.2.100–04). This image stands in stark contrast to that of Portia as the golden fleece, but the spiritual significance of gold and the purity of romantic love are both called into question by the fact that Bassanio seeks both her and her wealth.

The value system of noble Belmont, one that values character and emotional sincerity over material wealth, is challenged because material wealth is necessary for the maintenance of emotional bonds; this challenge is expressed in the battle between the two figures who compete as the play's protagonists: Antonio and Shylock. They are, in a sense, each other's *alter ego*. Shylock represents the debased raw desire for money, unveiled by status or traditional noble insouciance. His possessiveness toward his daughter, his simultaneous loss of his daughter and of his ducats, and his explicit equation of the two – "My daughter, my ducats" – reveals what is hidden in the idealized world and quasi-magical world of Belmont, where Portia's magical father has succeeded in maintaining control of both his daughter and his ducats.

The mutual hatred of Antonio and Shylock expresses the radical incompatibility involved in the aristocratic self-deceptive attitude toward money. Just like Shylock, the merchant Antonio is involved in a money economy, but he is given an aura of nobility in being called the "royal merchant." This aristocratic veil over his mercantile activity appears in his unconcern about his own welfare as he risks himself for the young but impoverished nobleman Bassanio and in the strange melancholy that surrounds him. The melancholy has no overt explanation, but an analysis of the language and action reveals that it derives from the same kind of covert connection between love and money that appears in the casket motif. Just as the casket scene reveals anxiety that monetary concerns might contaminate love, so do Antonio's answers to his fellow merchants when they ask why he is melancholy. When they suggest that he is melancholy because he cannot cool his soup or go to church without bringing to mind the rocks upon which the winds might drive his ships, Antonio denies that all his wealth is at hazard. He also denies their suggestion that he grieves for Bassanio's imminent departure.

However, the action refutes both denials, for were all Antonio's wealth not at hazard he would have been able to finance Bassanio without making the bond with Shylock; and later, he would have been able to repay his debt to Shylock. And were he not grieving for Bassanio he would not later cast himself as competitor with Portia for Bassanio's love. He does so in the trial scene by using his predicament as a means by which to draw Bassanio away from Portia. He explicitly contrasts his self-sacrificing love to Portia's when he tells Bassanio to "[s]ay how I loved you, speak me fair in death; / And, when the tale is told, bid her be judge / Whether Bassanio had not once a love" (4.1.273–5). He again casts himself as Portia's rival when he urges Bassanio to part with Portia's ring, requesting that Balthazar's "deservings and my love withal / Be valued 'gainst your wife's commandement" (4.1.448–9). Love and money therefore are intimately connected, for Bassanio's need for money to win Portia and her great wealth drains Antonio's coffers, leaving him vulnerable to Shylock's animosity. It would seem that Antonio is so melancholy as to refer to himself as a "tainted wether of the flock" (4.1.114) because he cannot acknowledge that the primary way he expresses his love for Bassanio is by giving him money to court Portia.[34] He also cannot acknowledge that as a merchant who buys cheap and sells dear, he values money as much as does Shylock, whose love for money he despises.

The underlying similarity between the apparently opposite Shylock and Antonio emerges in other ways. Antonio cannot understand why he is melancholy. He admits that it makes him a "want-wit" and adds that in this state of confusion "I have much ado to know myself" (1.1.6–7). It may well be that Antonio is melancholy because he is suppressing something about himself he would not want to admit. Shylock is taunted for his conflation of his daughter with his ducats, but from the first scene, Antonio too conflates currency with emotional bonds without realizing he does so. Shylock's alliterative complaint that envelops personal and financial losses ("O, my ducats! O, my daughter!") is anticipated by Antonio's own alliterative pledge to Bassanio of financial support in the first scene. "My purse, my person, my extremest means," he says, "[l]ie all unlocked to your occasions" (1.1.138–9). "Purse" and "person" sound so similar and flow so easily together in his speech, that it is easy to imagine Antonio is, like Shylock, seeing the emotional and material commingle. Moreover, Antonio's claim that his "person" is "unlocked" to Bassanio is a hollow promise since he has already admitted he doesn't understand himself, and it raises the question of how he can open himself freely for another when he himself cannot understand what lies within. Antonio's self-deception expresses itself precisely in the moment he claims to be "open" (a word that crosses the idea of financial generosity with the idea of honesty or transparency) to Bassanio. Finally, in the representation of Antonio's person as a container that can be "unlocked," Shakespeare prefigures the casket scene, in which Bassanio unlocks the riddle and opens the correct casket, thereby winning Portia. Bassanio truly wishes to "open" Portia, rather than Antonio, and Antonio's offer of complete generosity seems in light of this, almost pathetic.

The similarity between the enemies also appears in the fact that both are in the end comforted only by wealth, about which they have similar things to say. When he faces death at Shylock's hands, Antonio considers himself lucky that at least he will not, like many others, outlive his wealth and "view with hollow eye and wrinkled brow / An age of poverty" (4.1.267–8). When Portia informs Shylock that his "goods" will be taken from him for conspiring to harm Antonio, Shylock says with great directness, "[y]ou take my house when you do take the prop / That doth sustain my house, You take my life / When you do take the means whereby I live" (4.1.373–5). Antonio escapes the final humiliation that Shylock suffers, but the play excludes Antonio, along with Shylock, from the comedic celebration of multiple marriages. To the end Antonio remains an isolated and melancholy figure. These hidden links between the two figures who are on the surface so radically opposed reveal that the Jew is not as alien to Venetian society as Venetian society pretends that he is. For while he is repudiated, he is also cast as the incarnation of the mercantile values that characterize the Venetian state, the laws of which are framed to protect mercantile interests and in which Antonio is king of merchants.[35]

The uneasy ambivalence toward liquid wealth upon which mercantile activity depends, in contrast to the solidity of landed wealth, appears as well when we follow out the human drama. The light that plays on Shylock will not remain steady. It isn't clear whether he makes the bond with Antonio because it makes financial sense, or because he hopes that Antonio's ship will not come in and afford Shylock the occasion to kill him. One can sympathize with Shylock when, even in the process of borrowing money, Antonio says "I am as like to call thee so [a dog] again, / To spit on thee again, to spurn thee too" (1.3.128–9), and one can understand when he explains to Antonio's fellow merchants that he hates Antonio because he has "disgraced me, and hindered me half a million, laughed at my losses, mocked at my gains, scorned my nation, thwarted my bargains, cooled my friends, heated mine enemies; and what's his reason? I am a Jew" (3.1.51–5). "Hath not a Jew / eyes?" (3.1.55–6) he demands, arguing that in the circumstances to want revenge is as normal as it is to die when poisoned or laugh when tickled. On the one hand, the play shows Antonio's gratuitous malice giving Shylock ample cause for hatred, while on the other, the image of Shylock cutting a pound of flesh makes almost everyone's flesh creep.

A similar ambivalent light plays around Portia's figure. At times, she is a model of feminine submissiveness, first to her father, and then to Bassanio. Furthermore, she seems an incarnation of redeeming compassion when she hastens to Antonio's aid, and when she appeals to Shylock for mercy, which "droppeth as the gentle rain from heaven" (4.1.183). She is, however, also controlling and tricky, and her emotional bond with Bassanio seems to come at the cost of his bond with Antonio. Berger Jr. calls her Antonio's "competitor in noble deeds" (35),[36] and, according to Coppélia Kahn, we can account for that competition by seeing in it an anxiety that men "must renounce their friendships with each other" when they marry (106). She calls Portia a "strong, shrewd woman" (107) who feels "threatened" by Bassanio's love for Antonio.[37]

Even though Maus cautions us that "there is no textual evidence that Portia resents Antonio" (89),[38] in getting Bassanio to give "Balthazar" the ring at the close of the courtroom scene, Portia carries on the implicit rivalry that Antonio had initiated by claiming that Portia's love for Bassanio could not match his own self-sacrificing love. The performative, staged nature of this moment, as she prepares to reveal her charade, once more demonstrates the triangular relationship between herself, Bassanio, and Antonio. She produces the ring that Bassanio had given away, and Antonio, desperate to save his friend once again, assures Portia that Bassanio will "never more break faith advisedly" and says he is willing to be "bound again" to prove this (253). In response, Portia passes the ring to Antonio to give to Bassanio. She tells Antonio, "you shall be his surety. Give him this / And bid him keep it better than the other" (254–5). This new "surety" replays the financial bond that tied Bassanio to Antonio. Whether or not we can prove that Portia resents Antonio, Shakespeare leaves their relationship at least symbolically knotted with the same emotional entanglements we first saw, with Bassanio, still running a deficit, still caught up in the middle.

And what of Portia's appeal to Shylock's mercy in the courtroom scene, her plea that he simply forfeit the bond? She might have accomplished Antonio's release without appealing to Shylock for mercy by revealing the Venetian law that condemns to death strangers who plot against a Venetian life. By this appeal, she toys with Shylock's thirst for revenge by giving him false hopes for victory. She speaks with deep compassion, but she behaves with a certain cruelty.[39] We might view her toying with Bassanio with her ring trick as another form of her cruelty, her desire to humiliate.

The courtroom scene brings together these various motifs and contradictions. Portia dressed as a young lawyer has the charm and wit of Shakespeare's early heroines. She orchestrates all of the complex action, as Shylock and Gratiano take turns in cheering her on. Mixed light plays on her as, in the name of mercy, she toys with Shylock's thirst for revenge, and mixed light plays on Shylock as he demands his pound of flesh, but points out that slave-holding Venetian aristocrats own whole men and do not sit down to dinner with them. The utter humiliation in which Shylock leaves cannot dramatically be cancelled out, even by the portion of his fortune that he will be allowed to retain. Garber quite rightly says that the "question of instability, of things turning into other things – comedy into tragedy, Christians into Jews and Jews into Christians, women into men and men into 'women,' Venice into Belmont and Belmont into Venice" (146) has been the point of the play all along.[40] Nowhere is this uncertainty more powerful or ironic than in the courtroom, a place where truth is supposed to be derived from two different accounts of the same event.

The union of Bassanio and Portia comes to a properly romantic and comic conclusion, but the play's end is haunted by a kind of uneasiness. The two principal male characters, Shylock and Antonio, are excluded from the comedic celebration; Shylock has retreated from the action in bitter humiliation at the end of Act 4, and Antonio, who will presumably be a welcome hanger-on in Bassanio and Portia's court, is still melancholy, terming himself "unhappy" (5.1.238) that his trial – and the loss of Bassanio's ring to Antonio's "lawyer" – has caused friction between Bassanio and Portia. Even the union of the four lovers has some uncomfortable undertones, as Portia and Nerissa taunt Bassanio and Gratiano with having slighted them by giving their rings away. Of course, it is all in fun, and it is funny, but the gigantic figure of Shylock, and all the disturbing resonances of the issues he raises about the basis of Belmont's happiness cast a shadow over the scene. The play clearly has a comic structure, but it is as though Shakespeare deliberately calls that comic structure into question through the overwhelming figure of Shylock, for whom there is no place in Belmont.

Notes

1 *Being and Having in Shakespeare*. Oxford: Oxford University Press, 2013.
2 *Shakespeare and Venice*. Burlington, Virginia: Ashgate, 2010.
3 "The Counterfeit Order of *The Merchant of Venice*." In *Representing Shakespeare: New Psychoanalytic Essays*. Eds. Murray M. Schwartz and Coppelia Kahn. Baltimore: The John Hopkins University Press, 1980. 54–69.
4 "Love in Venice" *Shakespeare Survey* 44 (1992): 41–53.
5 Charles Edelman writes that there is a "yearning, shared by all students of the play, to reconstruct somehow the first Shylock, about whom there is no reliable contemporary information whatsoever" ("Which is the Jew?" *The Cambridge Shakespeare Library: Shakespeare's Times, Texts, and Stages*. Ed. Catherine M. S. Alexander. Cambridge: Cambridge University Press, 2003. 444–451, 444).
6 *Shakespeare and Modern Culture*. New York: Anchor Books, 2008.
7 *Shakespearean Motives*. New York: Palgrave Macmillan, 1988.
8 New York: Riverhead Books, 1998.
9 John Gross. *Shylock: Four Hundred Years in the Life of a Legend*. London: Chatto & Windus, 1992. Gross writes that Edwin Booth's portrayal of Shylock in 1867 gave an "overall impression of evil," ultimately "denying Shylock even the right to be considered a human being" (124–125).
10 Actor Ian McDiarmid, who played Shylock, seems to brush aside any question of anti-Semitism in a 2014 interview: "Well of course it's not anti-Semitic, we wouldn't be doing it if it was" (Claire Allfree "Ian McDiarmid's Merchant of Venice" www.independent.co.uk. para. 1).
11 Halio, "Introduction," *The Merchant of Venice*. Oxford Shakespeare. Oxford: Clarendon Press, 1993.
12 Gross, *Shylock*.
13 Gross, *Shylock*. Dismissive of this production, Gross describes the "authentic" Jewish details like the *Kaddish* as ringing "particularly false" (303).
14 *Shakespeare and Outsiders*. Oxford: Oxford University Press, 2013.
15 *Shakespeare and Outsiders*. Novy suggests that audiences of Shakespeare's time would have been familiar with the trauma caused by religious persecution given Mary's attack on Protestants and, in turn, Elizabeth's attack on Catholics in the tumultuous years following the death of Henry VIII.

16 *Shakespeare and the Jewish Question.* Baltimore: Johns Hopkins University Press, 1997.

17 *Shakespeare and the Jewish Question.*

18 *Shylock is Shakespeare.* Chicago: University of Chicago Press, 2006.

19 James O'Rourke identifies racist and homophobic stereotypes in relation to Shylock and Antonio to argue that the play is an "antiracist response to the hanging" of Ruy Lopes ("Racism and Homophobia in *The Merchant of Venice*" *ELH* 70.2 (2003): 375–397. 375).

20 *A Fury in the Words: Love and Embarrassment in Shakespeare's Venice.* New York: Fordham University Press, 2013.

21 *A Fury in the Words.*

22 *Blood Relations: Christian and Jew in* The Merchant of Venice. Chicago: University of Chicago Press, 2008.

23 New York: Columbia University Press, 1996.

24 *Blood Relations.*

25 *Blood Relations.*

26 *A Theater of Envy.* Girard believes that if Shylock is "rehabilitated" at all from villainy, it is because "the Christians are even worse than he is" and "the 'honesty' of his vices makes him almost a refreshing figure compared to the sanctimonious ferocity of the other Venetians" (248). Garber says that the "now-current" reading that the Christians are "as bad as the play's Jews or worse, and that Shakespeare saw that and put it into his play – even if true doesn't really resolve the issue" that the play is worrying to us (*Shakespeare and Modern Culture*, 128).

27 *Christopher Marlowe: Renaissance Dramatist.* Edinburgh: Edinburgh University Press, 2008.

28 *Christopher Marlowe and the Failure to Unify.* Farnham, Surrey: Ashgate, 2015. Yaffe notes that Barabas "abandons all pretense of deferring to a standard of behavior beyond his own self interest as he sees it" (*The Jewish Question*, 38).

29 In comparing Marlowe to Shakespeare, Yaffe suggests "Marlowe's Machiavellian approach to the theologico-political situation of his Jewish character strikes one as inferior to Shakespeare's" (*The Jewish Question*, 35).

30 For more on Barabas and his differences from Shylock, see the chapter entitled "Where Does He Come from?" in Gross's *Shylock*.

31 *Shakespeare and Venice.*

32 In addition to troubling anti-Semitic elements, the play contains a troubling racist moment when Portia expresses relief that the dark-skinned Prince of Morocco is unable to win her. For more on this, see Ania Loomba's chapter "Religion, Money, and Race in *The Merchant of Venice*," in *Shakespeare, Race and Colonialism*. Oxford: Oxford University Press, 2002.

33 Freud, analyzing the casket scene, writes that there are "concealed motives" behind each suitor's decision on which casket to choose (*The Standard*

Edition of the Complete Works of Sigmund Freud. Trans. James Strachey. Vol. XII. London: The Hogarth Press, 1958. 291) and that the caskets are symbols of women. The suitors' ostensible ability to choose between them represents fate or death under the guise of life and choice. Belsey reads in the casket device what is essential about desire: "[r]iddles tease, torment, elude, challenge, and frustrate. Once the answer is known the riddle ceases to fascinate, just as desire evaporates once the otherness of the other is mastered" ("Love in Venice," 77).

34 Marianne Novy writes that Antonio pretends to a "self-effacement and self-sufficiency," but in the end cannot hide his "need for a mutuality of relationship" with Bassanio (*Love's Argument*, 68-9). In his negative view of Antonio's ostensible charity, Harry Berger Jr. describes Antonio as using "negative usury," which "consists of giving more than you take in a manner that makes it possible for you to end up getting more than you gave" (*Fury in the Words*, 29). Its aim, then, is to "embarrass the victims of donation by placing them under a moral debt they can't easily pay off" (29). He terms this strategy "mercifixion."

35 Novy writes that Antonio makes of Shylock the "double who shares and exaggerates his mercantile profession and marginal social status" (*Love's Argument*, 70).

36 *Fury in the Words*.

37 "The Cuckoo's Note: Male Friendship and Cuckoldry in *The Merchant of Venice*." In *Shakespeare's Rough Magic: Renaissance Essays in Honor of C.L. Barber*. Eds. Peter Erickson and Coppélia Kahn. Newark: University of Delaware Press, 1985. 104–112. While Yaffe describes the situation as a "love triangle" (52), he views Portia favorably overall. See also Edward J. Geisweidt, "Antonio's Claim: Triangulated Desire and Queer Kinship in Shakespeare's *The Merchant of Venice*." *Shakespeare* 5.4 (2009): 338–354; Steve Patterson, "The Bankruptcy of Homoerotic Amity in Shakespeare's *The Merchant of Venice*." *Shakespeare Quarterly* 50.1 (1999): 9–32.

38 *Being and Having*.

39 Novy notices the contradiction between Portia's wit and cruelty, writing that even though Portia falls "short by traditional standards of perfect charity, she succeeds by the standards of romantic comedy" (*Love's Argument*, 71). Yaffe, however, believes Portia pleads for Shylock's mercy because she wants to offer him "every possible opportunity to extricate himself from the harsh legal predicament" (*The Jewish Question*, 76).

40 *Shakespeare and Modern Culture*.

4

Richard II

Though it is commonplace to caution that one should not look to Shakespeare's plays for historical knowledge, one can overstate the caution, for though specific events are altered, the issues around which Shakespeare builds his dramas are the same issues that concern historians of the period – the legitimacy of succession, the contest between traditional sources of power and the rise of a new class of courtier, the problems of financing the crown and of consolidating the power of the monarchy, and the tenuous bond of duty that unites the King and his subjects. Shakespeare wrote ten plays we now consider the history plays, plays devoted to the representation of English history. The major series of such plays, the "second tetralogy," includes *Richard II, Henry IV* parts *1* and *2*, and *Henry V*, all of which were written between 1595 and 1599. The four plays tell the story of Bolingbroke's usurpation of his cousin Richard's throne, the problems he encounters as King when those who helped him to the crown want to overthrow him, his success in maintaining his power and passing it on to his son, who becomes Henry V, and Henry V's consolidation of the Lancastrian line.

The history plays are particularly interested in the disjunction between the King's belief in his role as God's substitute and his experience of his vulnerable body and a shifting, mutable identity that is anything but divine. Royal power in Shakespeare's time was believed to encompass but go well beyond the King himself – his body, his humanity. It was understood, as Peter Lake explains, that the "authority of the prince in his kingdom" was a "direct creation of God" (247) and "the royal person and will are embodiments of divine authority on earth" (248).[1] One way to conceptualize a human fulfilling a divinely ordained role was to imagine that that the King had two bodies – the natural, fallible body and the body politic, the latter being the divinely crafted, infallible state that outlived any one ruler. Yet, as Tim Spiekerman observes, the idea that kings have "divine authority" and an infallible body politic requires a "curious combination of the highest political principles with the lowest practical result" because, as *Richard II* demonstrates, it "becomes the basis for the most

Thinking About Shakespeare, First Edition. Kay Stockholder, revised and updated by Amy Scott.
© 2018 John Wiley & Sons Ltd. Published 2018 by John Wiley & Sons Ltd.

arbitrary and pernicious tyranny" (73).[2] Through the staging of Richard's politically unwise decisions, Shakespeare demonstrates that "royal power itself is dangerously unstable" (24) and is influenced by "human rules and precedents."[3] These issues were pertinent to the plays' original audiences, who would find in the chronicle materials as crafted by Shakespeare the images of contemporary political and personal concerns and uncertainties.[4]

Richard II has a double source of interest. As a history play, it involves us in the process by which the self-indulgence and histrionic posturing of Richard II plays into the hands of the usurper Bolingbroke. This layer of the play contrasts Richard's flamboyant character to the steady, astute, and somewhat mysterious character of Bolingbroke. The dramatic opposition between the two characters reveals that royal power is by no means divine or absolute, dependent as it partly is on the changeable affections and personal idiosyncrasies of individual men and women – of the King *and* the subjects whom he rules. The historical dimension of the play moves into a tragic realm as we follow the defeated Richard out of the battles and power struggles and into the privacy of his personal confrontation with his vulnerable body and his preparation for death.

Scholars continue to observe the irony that Richard himself becomes a compelling and tragic figure once Bolingbroke strips him of his royal power. There are, though, different interpretations of Richard's identity at the close of the play. Has he uncovered a primal identity that his kingship covered up or distorted? Has he discovered a new identity wholly separate from his previous one? Has he lost identity altogether and enacted a dissolution of his "self," thereby countering the idea that a static, essential "self" exists? For some readers, Richard's state of political powerlessness seems to be a prerequisite for his final self-knowledge and humanity.[5] Robert M. Schuler sees in Richard's contemplation of himself in the mirror at the end of the play a "courageous determination to confront his own moral being, his own demons" (152), by which he achieves an "eleventh hour redemption as a human being" (172).[6] Jonathan P. Lamb suggests that over the course of the play, Richard is "not losing but gaining a coherent sense of self in a movement to "Stoic personal empowerment" (124).[7] Katherine Eisaman Maus attributes the audience's fascination with Richard to his solitary and introspective presence at the end of the play, when he must "play all roles himself" (31). In her view, this state of "subjective complexity" (32) has the effect of making him as "theatrically fascinating" as Hamlet (30).[8]

Conversely, in a complex discussion of Richard's performativity as "messianic performance," Donovan Sherman suggests that Richard wants to "perform himself into occlusion, invisibility, even nonbeing" (30). He is, Sherman contends, a "bare body" (26) through which Shakespeare paradoxically enacts a "fantasy of total disembodiment" (44) and "radical self-abnegation" (48). Sherman contends that this occlusion parallels the process of theatricalization itself, which is "dependent on mobilizing forms" only to remind us that it is a "no-thing" (48).[9] John J. Joughin charts a middle road between Richard's being or nonbeing at the end of the play. He finds in Richard a "'self' hovering on the point of collapse as the unstable fiction that it "actually is" (para. 14) and one that paradoxically creates a "new found autonomy" (para. 15) in this self-conscious, "compulsive" need to tell us what he is not.[10] Joughin reads in Richard's words "paradoxical tropes of self-erasure *and* omniscience" (para. 19, my italics). These tropes help depict the experience of being a "bare body" – that is, a person stripped of all political power, and social entanglements, and human relationships. It is a state of utter isolation but one, perhaps, of new wisdom.

Lake sees Richard's performativity as a function of the role of divine authority because the King must "display" and "deploy" his "person and will" in "symbolically charged arenas of power" (248) in order to ensure his subjects endorse the fiction.[11] According to Lake, "Richard is shown to be both a past master at, and the prisoner of, this sort of monarchical performance" (248).[12] Because Richard is so "enamoured" of his "his image of himself as God's anointed," he "never sees his political circumstances as a result of his own mistakes" (250) and cannot, therefore, reverse the chain of events that lead to Bolingbroke's usurpation. Naomi Conn Liebler writes that rituals in the play, those acts of power that help a king "perform" his divine authority, have been "evacuated of meaning" (85).[13] Even if we read Richard's self-searching after he has been divested of the crown as his desperation to cling to "monarchical performance," there is no doubt that at this point, Richard has lost his original "arena of power." In light of shift, Richard's performative qualities – what they hope to accomplish and what they do indeed accomplish – are recalibrated.

Conn Liebler is undoubtedly right that Richard's character is never truly "resolved as preeminently negative" (85), nor is it easy to ascertain what kind of self Richard is left with at the end of the play. Shakespeare brings Richard back from the brink of nothingness and utter villainy by making the play's audience subjects of Richard's performative sway and making the theater itself the new "arena of power." In affording Richard "celebrated verbal puissance" (136)[14] at the end of the play, Shakespeare makes it possible us to transfer our loyalties from Bolingbroke to Richard, to see the play as Richard's tragedy even if we cannot forget he has also been its tyrant and a fool.

The shifting of our loyalties from Bolingbroke to Richard, and back again, simulates the transfer of power and loyalties from one King to another; indeed, the continual instability of loyalty is a persistent concern in Shakespeare's historical plays as a whole. One theory at the time of Shakespeare's writing was that historical events like the ones Shakespeare dramatized were part of a providential design: God "stepped in to discipline sinners and bestow blessings on the righteous and good" (2).[15] History, then, would serve as a record of God's "purposes and intentions" (2).[16] At the same time, early moderns also saw throughout history the continual rise and fall of kings on Fortune's wheel – a pattern modeled after Boccaccio's work *De Casibus Virorum*

Illustrium.[17] Shakespeare had already dramatized this cycle of rise and fall of kings in the *Henry VI* plays, which "had depicted the pattern of power seekers disobeying and being disobeyed, robbing and being robbed" (176).[18] In the second tetralogy, however, beginning with *Richard II*, as Paul Budra perceptively observes, Shakespeare "does not so much body forth the *de casibus* structure in its own form as reflect upon it" (82).[19] So too, this reflection also implicitly challenges the idea that the events of the past were part of God's plan to establish the Tudor dynasty. In *Richard II*, Shakespeare makes Bolingbroke the initial "avenger" of wrongs committed by an almost tyrannical King, but these same acts of vengeance are read as crimes in the *Henry IV* plays. The overall sense of Shakespeare's histories is that many men may have a claim to the throne, and the task of deciding which claim is the "true" or divinely ordained one is impossible. As Harry Berger Jr. points out, "no linear succession can descend or ascend, for the genealogical positions are continually being shuffled, exchanged, reoccupied in the Henriad's symbolic economy" (97).[20] The "shuffling" of both loyalties and claims to the throne allows Shakespeare to question the nature and extent of political power.

The beginning of *Richard II* introduces us to a double-layered drama with Bolingbroke's accusation that Mowbray was responsible for the death of the Duke of Gloucester, Richard's Uncle and York's brother. The first layer is that staged by Richard for his on-stage audience, and the second is the one that everyone on the stage, and presumably Shakespeare's original audience, knows to be going on behind the scenes. Bolingbroke's charge of treason against Mowbray, including the accusation that "he did plot the Duke of Gloucester's death" (1.1.100), is a covert bid to unsettle Richard, since it was widely known that Mowbray killed Gloucester on Richard's orders, a detail Gaunt makes explicit in the following scene when he discusses the Duke's murder with his widow. In this scene, Gaunt lays the blame squarely on Richard, connecting the role of king to God. "God's is the quarrel," he tells the Duchess, "for God's substitute, / His deputy anointed in His sight, / Hath caused his [Gloucester's] death; the which if wrongfully / Let heaven revenge, for I may never lift / An angry arm against His minister" (1.2.37–41). The effect of Gaunt's statement is to critique Richard – whose actions are hardly divine – at the same time that it also recognizes the powerlessness of those subjects who respect and fundamentally endorse the notion that the King is God's minister on earth. York will be one of those subjects trapped between his respect for Richard's God-given right to be King and his awareness that Richard has been financially incompetent and unjust to his subjects.

When it is clear to Richard that he cannot get either Bolingbroke or Mowbray to back down from their mutual challenge, he stages the elaborate trial by combat – one of those "arenas of power" – in which God is supposed to ensure that victory goes to the just.[21] While the play does not make Richard's motivation for this kind of resolution to the debate explicit, it is clearly designed to display his authority. Richard presents himself as above the argument, informing Mowbray that "impartial" are his "eyes and ears" (1.1.115); this elevated position above the fray helps Richard cultivate that impression that the King stands in for God. Richard resorts to the lists at Coventry, then, to stall for time and to display his divinely ordained power. Richard takes position over the combatants on a raised throne, descending only to bestow an embrace on Bolingbroke in a rather calculated bid to seem affectionate. In reality, it is not in Richard's interest for either man to win; should Mowbray win, and with Bolingbroke gone, Mowbray could constitute a threat to Richard. Furthermore, Richard would hardly want Bolingbroke to win if his challenge to Mowbray is a covert challenge to his own power. Therefore, it makes sense that he should make a display of his royal power in order to be rid of two potential enemies at one stroke. After Richard stays the lists and banishes the two men, Bolingbroke draws ironic attention to the association of Richard with God by echoing the Lord's prayer when he responds to his banishment, saying simply "[y]our will be done" (1.3.144). Presumably Richard then yields to Gaunt's plea for his son and shortens the length of banishment in order to placate him and to make a public display of mercy, that same calculated tenderness that brought him down from the throne to embrace Bolingbroke. But Richard's subsequent ruminations on Bolingbroke's popularity with the crowds and his speedy decision on Gaunt's death to seize Bolingbroke's lands suggest that he has plans to ensure that Bolingbroke never returned. The lists scene generates a deep irony that exposes the limits of kingly power, the wide gulf between the idea of the king as God and the reality of the king as a fallible human. The irony arises because Richard flamboyantly displays his power in the exercise of divine will and mercy that instead leads him to an experience of utter impotence at the hands of the very man that he hoped never to see alive again.

While the scene reveals a world of political machination that depends on the fragile sense that royal power is absolute, it also has wider and more emotional resonance. We see the suffering such power entails in Mowbray's moving speech on the loneliness of exile, "which robs my tongue from breathing native breath" (1.3.173), and when Gaunt reminds his monarch that even his power cannot forestall death, which Gaunt foresees will overtake him before his son returns, royal power is set in the wider context of life and death beyond all human control. All men and women, even the king, are subject to the limits of their mortal bodies. This commentary foreshadows the powerful tide of events that Richard has by his arbitrary action unleashed, and which will at the end carry him away. Gaunt reminds Richard, "[t]hou canst help time to furrow me with age, / But stop no wrinkle in his pilgrimage; / Thy word is current with him for my death, / But dead, thy kingdom cannot buy my breath" (1.3.229–32). So while Richard can use his royal power to end lives, death is ultimately more powerful than he in that the King cannot reverse time's effects, and he himself is subject to time's unwavering movement toward death.

Before depicting Richard's death, Shakespeare leaves us in no doubt that Richard is a bad King, personally vicious to the dying Gaunt who tries to reform him, as well as heedless of any effort to make him understand his Kingship as anything other than a means for personal gratification. With patriotic fervor, Gaunt contrasts the glories of old England, "this other Eden, demi-paradise" (2.1.42), to the horrors that follow from conceiving England's sacred land merely as a source of revenue, through leasing or sale as was common in Shakespeare's day, rather than as an inviolate trust.

It is this image of Kingship that Gaunt has in mind when, evoking England's former glory, he says that it "[i]s now leased out" (2.1.58), and says to Richard, "[l]andlord of England art thou now, not king" (2.1.113). In this accusation he raises an issue that was more pertinent to the time of the play's performance than to Richard's time. The historical divide is visible in the pejorative coloring he gives to the term "landlord," for the historical Gaunt would not have so used the term, and that the dramatic Gaunt does reveal the inroads commercial conceptions had made on traditional notions of landholding between Shakespeare's day and the time of which he writes. In a feudal, or pre-commercial, system of land tenure, the King was conceived of as lord of the land that comprised his country, just as nobles were lords of the land over which they presided, theoretically at the pleasure of the King. It is clear from Gaunt's use of the term not only that it has lost its traditional meaning, but that he no longer knows it. His use of it suggests instead a commercial relation in which a landowner no longer regards himself as divinely appointed to husband his land and to care for those who till its soil as a father looks after his children; the land has become instead a source of revenue, just as Richard regards his country. It is ironic that Shakespeare should have his idealized representative of an older order, in which landholding was conceived in analogy to the rights of a King over his kingdom, use the term "landlord" as a contrast rather than an analogue to a monarch. In having Gaunt condemn the loss of traditional values with a term the use of which illustrates, without his awareness, the very debasement that he deplores, Shakespeare subtly reveals the difference that had developed between his time and the older order to which he compares it.[22]

Richard's management of the country, his failure to control the nobles and satisfy the commoners, is critiqued in the garden scene in which the gardener gives orders to his underling to:

> Go bind thou up young dangling apricots,
> Which, like unruly children, make their sire
> Stoop with oppression of their prodigal weight.
> Give some supportance to the bending twigs.
> [*To the other.*] Go thou, and like an executioner
> Cut off the heads of too-fast-growing sprays
> That look too lofty in our commonwealth.

All must be even in our government. ...
You thus employed, I will go root away
The noisome weeds which without profit suck
The soil's fertility from wholesome flowers. (3.4.29–39)

As if the contrast between the old order and the new, the contrast between how Richard should rule and how he has ruled, were not sufficiently driven home, the gardener's man makes explicit the connection of an unweeded garden to a poorly managed kingdom by asking why they should "[k]eep law and form and due proportion" in their small estate:

When our sea-wallèd garden, the whole land,
Is full of weeds, her fairest flowers choked up,
Her fruit trees all unpruned, her hedges ruined,
Her knots disordered, and her wholesome herbs
Swarming with caterpillars? (3.4.43–7)

When the gardener later hears that Richard's favorites have been killed and Richard himself displaced by Bolingbroke, he laments that if Richard had "trimmed and dressed his land," he might have tasted the "fruits of duty" (3.4.56, 63). The gardener offers a clear critique of authority that fails to cultivate the bond between King and subjects.[23]

The garden allegory highlights the delicate balance the King must strike when protecting his power: the feeling of duty or loyalty that should preserve the King's power and the state's health by binding his subjects to him does not simply grow on its own; it must be groomed with just and affectionate treatment. Over the course of the play, the bond of loyalty is strained to its limits by Richard's mishandling of political and personal relationships. Duty toward the King is often described in the play as "tender." This word nicely illustrates the fragility of duty; like a new shoot, or a "dangling apricot," loyalty is not guaranteed to survive. With the word "tender," Shakespeare also indicates an emotional aspect of a subject's duty to his or her King. Loyalty requires a feeling of affection, often described in the play as the engagement of the heart, between the subject and the King. This more emotional connection is harder to define and control, and the play makes clear that Richard has failed to maintain that critical feeling of affection with those nobles who eventually wrest power from him.

In *Richard II*, the impermanence of dutiful bonds is ironically expressed in the character of Harry Percy, son to the Bolingbroke supporter Northumberland. The young Percy transfers his loyalty from Richard to Bolingbroke with impressive words:

My gracious lord, I tender you my service,
Such as it is, being tender, raw, and young,

> Which elder days shall ripen and confirm
> To more approvèd service and desert. (2.3.41–4)

Percy plays upon the idea of duty when he uses the word "tender" as a verb meaning "to offer" and then as an adjective meaning "youthful." He furthermore anticipates the gardener's metaphor in terming duty a young fruit that must be cultivated over time in order to mature and bring rewards. The deep irony of this delightful expression of duty is that Harry Percy will lead a rebellion against Bolingbroke as King in *1 Henry IV*.

While "tender" duty has emotional resonance, "tendering" a service has financial or legal implications. Once again, as in the *Merchant of Venice,* the overlap of emotional and contractual domains charts the limits of both. Richard's seizure of Bolingbroke's land after Gaunt's death depicts the power of material interests to erode the foundations of monarchy and the damaging effects of corruption on the rather fragile covenant of loyalty to which subjects of the King are sworn. There can be little less tender than Richard's ruthless seizure. The action turns on this point, for not only does Richard here give Bolingbroke an excuse to return to England to reclaim his birthright, he also enrages the nobles and prepares them to join Bolingbroke. The whole structure of the play can be seen to illustrate the moral York points when he cautions Richard:

> Take Hereford's rights away, and take from Time
> His charters and his customary rights;
> Let not tomorrow then ensue today;
> Be not thyself; for how art thou a king
> But by fair sequence and succession? (2.1.195–99)

York suggests that in claiming Bolingbroke's inheritance, Richard has undermined the very concept of succession upon which the state relies – and in doing so, he has undermined his own claim the throne. In a larger sense, the history plays reveal that "fair sequence and succession" depends, like concepts of truth or justice, on individuals' often shifting interpretations of the facts. As the tide of events turns against him, Richard's invocation of the principle of Divine Right is an illustration of the way in which such a belief can corrupt the mind of the King who holds it. Instead of turning his mind to the action the times require, Richard deceives himself about the gravity of the situation by assuming that God will protect him. The structure of the scene depicting Richard's return to England (3.2) emphasizes Richard's decline and turn inward, for just as Richard begins to attend to Aumerle's and Carlisle's hints that he ought to take action, Scroop comes with the news that Bushy and Green are dead. Richard once again sinks into his experience of defeat; he rallies briefly under the encouragement of his followers, only to resign himself completely when Scroop gives him a final blow with the news of York's defection.

This structure also gives us a double view of Richard, for we first see his self-dramatizing nature as the tides of bad news roll in, but by the time Richard closes the scene with, "[d]ischarge my followers. Let them hence away, / From Richard's night, to Bolingbroke's fair day" (3.2.217–18). It is clear that the game is up, and would be even if Richard were not inclined to wallow in sad tales. Though his stance is self-defeating, when Richard reflects on the limitations of kingly power in relation to death, he carries forward the theme that Gaunt initiated. His words simultaneously show his self-reflection and function as a commentary on the entire action:

> ... For within the hollow crown
> That rounds the mortal temples of a king
> Keeps Death his court, and there the antic sits,
> Scoffing his state and grinning at his pomp,
> Allowing him a breath, a little scene,
> To monarchize, be feared, and kill with looks,
> Infusing him with self and vain conceit,
> As if this flesh which walls about our life
> Were brass impregnable. (3.2.160–168)

Richard now uses his characteristic self-dramatization to understand his own relation to his role, and to come to terms with the difference between his mortal human body and his image of that body as the immortal body politic. The closer Richard comes to defeat, the more interesting and dignified a figure he becomes. He no doubt accepts defeat too easily, but he knows exactly what is going on; he calls a spade a spade, and is not deceived by Bolingbroke's assurances that he has returned to England only for his inheritance. Perhaps the most telling exchange between the two men occurs when Richard has, like "the blushing discontented sun" on "his bright passage to the occident" (3.3.63, 67) descended from the balcony to the base court. Richard asks Bolingbroke, "[s]et on towards London, cousin, is it so?" and to his "[y]ea, my good Lord" responds, "[t]hen I must not say no" (3.3.208–10). There is a perfectly clear understanding between the two men, and though Richard in part brought his defeat upon himself, in defeat he acts with both dignity and self-understanding. He may have been close to whining as he felt the turn of events undermining his power base, but he does not do so once it is gone.

The drama of Richard's struggle to understand his identity when stripped of his social role continues through the deposition scene (4.1). Once again, his speeches are self-dramatizing and inward-turning, as though he is audience to his own story, but his self-absorption at the same time probes at the mystery of the relation of his person to the role he plays. As he reflects upon himself in the process of giving up the crown and breaks his "brittle" mirror image, he earns Bolingbroke's mocking comment that Richard's grief seems just a show of real sadness: "The shadow of your sorrow hath destroyed / The shadow of your face" (4.1.293–4). Yet it is precisely through his theatrical reflections on his condition that Richard also finally acknowledges the widening gulf between his body natural and his body politic. At this point in the play, Richard becomes, as Sherman effectively puts it, "an irreducible irritant of tangibility chafing against the symbolic fabric of his surroundings" (27).[24] This process continues as, imprisoned in Pomfret Castle after his deposition, he meditates on the same subjects, struggling to find some firm ground on which to rest, and encountering himself as "nothing" beneath all the roles his imagination can generate. Through this meditation on the hollowness of his royal role, Richard reaches his body's truth and a much deeper understanding of his dependence on others' to maintain his power. Before he murders Richard, Exton recounts hearing Richard say "[h]ave I no friend?" twice (5.4.4). Exton's revelation is followed by Richard's contemplation on his imprisonment, where, in his loneliness, he imagines the prison as a world and his thoughts as people in the world. But these thoughts, he discovers are "[i]n humours like the people of this world, / For no thought is contented" (5.5.10–11). At the point when Richard turns most inward and is most alone, he reveals a heretofore absent understanding that unpredictable and changeable forces, defined as people's "humours," can serve as engines of action. In *imagining* a kingdom and peopling it from within himself, he gives up any claim he once had to royal power over real people, understood as superior to his subjects because derived from God. He may have created this kingdom, but it is a "scene of disappearance" (44).[25]

Finally, Richard shifts to another metaphor for his mind and body; he imagines his mind as a recorder of time: "[m]y thoughts are minutes, and with sighs they jar / Their watches on unto mine eyes, the outward watch / Whereto my finger, like a dial's point, / Is pointing still in cleansing them from tears" (5.5.51–5). He demonstrates a heightened and self-aware sensation of grief, allowing his experience of the world and time's passage to dwell within and overlay his natural body. It is not just that he understands he is subject to time, but rather that he sees his body *as* time, an imagined fusion that signifies a complete acknowledgment of the mortality and humanity he had denied and repressed when he was King. When he suspects he will be poisoned moments later, Richard suddenly turns on his keeper and, however futilely, fights for his life as the murderers come to kill him.

This richly elaborated drama of Richard's self-consciousness renders him a polar opposite to Bolingbroke, about whose interior life we know almost nothing. By having Bolingbroke remain equally opaque to both his off- and on-stage audiences, Shakespeare lets us know what it feels like to deal with such a person. Like a true Machiavellian, Bolingbroke keeps his own counsel.[26] It might be that his challenge to Mowbray constituted his first bid for kingship; he might have had that in mind from the time he returned with an army, or he might have decided to take the crown once Richard came down from the balcony.

The point is that we do not know, but we do know that the fiction of his demanding only his birthright provides the defecting nobles with the excuse they need to join his party. Richard loquaciously expresses his inner state, while Bolingbroke silently waits, listens, courts popular support, and gauges the realities of power. The difference between the two men is most marked by the contrast between the judgment scene staged by Richard, and the one over which Bolingbroke presides in cool silence while Aumerle and Fitzwater accuse each other of treachery and throw down their gages in challenge. Bolingbroke sidesteps the entire issue by saying that he will settle it after he has recalled Mowbray, and the whole issue of Gloucester's death evaporates when Carlisle announces that Mowbray has died.

While this action raises questions about the nature of kingship and the basis of its legitimacy, it also represents the crisis of loyalty such perturbations among the great entail for those beneath them. This issue is articulated most graphically in the figure of York and his relation to his family. Of all the nobles, York is the most loyal to Richard, as well as the most outspoken in his criticism, and in this he is the perfect courtier. Richard's careless arrogance is nowhere more pointedly depicted than when Richard designates York as his substitute upon his departure for Ireland. York warns Richard that if he "wrongfully seize[s] Hereford's rights" then he will "lose a thousand well-disposèd hearts," and York's own "tender patience" will also suffer (2.1.201, 207). Richard ignores York's fulsome condemnation and immediately places his power in the hands of the very man who has just admitted his loyalty is wavering. He "creates" York the Governor in his absence, reasoning that York is "just" and has always "loved" Richard (2.1.221). Richard fails to understand that it is precisely York's sense of justice that makes him break faith, however slowly and reluctantly, with his King. Richard both ignores York and takes his fidelity for granted, failing to understand that York's "tender" duty must be cared for – in acknowledging his objections at the very least. Fiercely committed to the duty he owes Richard as King, York condemns those who forsake Richard even while he feels that Bolingbroke has justice on his side. He rebukes Bolingbroke for breaking his vow by returning to England, but reveals his divided mind when he says that he would, if he could, make Bolingbroke and his party "stoop / Unto the sovereign mercy of the king" (2.3.156–57), but that since he is powerless, he will "remain as neuter" (2.3.159). However, a moment later he invites Bolingbroke to spend the night at Berkeley castle, in effect, turning it over to him. That is as close as we come to seeing the moment at which York transfers his loyalty and violates his announced principle of fidelity to his King.[27]

Shakespeare here raises the question of whether subjects are obligated to be loyal to the King no matter what his actions, for York believes that he owes his loyalty to the crown despite Richard's grievous faults. But loyalty to the crown entails loyalty to the man who wears it, and after a certain point Richard clearly no longer does. The play does not provide a solution to this problem, but it does represent the psychological consequences that follow from it, for York acts like a guilty man when he pleads with Bolingbroke, now Henry IV, to execute his son, Aumerle, for having taken part in a plot to reinstate Richard. Shakespeare also shows the divisive effects of public conflicts on private life when York vies with his wife to dissuade the King from granting Aumerle mercy. In pardoning Aumerle, Henry acts rationally, for he thereby wins his loyalty, but, as usual, we do not know his motives. He might pardon Aumerle from a merciful impulse, or he might do so as a clever political act that would win him with little cost a loyal ally and gain him a reputation for mercy. On the whole Henry seems inclined to kill as few people as possible, but he seems to have taken a page from Machiavelli's book when he hints to Exton that he would be happy to be rid of Richard, and then repudiates him for obliging. The play closes with Henry's lament for Richard's death, but Richard's death secures Henry's hold on the throne, and allows him to appear suitably mournful in public as he follows Richard's "untimely bier" (5.6.52). Furthermore, as we will see at the opening of *1 Henry IV*, the trip to the holy land that Henry proposes in order to wash off the guilt of usurping the throne also has a quite pragmatic function as a means by which to divert the attention of discontented subjects.

Richard II counterpoints Bolingbroke's cunning efforts to secure his power with Richard's descent into personal tragedy. While we are given no reliable glimpse of Bolingbroke's inner state, we are invited into the depths of Richard's struggle to understand his own identity, and to come to terms with the realization that he is merely human and mortal, that his body natural is distinct from what was his body politic:

> Sometimes am I king;
> Then treasons make me wish myself a beggar,
> And so I am. Then crushing penury
> Persuades me I was better when a king;
> Then am I kinged again, and by and by
> Think that I am unkinged by Bolingbroke,
> And straight am nothing. But whate'er I be,
> Nor I, nor any man that but man is,
> With nothing shall be pleased till he be eased
> With being nothing. (5.5.32–41)

Richard's experience of his own mortality, and of the sense of nothingness that lies beneath all roles and public action, casts ironic light on the grandeur that had once been his, and that now is Henry's. It is ironic, too, that Richard's willingness to probe to the bottom of his sense of selfhood prepares him to die fighting – simply for his life rather than for the crown.[28] In other plays, we will find different versions of this meditation on the shifting sands of human identity that underlie the seeming solidity of the political world, as well as on the sheer love of being alive, most powerfully illustrated by Falstaff.

Notes

1 *How Shakespeare Put Politics on the Stage: Power and Succession in the History Plays.* New Haven: Yale University Press, 2016.
2 *Shakespeare's Political Realism: The English History Plays.* Albany: State University of New York Press, 2001. See also Ingy Aboelazm, "A Poised Crown: Rival Monarchs in *Richard II.*" *Interactions* 23.1–2 (2014): 1–12.
3 Katherine Eisaman Maus. *Being and Having in Shakespeare.* Oxford: Oxford University Press, 2013.
4 Much critical attention has been directed to the commission of a performance of a play called *Richard II* (possibly Shakespeare's play) in February 1601. The commissioners were purportedly the followers of the Earl of Essex, who staged an unsuccessful uprising against Queen Elizabeth the following day. Presumably the followers viewed Elizabeth as Richard II and Essex as Bolingbroke and meant to stir up support for their rebellion. See Paul Hammer, "The Smiling Crocodile: the Earl of Essex and Late-Elizabethan 'Popularity.'" In *The Politics of the Public Sphere in Early Modern England.* Eds. Peter Lake and Steven Pincus. Manchester: Manchester University Press, 2007. 95–115; Jonathan Bate, *Soul of the Age: A Biography of the Mind of William Shakespeare.* New York: Random House, 2009; Alexandra Gajda, *The Earl of Essex and Late Elizabethan Political Culture.* Oxford: Oxford University Press, 2012.
5 Irving Ribner says that "Richard's downfall as a king leads to his regeneration as a man" (*Patterns in Shakespearean Tragedy.* London: Methuen, 1960. 46).
6 "Magic Mirrors in Richard II." *Comparative Drama* 38.2/3 (2004): 151–181.
7 "The Stylistic Self in *Richard II.*" *Medieval and Renaissance Drama* 28 (2015): 123–151.
8 See John J. Joughin: "In many respects, the dramatic prototype for Hamlet is already drawn in Shakespeare's *Richard II* and, unsurprisingly perhaps, critics are frequently attracted to Richard and Hamlet in a similar vein, often again in terms of plotting the emergent subjectivity of each, a condition which Richard casts in terms roughly analogous to Hamlet" ("The Inauguration of Modern Subjectivity: Shakespeare's 'lyrical tragedy' *Richard II,*" Revue Electronique sur le Monde Anglophone 2.2 (2004): 22–34. para. 6).
9 "'What more remains?': Messianic Performance in *Richard II.*" *Shakespeare Quarterly* 65.1 (2014): 22–48.
10 "The Inauguration of Modern Subjectivity."
11 *How Shakespeare Put Politics on the Stage.*
12 *How Shakespeare Put Politics on the Stage.*
13 *Shakespeare's Festive Tragedy: The Ritual Foundations of Genre.* London: Routledge, 1995.
14 Lamb, "Stylistic Self."

15 Alexandra Walsham. *Providence in Early Modern England*. Oxford: Oxford
   University Press, 1999. One notable reading of Shakespeare's history plays as
   contributors to an idea of providential design (the idea that the course of
   human history was leading to the establishment of the Tudor dynasty) is E.M.
   Tillyard's *The Elizabethan World Picture*. As James N. Loehlin notes, however,
   "[m]any critics have argued that Shakespeare [...] took a more complex and
   multi-vocalic view of medieval history than the providential view" (*Henry IV:
   Parts I and II*, Houndmills: Palgrave Macmillan, 2008). For a description of
   these competing interpretations of Shakespeare and the Tudor myth, see
   Phyllis Rackin's *Stages of History: Shakespeare's English Chronicles*. Ithaca:
   Cornell University Press, 1990, pages 40–85.

16 *Providence in Early Modern England*.

17 For more on this tradition, see Paul Budra, *A Mirror for Magistrates* and the
   de casibus Tradition. Toronto: University of Toronto Press, 2000.

18 Schuyler, "Magic Mirrors."

19 A Mirror for Magistrates *and the de casibus Tradition*. As Jan Kott observes,
   in *Richard II*, we can read the seeds of a "new tragedy" that the *Henry IV* plays
   depict (13). Once he becomes Henry IV, Bolingbroke's acts of "vengeance" are
   read instead as crimes that stir another generation of rebels to seek vengeance.
   In *Richard II*, Kott says "[t]he cycle has been completed" and at the same time,
   "[t]he cycle is beginning again" (*Shakespeare Our Contemporary*, 13).

20 "Hydra and Rhizome." In *Shakespeare Reread: The Texts in New Contexts*.
   Ithaca: Cornell University Press, 1994. 79–104.

21 For a description of the meaning and use of the trial by combat ritual, see
   Conn Liebler, *Shakespeare's Festive Tragedy*, 61.

22 John Gillies discusses the degradation of a "transcendental order of value" of
   property to a "purely mercenary" one in relation to *Richard II* and several
   other plays ("The Scene of Cartography in King Lear." In *Literature, Mapping,
   and the Politics of Space in Early Modern Britain*. Eds. Andrew Gordon and
   Bernhard Klein. Cambridge: Cambridge University Press, 2001. 109–137.

23 Conal Condren argues that the gardener describes an ideal form of
   government, but the play never enables the audience or reader to confirm
   whether this is the correct view of government and rule ("Skepticism and
   Political Constancy: *Richard II* and the Garden Scene as a 'Model of State'."
   The Review of Politics 78.4 (2016): 625–643.

24 "Messianic Performance."

25 "Messianic Performance." Maus makes a similar point that "the conditions for
   self-realization are also the conditions in which the self cannot, apparently,
   exist" (*Being and Having*, 32).

26 See Irving Ribner, "Bolingbroke, a True Machiavellian." *Modern Language
   Quarterly* 9.2 (1948): 177–84. See also Spiekerman, *Shakespeare's Political
   Realism* (especially pages 60–69).

27 Robert Ornstein calls York an "odd specimen of Tudor orthodoxy" and says that in *Richard II* we see the "enormous difficulty" of "political loyalty" (*A Kingdom for a Stage* excerpted in *Richard II: Critical Essays*. ed. Jeanne T. Newlin. London: Routledge, 1984).

28 Martha Tuck Rozett says that at this moment, Richard becomes "an actively heroic figure for the first time in the play" (*The Doctrine of Election and the Emergence of Elizabethan Tragedy*. Princeton: Princeton University Press, 1984. 288).

5

The *Henry IV* Plays

1 Henry IV is structured around the convergence of three distinct plot lines that interrelate under the umbrella of a fourth. The three plots are the struggle between King Henry and the conspirators against his rule, the conspirators' manipulation and fatal abandonment of the young Hotspur, and the comic story of Falstaff, which for many becomes less comic as he moves from the tavern to the battlefield. The fourth plot line involves Hal's relation to Falstaff, to his father the King, and to the realms of power. These multiple plot lines give the play an entirely different feel from the more concentrated *Richard II*, but, like the earlier play, *1* and *2 Henry IV* also raise urgent questions concerning the nature of the bonds that hold subjects faithful to a King and the forms of affection that ensure friends and relatives are loyal to each other. The plays also stress that although the King's power seems to dominate his subjects from the top down, his power is also dependent on others, built as it is on the idea of exchange – exchange of one King for another through succession, exchange of favors to mollify supporters, and exchange of shame for honor in the case of Henry's son Hal. Finally, they add a new dimension by pitting the Elizabethan concept of idealized and abstract honor against a earthy physicality and realism. This conflict works to further develop the existential concerns that emerge at the end of *Richard II*.

The serious business of history as represented in *1* and *2 Henry IV* has a public and a personal side, the latter being primarily and, perhaps surprisingly, comic. I will consider the serious public issues first. These concern the disputes that follow Henry's ascension to the throne and the efforts of the disaffected to take it from him. Just as Carlisle and others had predicted in *Richard II*, dissension does indeed follow from Henry's usurpation of King Richard. While many characters interpret the wars that follow as a sign of God's displeasure with usurpers, as those who predicted them did, the play also encourages us to see such dissension from a Machiavellian perspective as an inevitable consequence of gaining a throne by depending on others' often fleeting sense of loyalty.

The fragility of the bond between King and subject is raised at the play's beginning when Henry says that "majesty might never yet endure / The moody

Thinking About Shakespeare, First Edition. Kay Stockholder, revised and updated by Amy Scott.
© 2018 John Wiley & Sons Ltd. Published 2018 by John Wiley & Sons Ltd.

frontier of a servant brow" (1.3.18–19). Henry realizes that to be a King, one must retain control over unpredictable and emotional individuals whose sense of affection for him will necessarily change once he is in a position to command them; in the seemingly unavoidable deterioration of affection for the King once he begins to view his subjects as "servants," those who helped make him attain the kingship begin to resent his ascendancy over them. Both parties to the dispute know this, and the knowledge lies behind the play's opening in which we see Henry in the midst of making a political speech. After creating an elaborate image of the horrors of civil wars and of the blessings of peace to follow, he reiterates his promise to launch a crusade to the Holy Land. This project is apparently jeopardized when Westmorland announces that Mortimer has been taken by Glendower, and, worse, that Hotspur has won a battle against the Scots but refuses to turn over his prisoners to the King. Upon hearing this news, Henry says that "[i]t seems then the tidings of this broil" at home (1.1.47) must suspend his crusade to the Holy Land. But this show of Henry's devotion to the crusade and his seemingly spontaneous decision at the news that the crusade must be postponed has been staged by him and his cronies, a fact that is revealed when Henry says that he has *already* sent for Hotspur to answer the charges against him. From the outset of the play, we are fully in the political world of power, deception, and strategic manipulation; we should keep this in mind when we assess the character of Prince Hal.

The serious personal business of the play centers on Hotspur. From the very first he is set apart from the other conspirators by Henry's admiration for his noble, warlike virtues, which Henry contrasts to the profligate ways of his own son, Prince Hal. Upon hearing of Hotspur's martial accomplishments from Westmoreland, Henry laments:

> Yea, there thou mak'st me sad, and mak'st me sin
> In envy that my lord Northumberland
> Should be the father to so blest a son –
> A son who is the theme of honor's tongue,
> Amongst a grove the very straightest plant,
> Who is sweet Fortune's minion and her pride,
> Whilst I, by looking on the praise of him,
> See riot and dishonor stain the brow
> Of my young Harry. O, that it could be proved
> That some night-tripping fairy had exchanged
> In cradle clothes our children where they lay,
> And called mine Percy, his Plantagenet!
> Then I would have his Harry, and he mine. (1.1.77–89)

This fanciful aside from Henry's main preoccupation in the scene picks up themes from *Richard II* and extends them. In praising Hotspur for being the "straightest" plant, Henry means that one should not deviate from the natural course of growth, a detour that Hal glories in when, as the Prince of Wales, he spends more time in the tavern than in Henry's court. The metaphor uses the natural world to explain human character, much in the way that the garden serves as a metaphor for political management in *Richard II*. In this speech, Henry furthermore introduces the crucial idea of exchange, or transfer. He wishes that Hotspur and Hal could have been switched at birth, and extending this idea, as the play unfolds, characters insist that Hal must exchange his shame for Hotspur's honor in order to correct the deviation in his growth and himself become the "straightest plant" in the grove; both men cannot flourish together. The restoration of Hal's honor, which has been languishing due to his association with Falstaff, requires that he triumphs over Hotspur and *takes* his honor.[1] Henry notes that Hal and Hotspur are two sides of the same coin when he remarks that they are both named "Harry." Exchange, ideally, is an act in which items of equal value change hands. And while Hal and Hotspur do share the same first name, while Hal does eventually see himself as taking Hotspur's honor, the play shows that a exact bond, equality between people, is an impossible ideal.

In a wider sense, the scene turns on an exchange of another kind: of the transfer of political prisoners from Hotspur to the King. Hotspur refuses to give to Henry the prisoners he has won in battle. When summoned to the King, Hotspur reveals that he will only turn over the prisoners if Henry frees Hotspur's imprisoned brother-in-law Mortimer. Henry reacts badly to the idea that he should negotiate, as if on equal terms, with his subject, or his "servant," and the entire "broil" leads to the full-blown rebellion.

Hotspur's role as a noble enemy is maintained throughout the scenes that show us the conspiracy, for Hotspur's motives are clearly distinguished from those of his elders (not, of course, that he is cast in a stereotypical heroic mold).[2] Hotspur's general obstreperousness and impetuous ardor in the quest for martial honor render him an admirable if humorous figure, and, then, as Northumberland and Worcester capitalize on Hotspur's naive nobility to manipulate and then betray him, he begins to acquire shades of tragic grandeur. Faithful to a somewhat feudal conception of honor, Hotspur feels demeaned both by his kinsmen's betrayal of Richard and by their humiliation in the face of Henry's assertion of his regal prerogative. Even though Hotspur joins their conspiracy, his outrage at their violation of family honor protects his figure from the obloquy that besmirches them. Shakespeare fills out this complex character by including scenes of both loving banter with his wife and eloquent camaraderie with "the Douglas." Hotspur's ardent loyalty make him an excellent second in command, but his lack of the more calculating skills do not suit him for leadership.

Hotspur's devotion to the feudal idea of honor is sincere, but Shakespeare suggests that because it suppresses the physical reality of his bodily needs, it comes at a cost. The first indication that Hotspur will be betrayed comes early when he reads a letter from an unknown person who writes that he is withdrawing from the campaign and warns him of more impending desertions. Undaunted by this warning, and confident in the support of Mortimer, Glendower, and Douglas, Hotspur easily dismisses "such a dish of skim milk" (2.3.32). This bold confidence does not come as easily as Hotspur makes it seem, though, as his wife Kate reveals. She comes upon him after he has read the letter and asks, "[t]ell me, sweet lord, what is't that takes from thee / Thy stomach, pleasure, and thy golden sleep? / Why dost thou bend thine eyes upon the earth / And start so often when thou sit'st alone? / Why hast thou lost the fresh blood in thy cheeks" (2.3.39–43). The letter's business may be a "dish of skim milk," but it turns out that Hotspur, having lost his appetite, does not have the stomach for anything. Kate then reveals that when he does fall into "faint slumbers" (2.3.47), Hotspur speaks agitatedly in his sleep about the political chaos. Kate brings to life a touchingly vulnerable Hotspur, his body betraying the signs of anxiety that his character's devotion to honor and heroism will not permit him to express. Here we see the battle between elevated ideals and base realities play out on the body of the play's noble enemy. Unlike Hal, Hotspur refuses to indulge in bodily comfort, so committed is he to the pursuit of his ideals.

To deepen the pathos of Hotspur's impending fate, Shakespeare then gives us an intimate glimpse into Hotspur's marriage. Hotspur deprecates Kate's "womanly" curiosity in conventional ways, claiming he doesn't love her when she pleads to be informed about the military actions he has in the works. He is, in keeping with his warrior values, a macho husband, and he puts his love for her second to the business of war and honor, but he clearly has an intimate and affectionate relationship with his wife, engaging in witty wordplay with and being addressed as "you paraquito" by Kate (2.3.85). Even her complaints sustain the scene's warm tone:

> Do you not love me? Do you not, indeed?
> Well, do not, then, for since you love me not
> I will not love myself. Do you not love me?
> Nay, tell me if you speak in jest or no. (2.3.96–99)

Though he remains adamant that women are not to be trusted with secrets, the scene concludes with his declaration to keep Kate by his side: "Whither I go, thither shall you go too. / Today will I set forth, tomorrow you" (2.3.114–15). In their last scene together (3.1), Hotspur has his head in Kate's lap, while their friendly sparring continues. It is almost as if he is seeking physical comfort from Kate even as he denies that he requires or indeed values it.

Hotspur's exchange with Douglas at the opening of the scene that depicts the turn of his fortunes adds to the poignancy of these expressions of affection in the context of the coming tragedy. Hotspur defies those who might think that he flatters Douglas in praising his courage, and says "a braver place / In my heart's love hath no man than yourself" (4.1.7–8), to which Douglas responds, "[t]hou art the king of honor" (4.1.10). Though Hotspur pushes aside his body's frailties, as his defeat in battle looms he is haunted by the idea that mortal bodies are indeed vulnerable. The first announcement is that Northumberland, Hotspur's father, cannot join the battle because he is ill, and no one else has been appointed to lead his forces. We will find out in the prologue of *2 Henry IV* that Northumberland was in fact "crafty-sick" (37). His betrayal of his own son is especially appalling in that, as his letter makes clear, he knows that the King's awareness of the plot makes it impossible for Hotspur to withdraw. Hotspur is distressed, saying that his father's illness "doth infect / The very life-blood of our enterprise" (4.1.27–28), but his optimism – or desire to ignore the limits of his capabilities – soon reasserts itself when he says that his forces will benefit from his father's absence, for now they will not be risking all "on the nice hazard of one doubtful hour" (4.1.48). His confidence is no sooner restored than Vernon brings news that the King's already sizable forces have been swelled by the addition of those following Prince Hal. Once again he is daunted, the imagery of illness reappearing when Hotspur, commenting on Vernon's glowing description of Prince Hal in arms, says that "[w]orse than the sun in March / This praise doth nourish agues" (4.1.111–112). However, as before, Hotspur glosses over his feeling of sickness by evoking the images of war on which he thrives and by reflecting on the glorious victory that awaits him. Finally, he is told that Glendower will not come. For the first time the wellsprings of Hotspur's copious words go dry, and his only response is to ask, "[w]hat may the King's whole battle reach unto?" (4.1.129). His heroism acquires a sober dignity when, no longer heedless of danger, he dismisses the answer to his question and says, "[c]ome, let us take a muster speedily. / Doomsday is near; die all, die merrily" (4.1.133–34). He doesn't whine; he doesn't complain; and now he doesn't deceive himself. He goes into battle with full knowledge of the odds, and without demur follows through on his early promises, however hot-headed or unwise they were. Later in the play, as Hotspur languishes in the grips of impending death after Hal defeats him, he clings to this tragic heroism. The "proud titles" Hal won from him, he says, "wound" his thoughts "worse than [Hal's] sword [his] flesh" (5.4.79–80). Hotspur's courage and his relentless pursuit of honor, which suppress the evidence that his physical body is indeed vulnerable, give tragic depth to this inevitable defeat.[3]

Hotspur's refusal to wallow in physical pain, even at the point of death, contrasts sharply with Falstaff's commitment to comfort even as he moves from tavern to battlefield. These two are developed with near-perfect symmetry. The difference between Hotspur's life of high enterprise and Falstaff's life of self-indulgent pleasure emerges at that early moment in the first scene when Henry IV laments that his son is not Harry Hotspur, whose martial reputation brings him honor, rather than Prince Hal, whose image is stained by the "riot and dishonor" associated with Falstaff. The succeeding action magnifies both images, but it maintains the balance as we witness alternating scenes of almost equal dramatic force in which Hotspur and Falstaff slowly approach the battlefield on which Hotspur will die and Falstaff will feign death to preserve life.[4]

Falstaff has enjoyed a long popularity with audiences even while other characters certainly ridicule, pity, and reject him.[5] Views of his character vary widely. Many can agree that he reminds us of an insistent corporeality underlying human affairs and stands opposed, therefore, to figures like Hotspur. H.E. Toliver says that Falstaff is a "champion of anti-chivalric flexibility" who "translates moral distinctions downward to purely physical phenomena, and in doing so indirectly affirms the relentless natural law to which he eventually falls" (149).[6] But there is more to Falstaff than this rather bleak reading. H.C. Goddard writes that critics who despise Falstaff have failed to give themselves over to the magic of theater and have failed to recognize his charm, that "he is what we long to be: *free*" (113). This lends to the character an immortal quality, according to Goddard, because Falstaff is free to "create" with his imagination (114).[7]

Godard may go too far, but he does identify something of the character's richness. While W. Farnham acknowledges Falstaff's association with the natural, he adds that he has a "lively understanding of his own grotesqueness as a man and beast together, and of its relation to a general human grotesqueness with reaches of high and low greater than his own" (161).[8] Falstaff's seeming "freedom" from considerations of status and aspiration enables him to offer a comic deflation of the political rhetoric and aspirations outlined in the play, a deflation that itself functions as a simultaneously serious critique. M. Platt contends that "we love Falstaff for his wit" which "disenchants" idols like ambition and wealth for us (186).[9] For this reason, it is essential that Falstaff's comic perspective penetrate Hotspur's realm of idealistic honor – this collision allows us to contemplate the allure and deficiencies of both approaches to life.

Each line of action carefully balances the sympathy for these diametrically opposed figures. As Hotspur is associated with high public action, Falstaff's first appearance associates him with the private underside of life. Hal refuses to tell Falstaff the time of day because the time of day is irrelevant to the life of cups and sack, capons, and fair, hot wenches. Falstaff accepts Hal's description, and revels in his self-image as one apart from the world's serious business and free of its laws. He makes himself into a kind of natural force, existing beneath the orderly daylight world governed by "old father Antic the law" (1.2.59), and is instead "governed, as the sea is, by our noble and chaste mistress the moon, under whose countenance we steal" (1.2.28–29). To dismiss the law, the organizing principle of any social organization, as "antic," as mad or buffoon-like, is to prize the immediate moment itself and to attend primarily to the body's needs in that moment. Falstaff's mighty embrace of the uncertainty that haunts all claims of absolute value represents a comic challenge to the world of serious or tragic enterprise.

In his banter with Falstaff, Hal encourages him to elaborate the ways in which he will benefit from lawlessness of every kind, but he also stands slightly apart from him. Shakespeare builds ambiguity into their relationship by articulating their friendship almost exclusively through their short, witty exchanges. He never allows Hal a decisive victory, and Falstaff has the last word in the battle of wits when he turns the moral tables in defending his life of petty crime with the claim that "['t]is no sin for a man to labor in his vocation" (1.2.102–3). The comic Gadshill robbery parallels Northumberland and Worcester's planned insurrection, and Hal and Poins' ruse to expose Falstaff parallels and parodies Northumberland and Worcester's betrayal of Hotspur. The robbery episode is replete, so to speak, with images of Falstaff's flesh and gives dramatic weight to his dedication to physical comfort and safety. But as a strategy to embarrass Falstaff it fails, for Hal can only throw up his hands before Falstaff's claim that instinct, like that of the lion who will not attack a true prince, prevented him from fighting Hal. No insults and no proof of cowardice, lying, or cheating can shame Falstaff, because he cares more about life and pleasure than he does about the standards by which others judge him, and, moreover, he derives pleasure from parodying those very standards.

Fuller and more ambiguous implications of Falstaff's comic world appear as the action moves out of Eastcheap and closer to the battle. When Hal prepares to reconcile himself to his father and to go into battle, Falstaff suggests himself as a stand-in for the King in a practice interview. The comic vignette, as Falstaff and Hal take turns playing the King and each other, has portentous undertones, for the choice Hal makes of who is to be his symbolic or ideological father matters greatly to the country. The tide turns when Falstaff playing the King, says that to banish "plump Jack" is to "banish all the world" (2.4.474), and Hal responds, "I do, I will" (2.4.475). Darker shades accumulate when Falstaff regards his foot soldiers as so much cannon fodder, and his command as an opportunity to line his pockets. Furthermore, Falstaff's teasing of Hal on the battlefield by giving him a bottle instead of a pistol seems out of place, inappropriate. The collision of the comic and tragic strains here complicate the idea that any character, or person, can adhere entirely to one or the other. Serious matters accumulate moments of comic absurdity, and jokes that are funny often contain insight into serious matters.[10]

However, although Falstaff violates a sense of obligation to duty and heroism, he seems to defy condemnation because he never dislikes himself; he is aware of the grim realities of war that lie underneath Hotspur's vision of glory and quite rightly wishes to preserve his life. In fact, when Hal finds Falstaff's soldiers a group of "pitiful rascals," Falstaff responds that they are "food for powder, food for powder" and, making a pun of "pitiful," adds that they will "fill a pit as well as better. Tush, man, mortal men, mortal men" (4.2.63–6). While Falstaff on the surface seems offensively uncaring of the fate of his soldiers, his manner of expressing this grim reality of war, the ruminative, repetitive wording could be played as an almost sad thoughtfulness and a philosophical penetration into the hollowness of the abstract ideals that are causing the battle and leading to needless death. The "great" and the "pitiful" are imagined together in this morass, simply as bodies filling the ground.

Falstaff's insight into the uselessness of Hotspur's devotion to honor reaches its depth two scenes later when the Prince urges Falstaff to say his prayers before the battle. Picking up the idea of praying, Falstaff wishes those prayers were for "bedtime" and "all well" instead of prior to battle (5.1.125). On the one hand, we could read Falstaff as unforgivably cowardly in this moment. Yet, on the other hand, he not only reveals a poignant fear of death, expressed as a child-like vulnerability, but also demonstrates a refreshing openness about this fear. This leads to his challenge to the idea of honor, that it is useless and hollow in the face of physical realities:

> "Can honor set to a leg? No. Or an arm? No. Or take away the grief of a wound? No. Honor hath no skill in surgery, then? No. What is honor? A word. What is in that word 'honor'? What is that 'honor'? Air."
> (5.1.131–135)

To some extent, Hotspur will argue against this at his death when he claims that he feels the loss of honor more keenly than his wounds. But Falstaff is exactly right: Hotspur's honor does not "take away" or somehow repair a physical wound. This reality, if embraced, can be liberating or utterly devastating. And, as Peter Lake points out, Falstaff's words about the "emptiness of honor" match up with "the role 'honor' has been shown actually playing in the framing, conduct and legitimation of the rebellion" (301).[11] Lake reminds us that Hotspur is "duped by his father and his uncle Worcester into fighting a battle he is all but doomed to lose" (301).[12] Hotspur's adherence to honor is notable because it is so absent from those who are supposed to be supporting his cause.

Falstaff and Hotspur represent diametrically opposed perspectives. The contrast between Falstaff and Hotspur is sharpened when, with Falstaff's conclusion that "[h]onor is a / mere scutcheon" (5.1.139–40) still in our ears, we hear Worcester in double treachery explain to Vernon that they must conceal from Hotspur the King's offer of pardon: "We did train him on, / And, his corruption being ta'en from us, / We as the spring of all shall pay for all" (5.2.21–23).

Falstaff's self-termed "catechism" against honor derives its force from the incontestably literal facts on which it is based. Words are air, honor is a word, and it cannot heal a wound. It would be a mistake, though, to dismiss the concept of honor he attacks. We may agree with Falstaff, but for the Elizabethans the word suggested foundational values, even though it was in the process, as we shall see in *Hamlet*, of being relocated, as it were, from a martial to a more interiorized realm. It is not the word that springs most readily to our lips, but Falstaff's catechism applies equally well to other value-laden terms such as integrity, courage, and truthfulness. Yet, the intangible values, so important to Elizabethans, that are evoked by words can pale beside the sheer physicality of Falstaff's living bulk. While Hotspur's nobility shines against the background of his kinsmen's dishonorable actions, it is consistently contrasted to Falstaff's earthy realism and pragmatic dedication to sheer survival. While Falstaff feigns death to avoid being killed, the mortally wounded Hotspur lying near him says:

> O Harry, thou hast robb'd me of my youth! [...]
> But thoughts, the slaves of life, and life, time's fool,
> And time, that takes survey of all the world,
> Must have a stop. O, I could prophesy,
> But that the earthy and cold hand of death
> Lies on my tongue. No, Percy, thou art dust,
> And food for –   (5.4.77–86)

As his life seeps out with his blood, Hotspur, illustrating the process by which abstract values fade before the reality of death, reflects that though he cares more for his honorable titles than for his body, honor is nonetheless merely a thought, and as such it is the body's slave, subject like all else to time. Falstaff's credo seems confirmed when death's cold hand not only gives Hotspur's budding honors to Hal's garland, but allows Hal to take from Hotspur's mouth his last word – "worms" – on the ironic light that death sheds on human aspiration. It is as though Hotspur's dying words have confirmed Falstaff's claim that Hotspur's dead body merely counterfeits a man, while "to counterfeit dying, when a man thereby liveth, is to be no counterfeit but the true and perfect image of life indeed" (5.4.117–19). The strangeness of the dead body, this "counterfeit of man," seems to affect Falstaff, causing him – and perhaps the audience – to consider its awfulness rather than the nobility of the principles for which it once fought. Blount's dead body stirs Falstaff's rumination on honor again as he comes across the body and addresses it as if it were living: "Soft, who are you? Sir Walter Blunt. There's honor for you. Here's no vanity!" (5.3.32–3). In referring to vanity, Falstaff astutely connects the pursuit of honor to the desire to appear admirable to others, a much less idealistic motivation for acting courageously. The mortal body will ultimately thwart anyone's attempts to appear admirable – its insistent materiality disturbs idealistic thinking.

The play provides no argument to allay the force of the sheer spectacle of Hotspur's own dead body, further dishonored when Falstaff, the living "huge hill of flesh" (2.4.241) who "will swear truth out of England" (2.4.303), claims credit for killing him. The convergence of Hotspur's and Falstaff's two plot lines is cataclysmic. The opposition between them has structured the entire action; the values inherent in each have been developed with equal power, with equally self-confirming fullness, and with equal dramatic force. Gradually, the values inherent in each trajectory infiltrate the other and compromise its purity. Because neither one can answer the other, and neither one is given sufficient dramatic force to overwhelm the other, the grand structures of history, politics, the ideology of rule, and heroic action are undermined, as are the fun and fellowship of ordinary existence. As we will see later, the concerns of "mortal men, mortal men" that shadow the epic sweep of the history plays reappear in the major tragedies and late romances, and it never ceased to haunt the imaginations of Shakespeare's major characters.

Hal's story is more elusive than Hotspur's and Falstaff's, for as was the case with his father in *Richard II*, we are never quite certain of what he is up to. If we take him seriously when he compares himself to the sun, biding its time to emerge so that, "[b]eing wanted he may be more wondered at / By breaking through the foul and ugly mists / Of vapors that did seem to strangle him" (1.2.195–7), we see a person who out of policy stays away from his father's tainted court and also looks down upon those with whom he passes his time in seeming fellowship. If one sees him in this way, then one cannot see the play as about the education of a prince, because Hal by his own account has nothing to learn. However, most people do not see Hal as so cold a figure. These critics emphasize the camaraderie between him, Falstaff, and the others, and they see Hal as educating himself about the life of his people as a preparation for assuming command.

A director can create an atmosphere of affection between Falstaff and Hal or a sense of Hal keeping Falstaff at arm's length as he amuses himself with his attempts to wheedle his way into intimacy. The play offers material for both readings. Harry Berger Jr. considers the bond between Falstaff and Hal "unresolved" and subject to "ongoing interrogations" (45)[13] precisely because each character is moved by feelings and inclinations of which they are not fully aware. Falstaff, Berger Jr. says, "wants to see how far Harry will let him go, to probe the limits of transgression, to expose himself to the risk of the rejection and punishment he half looks forward to" (41).[14] On the other hand, Hal's anger with and rejection of Falstaff is a "self-purging fury," a "defensive maneuver of self-exculpation" (43).[15] Berger Jr. writes of the "private war" being waged within both Harry and Falstaff, a battle with "contradictions, ambiguities, fissures and dislocations," that becomes exteriorized and displaced onto the "public war" that the play dramatizes (87).[16] However simple their relationship seems, Hal and Falstaff's intimacy offers each other a space to channel his darker desires and conflicting emotions, but this same intimacy is poisonous to a lasting friendship.[17]

Were I directing the play, I would try to combine the images of distance and intimacy, repulsion and desire, between the two characters in order to suggest something of the rich inner lives suggested by Berger Jr. and to hint at Falstaff's challenge to Hal's sense of self. Hinting at these features would preserve rather than dispel the ambiguity. I would take Hal's speech seriously, and try to portray a person who never doubts that he would banish all the world to solidify his political base, but I would want to suggest in subtle gestures that he might feel some sadness or uncertainty about the distance from his fellows at which he must hold himself if he is to accomplish his purposes.

A related ambiguity haunts the story of Hal's relationship to his father, Henry IV, an ambiguity achieved partly through Hal's relationship to Falstaff. Hal claims his plan, in spending time at the tavern, is to "so offend to make offense a skill, / Redeeming time when men think least I will" (1.2.210–11). If we believe Hal, this premeditated manipulation of opinion shows him as craftier than his father. Hal's feelings toward his father remain obscure when, having been told that his father wants to see him, he allows Falstaff, as a kind of Lord of Misrule, to play his father in a skit in which they parody Hal's later meeting with Henry.[18] In this complex play-within-the-play, Hal reveals complicated feelings for both men. Playing King Henry, Falstaff praises himself and says that because "the tree may be known by the fruit, as the fruit the tree," he sees "virtue in that Falstaff" (2.4.423–5). While Falstaff endorses here the idea that one's actions reveal one's true self, Hal's devotion to Falstaff and his "riot" is, by his own admission, an attempt to deceive people about his true self. Seeming to want no part of the jest that Falstaff is visibly virtuous, Hal does not allow Falstaff to continue, and, in what we might call a theatrical usurpation, he then takes on his father's role and casts Falstaff as himself. The ambiguous nature of the relationship between Hal and Falstaff overlaps with the relationship between Hal and his father, so the events of the plays will see Hal in many ways striving to take the place of his father and banishing Falstaff from his favor.

In the moving scene in which Henry rebukes Hal and expresses his pain at having so deficient a son, Hal apologizes, saying "I shall hereafter, my thrice gracious lord, / Be more myself" (3.2.92–3), in a tone that can be interpreted as sincere or merely formal. Moreover, it should strike us that Hal here does not commit to changing himself, but to revealing more of the person he has always planned to be; this statement may well be part of his policy he expressed earlier to find the right occasion "again to be himself" (1.2.190). It will turn out that finding the "right occasion" for this is something of a challenge. When Henry accuses Hal of planning to "fight against me under Percy's pay, / To dog his heels and curtsy at his frowns, / To show how much thou art degenerate" (3.2.126–8), there is no question about the ringing tones in which Hal vows to "make this northern youth exchange / His glorious deeds for my indignities" (3.2.145–6). He is more outraged at the notion of being in Hotspur's shadow than he is at the suggestion that he might betray his father's cause. There is no doubt that he will not do so, but there is doubt about his inner feelings toward his father when, back with Falstaff, he says, "I am good friends with my father and may do anything" (3.3.181–2). Hal's strategy to shape others' impression of him bears fruit. Before the battle, Hal's opponent Vernon says that in challenging Hotspur to battle, Hal "chid his truant youth with such a grace / As if he mastered there a double spirit / Of teaching and of learning instantly" (5.2.62–4). Vernon goes on to say that "[i]f he outlive the envy of this day, / England did never owe so sweet a hope, / So much misconstrued in his wantonness" (5.2.66–68). Though Vernon and even Henry have accepted Hal's reformation, Hotspur is less convinced. He deflates the praise, saying dismissively to Vernon "Cousin, I think thou art enamourèd / On his follies" (5.2.69–70). The rest of the play shows us a Hal who appears to others as he promised to appear at the beginning, but his inner life, like Bolingbroke's, remains opaque. The "double spirit" Vernon imagines in Hal makes for a good description of the ambiguity of Hal's character.

Neither Falstaff's nor Hal's story ends in *Part One*. *2 Henry IV* repeats some of the pattern of *Part One*, alternating Falstaff's tavern scenes with those having to do with more plots against Henry's rule. The emphasis is different, however, for Hal moves more firmly into his father's orbit and is much less frequently with Falstaff. Furthermore, this play gives greater moral weight to the counterparts of the earlier Falstaff scenes. In a funny, but symbolical, scene that parallels the Gadshill episode, Falstaff pretends not to hear the rebukes of the Lord Chief Justice, whose voice signifies the might of the Law. The scenes depicting Falstaff's use of his powers of conscription have their counterparts in those that show us Falstaff promising wealth to Shallow, a corrupt justice of the peace, and to his other cronies as he races to Hal's coronation. "[T]he laws of England are at my commandment" (5.3.138) he exults, and that could not fail to send chills down the spines of an English audience. The triangular structure – the relationship between Hal, Falstaff, and Henry – of the first part has an echo here as well, for the scenes that show us Falstaff on the way to Hal's coronation alternate with those that show us the final reconciliation between Hal and his father.

This reconciliation is not without its tension, however. With Henry on his deathbed, Hal, thinking his father already dead, anticipates nature by taking the crown –"O polished perturbation, golden care!" (4.5.23) – from his father's bed and placing it on his own head:

> Thy due from me
> Is tears and heavy sorrows of the blood,
> ....
> My due from thee is this imperial crown,
> Which, as immediate from thy place and blood,
> Derives itself to me. *[He puts on the crown]*. Lo, where it sits,
> Which God shall guard. (4.5.37–8, 41–4)

His father wakes and misses his crown, and thinking that Hal wishes him dead, he rebukes him:

> Thy life did manifest thou lovedst me not,
> And thou wilt have me die assured of it.
> Thou hid'st a thousand daggers in thy thoughts,
> Which thou hast whetted on thy stony heart,
> To stab at half an hour of my life. (4.5.104–08)

Although Hal will be rightfully crowned through succession after Henry's death, his anticipation of his father's demise seems like an echo of the violent usurpation of Richard by Henry, a wish to appropriate the symbol of his power.[19] Here Shakespeare seems to mock Hal's determination to find the "right occasion" to reveal his true nature. After Henry anticipates the horrible fate that awaits England when "the fifth Harry from curbed license plucks / The muzzle of restraint, and the wild dog / Shall flesh his tooth on every innocent" (4.5.130–2), Hal protests the grief he felt on thinking his father dead, and gives the following account of how he had "upbraided" the burdensome crown that had deprived his father of life:

> 'The care on thee depending
> Hath fed upon the body of my father;
> Therefore, thou best of gold art worst of gold.
> Other, less fine in carat, is more precious,
> Preserving life in med'cine potable;
> But thou, most fine, most honored, most renowned,
> Hast eat thy bearer up.' Thus, my most royal liege,
> Accusing it, I put it on my head,
> To try with it, as with an enemy
> That had before my face murdered my father. (4.5.158–67)

Well, that isn't quite what we heard him say. Hal certainly omits from his account the exultation that is implied when, without too much difficulty, he leaves his grief for his father behind and puts the crown on his head as he speaks the last of the lines quoted above: "Lo, where it sits, / Which God shall guard." The scene is a brilliantly ambiguous rendering of the complex feelings between father and son and of the mixed motivations that power relations introduce into the heart of the family, despite the expectation that affection should spring naturally between members of the same family. Hal's awkward seizure of the crown before Henry's death, much like his boast to Falstaff that his father is his "friend," also underlines the fundamental theme of the plays that an unsettling of power relations between King and subjects occurs when one King succeeds another: the transfer of power from one to another exposes the difficult process of exchange.

As Henry nears death and Falstaff draws nearer London, Hal's brothers fear, as their father did, that when Hal becomes King Henry V he will despoil the country. The Chief Justice, who had the courage to rebuke the royal youth, fears for his life, but Hal enters to announce his reformation, which he illustrates by embracing the Chief Justice and directing him to chastise his son, should the Chief Justice have cause, as he did his father's son. The final meeting between Hal and Falstaff occurs when Hal, now Henry V, appears in his coronation march at the side of the Chief Justice, while Falstaff from the side of the road greets him with his old familiarity. Falstaff fails utterly to read Hal's reformation as the beginning of his own fall from grace. In fact, Hal repudiates him for this failure explicitly. When Falstaff addresses Hal as "my sweet boy" (5.5.43), Hal coldly replies, "[p]resume not that I am the thing I was, / For God doth know, so shall the world perceive, / That I have turned away my former self" (5.5.56–8). The brilliance of this put-down is that in it Hal never truly admits what he was or what he now has become – he simply notes that they are not the same. This is a clear admission that he is a "double spirit" without actually explaining what those spirits are. After this rebuke, Hal tells the Chief Justice to take him in hand and commit him to prison. This scene, which is commonly referred to as the rejection of Falstaff, is the most controversial scene of the two plays. Some people feel that Hal outrageously violates an old friendship, while others think that Falstaff is simply a scoundrel who has no place in the courts of Kings.[20] Coppélia Kahn writes that "Falstaff's regressive appeal is so dangerously strong for Shakespeare that he cannot afford to integrate it into Hal's character, and must, to Hal's loss, exclude it totally" (70).[21] Indeed, if Falstaff's attitude to life, however winning, is not seen as merely personal, but as representing a refusal to repress bodily needs in the service of abstract ideals, then Hal (who is bound as King to defend the integrity of public life and the body politic) must reject him, and that rejection paves the way for the portrait of the ideal King, which Shakespeare was to present – not, of course, without raising penetrating questions – in *Henry V,* the culminating play of the second tetralogy.

Notes

1 Bernard J. Dobski reads Hal as concerned with questions of "honor, of the origins, character and value of a lawful order, sacrifice in the service of which yields the praise of men and the glory of nations" long before he renounces Falstaff ("Friendship and Love of Honor: The Education of Henry V." in *Souls With Longing: Representations of Honor and Love in Shakespeare*. Eds. Bernard J. Dobski and Dustin A. Gish. Lanham: Lexington Books, 2011. 145).

2 While acknowledging Hotspur is the most "attractive of the rebels," Franziska Quabeck points out that "even honor constitutes a private motive" that cannot be a "just cause" for the rebellion (*Just and Unjust Wars in Shakespeare*. Berlin: De Gruyter, 2013. 120)

3 Peter Lake argues that Hotspur's notion of honor should not be viewed as a discredited part of the feudal past. He says Hotspur's values are "reaffirmed as attributes" at his death (especially in Hal's words over his enemy's body). *How Shakespeare Put Politics on the Stage: Power and Succession in the History Plays.* New Haven: Yale University Press, 2016.

4 For more on Hotspur's opposition to Falstaff, especially in terms of their approaches to honor, see Harold Bloom, *Falstaff: Give Me Life.* New York: Scribner, 2017; Norman Council, *When Honor's at the Stakes: Ideas of Honor in Shakespeare's Plays.* London: Allen and Unwin, 1973.

5 Falstaff's popularity is reflected in the fact that Shakespeare wrote another play for him, *The Merry Wives of Windsor.* Falstaff was reimagined in Orson Welles' 1966 movie *The Chimes at Midnight,* and Gus Van Sant's 1991 movie *My Own Private Idaho.* For more on Falstaff and a short recounting of historical figures and literary types from which his name and character may have derived, see Michael Jacobs, *Shakespeare on the Couch.* London: Karnac, 2008. pp. 77–78. Jacobs then describes psychoanalytic theories that can be applied to Falstaff, such as his subversion of the super-ego, his narcissism, and Hal's rejection of him as the desire to kill his father figure.

6 In *Falstaff.* Ed. Harold Bloom. New York: Chelsea House, 1992.

7 *Falstaff.* Ed. Harold Bloom.

8 *Falstaff.* Ed. Harold Bloom.

9 *Falstaff.* Ed. Harold Bloom. See also Hygh Grady. "Falstaff: Subjectivity between the Carnival and the Aesthetic." *The Modern Language Review* 96.3 (2001): 609–623.

10 See David Ellis "Falstaff and the Problems of Comedy." *The Cambridge Quarterly* 34.2 (2005): 95 – 108; Rudolf B. Schmerl. "Comedy and the Manipulation of Moral Distance: Falstaff and Shylock." *Bucknell Review* 10.2 (1961): 128–137.

11 *How Shakespeare Put Politics on the Stage.*

12 *How Shakespeare Put Politics on the Stage.*

13 "The Prince's Dog: Falstaff and the Perils of Speech-Prefixity." *Shakespeare Quarterly* 49.1 (1998): 40–73.

14 "The Prince's Dog."

15 "The Prince's Dog."

16 "Hydra and Rhizome." In *Shakespeare Reread: Texts in New Contexts.* Ed. Russ McDonald. Ithaca: Cornell University Press, 1994. 79–104.

17 Some account for the simultaneous closeness of and distance between Hal and Falstaff by noting their masculine and feminine energies. Jean Howard and Phyllis Rackin suggest that Falstaff takes up the "woman's part" in the *Henry IV* plays and is both "empowered and discredited" by this appropriation (*Engendering a Nation: A Feminist Account of Shakespeare's English Histories.* London: Routledge, 1997. 166). Valerie Traub suggests that the relationship between Hal and Falstaff carries resonances of "homoerotic desire" (59),

which is part of the histories' treatment of women and mothers as "objects to be desired, resented, and most importantly, feared" (52). This treatment, Traub argues, aims for the "elimination of women from the historical process" (53). It is notable that while Mistress Quickly and Doll Tearsheet frequent the tavern scenes, their lively energy is not mirrored or even contrasted with female presence in the scenes of the rebellion and Henry's court (*Desire and Anxiety: Circulations of Sexuality in Shakespearean Drama*. London: Routledge, 1992).

18 David Bevington links Falstaff's character to the Lord of Misrule, a figure who "presided over [...] occasions of permitted indecorum" in the holiday season before Lent ("Introduction," 33) in his edition of *1 Henry IV* (Oxford, Oxford University Press, 1987). For a description of the Lord of Misrule, see C.L. Barber's chapter on the figure in *Shakespeare's Festive Comedy: A Study of Dramatic From and Its Relation to Social Custom*. Princeton: Princeton University Press, 1959.

19 See Maurice Charney. *All of Shakespeare*. New York: Columbia University Press, 1993, pages 184–185. See also Michael Jacobs' psychoanalytic reading of the relationship between Hal, Falstaff, and Henry IV in *Shakespeare on the Couch*. London: Karnac, 2008, pages 75–94. Frederic B. Tromly also explores the relationship between Hal and Henry IV in *Fathers and Sons in Shakespeare: The Debt Never Promised*. Toronto: University of Toronto Press, 2010.

20 For a short summary of critics' readings of Hal's rejection of Falstaff, see Bernard J. Paris, *Character as a Subversive Force in Shakespeare: The History and Roman Plays*. Madison, New Jersey: Fairleigh Dickinson University Press, 1991. Paris observes that even those critics who agree that Hal must renounce Falstaff will admit that it results in a "regrettable narrowing of his personality" (72). Valerie Traub argues that Hal must reject Falstaff because the latter is a "fantasized pre-Oedipal maternal, against whom Hal must differentiate" (*Desire and Anxiety* 53). Similarly, Rackin and Howard note that Hal, in this moment, "produces a theatrical power purged of its feminine pollution" (166).

21 *Man's Estate: Masculine Identity in Shakespeare*. Berkeley: University of California Press, 1981.

6

Hamlet

More has been written about *Hamlet* than about any other single piece of literature. Not only has it been commented upon by poets and thinkers such as Coleridge, Goethe, and Freud, but it even has its own journal, *Hamlet Studies*, and every year dozens of articles and books are published on it. Almost every literary movement in some way co-opts the play, and every school of criticism undertakes an interpretation of it. *Hamlet* functions as a touchstone: to interpret it convincingly is to validate one's literary theory or approach. Even people who have read little or no Shakespeare know about the play by hearsay, and the character of Hamlet has so much apparent substance that his name signifies a certain kind of person. For many young people he functions as a literary liberator, because he seems so much like their secret selves – the person whom they feel themselves to be, unknown to their families and friends. The kind of secret kinship one can establish with such figures offers the assurance that one is, after all, part of the human race. As the play is considered the "central dramatic piece in Western cultural consciousness" (78),[1] one could say that Hamlet haunts our culture as much as he is haunted by his father's Ghost,

While Hamlet is one of the most compelling of literary creations, he is also one of the most elusive. Therefore, it is worth the effort to consider what it is about the play that makes it at once so popular, so compelling, and so puzzling. Maynard Mack articulates the questions that the play asks of us even as we see Hamlet working through them: "[w]hat […] is an act? What is its relation to the inner act, the intent?" (49).[2] The play generates its power by staging the characters' struggle with these questions, along with their questioning of the gap between what is known (and trusted) and what is unknown (and feared). This struggle leads to an atmosphere of paranoia, a widespread uncertainty about crucial bonds that should hold a family and state together.[3] As Susan Snyder points out, even Hamlet, a "role-player, manipulator, crafty madman, wit, and eiron [character in Greek comedy with ironic perspective]," voices "frustration" that his "superior awareness" leads only to an "existential nightmare of competing perceptions of reality" (91).[4] Stephen Greenblatt likewise describes the play as one of

Thinking About Shakespeare, First Edition. Kay Stockholder, revised and updated by Amy Scott.
© 2018 John Wiley & Sons Ltd. Published 2018 by John Wiley & Sons Ltd.

"contagious, almost universal self-estrangement" (212).[5] This self-estrangement derives from the straining of kinship and friendship bonds between nearly all characters in the wake of the death of Old Hamlet and the remarriage of Gertrude to Claudius.[6] Yet part of the allure of the play is that Hamlet makes the audience privy to a great deal of his experience through his lengthy soliloquies. He tells Gertrude that he has "that within which passes show" (1.2.85). He will spend the entire play sharing parts of "that within" to us without ever fully divulging the key to his moods and actions, revealing and continuously exercising what Ralph Soellner terms his "churning intellect" (174).[7]

Mack's question about what constitutes an act has direct bearing on several of the play's enduring mysteries: what delays Hamlet in getting his revenge on Claudius? What is Hamlet's tragic flaw, the one quality that leads to the nearly total destruction at the end of the play? [8] Is he crafty, insane, or a little of both? The theories marshaled to answer these questions are diverse and plenty, and tend to sound like diagnoses. They are summarized by Phyllis Rackin:

> Hamlet has been charged with procrastination, excessive conscientious-
> ness, an intellectual's incapacity for action, melancholy, subconscious
> lust for his mother, insanity and any number of other defects of character
> and personality. (47)[9]

Picking up where Rackin left off, Margreta de Grazia recounts the aforementioned theories and to them adds the "post-structuralist psychoanalysis" of Abraham and Žižek and the deconstructive reading by Derrida (170).

The theory that Hamlet harbors a "subconscious lust for his mother," suggested by Freud in *The Interpretation of Dreams* and outlined in greater detail in Ernest Jones's work *Hamlet and Oedipus*, has proved influential because it seems to explain why Hamlet's most intense anger and disgust is directed toward Gertrude rather than Claudius.[10] Jones dismisses the idea that Hamlet's deferral of revenge is due to "any sort of failure in moral or physical courage" (33).[11] He argues instead that Hamlet is motivated by subconscious desire to have sex with Gertrude and supplant his father. Hamlet's desire is only inflamed when Claudius takes the place of Old Hamlet because Hamlet must then endure a rivalry with yet *another* father. The thought of "incest and parricide combined is too intolerable to be borne" (70), Jones says, and this torment delays Hamlet's actions and shapes Hamlet's treatment of Gertrude and Ophelia. The latter, as an object of desire, becomes enveloped by Hamlet's disgust for his mother.[12]

Rackin admits that because the play is so inscrutable, "all our critical formulations [...] seem presumptuous" (67). De Grazia reminds us that when readers focus solely on Hamlet's "interiority" as a "vortical subject of the play" (5), they are likely to pass over key plot points and dialogue that speak to the play's very "worldly preoccupations" (204).[13] In light of de Grazia's warning, this chapter will make a reading of Hamlet's interiority not as a critical vortex, as if he were a patient on our couch, but rather as a source of knowledge about what happens to bonds between people in the midst of what Arthur Kirsch calls a "tremendous experience of pain and suffering" (17).[14] Kirsch is quite right that theories that "explain" Hamlet's actions, such as those that highlight the "Oedipal configurations of Hamlet's predicament," must not be "disentangled from Hamlet's grief" (21–2).[15] Hamlet's grief drives him to question and redefine concepts that give us a sense of our identity and help us relate to one another – concepts like revenge and honor. As John Joughin points out, Hamlet grieves not only his father but also that he is "deprived of mourning itself, a fate he feels bitterly and which surfaces as a recurrent preoccupation in the play as Hamlet is increasingly insistent in drawing a distinction between the mere theatricalization of grief and his own inability to mourn openly" (48).[16] This complex doubling of his grief – that he mourns for his father and mourns for his inability to mourn – permeates everything that Hamlet says and does.

However one accounts for Hamlet's delay in killing Claudius, one must acknowledge at least the uncertain nature of revenge in the play.[17] Shakespeare seems to be reconsidering the value of exacting revenge, wondering if it offers the desired compensations for injustice, for grief.[18] Snyder writes that "[g]enerations of critics have sought a consistent Hamlet, one whose conviction that he must take revenge is not at odds with his reluctance to take that revenge" (91).[19] Killing Claudius, Hamlet seems to immediately recognize, will not answer the question of "to be or not to be?" In fact, as Stephen Greenblatt reminds us, at the end of the play, there is no moment of "reckoning, however brief, in which the revenger [...] discloses the nature of the crime that he has now punished" (227).[20] He notes too that the Ghost at first calls for Hamlet to avenge him, but this request transforms to the command for Hamlet to "remember" him (1.5.91). Greenblatt reasons that "[s]ticking a sword into someone's body turns out to be a very tricky way of remembering the dead" (225), and intimates that the play may wear the clothing of a traditional revenge tragedy, but it contains something more within.[21] Similarly, Mack explains that Hamlet may resist revenge because "[t]he act required of him, though retributive justice, is one that necessarily involves the doer in the general guilt" (55).[22] Noting that the Ghost first appears "armed at point," and carrying a truncheon (1.2.199, 203), René Girard concurs, writing that in taking revenge, Hamlet knows he would then be entering a "long chain" of violence and criminality, making him no better than Claudius and "perfectly identical to all the other links" (273).[23] In Girard's estimation, Hamlet is "trying to fight" the call to revenge because it will swallow him in "overwhelming indifference" (276). Hamlet, then, is left in a state of "sick revenge" because he is "unable to take revenge and yet unable to renounce it" (286).[24] Hamlet will face evidence of yet another frightening chain of indifference when he confronts Yorick's bones in the graveyard and realizes that death is the ultimate leveler.

Yet the concept of honor, which we saw in *1 Henry IV*, demands that people avenge wrongs done to members of their family. Manliness and dignity, as well as honor, are all intimately connected with the obligation to avenge wrongs done to oneself or one's family. This honor is also deeply implicated in the martial code that Hamlet's father invokes. It is significant in this regard that the Ghost appears as a warrior, and that Marcellus and Horatio emphasize his martial heroism and his victory over Fortinbras. These details attribute to the Ghost a worldview and values similar to those of Hotspur. But Hamlet is of a different character altogether.

Some light is shed on the revenge question by comparing *Hamlet* to other revenge plays of the time. Like the first of its kind, *The Spanish Tragedy* by Thomas Kyd, the plays in this extremely popular genre typically place the revenge hero in a lower social rank than the person against whom he seeks revenge. This social inequality places the revenge ethos in opposition to a conception of justice that the law or the court should, but often fails, to make available. In this situation, the revenge code appears as a throwback to a feudal morality based on kin groups, one that was being supplanted by a conception of justice deriving from the centralized authority of the crown. In *Hamlet* this contrast between the revenge code of kin groups and the concept of justice associated with centralized authority does not arise, because Hamlet is of the same rank as his antagonist, and there is no one of higher authority to whom he can appeal for justice. Nonetheless, the contrast between the intellectual Hamlet and his warrior father is emblematic of a clash between feudal values and those appropriate to a centralized authority structure.

The play casts further doubt on a thoughtless commitment to the revenge code by building into its structure two parallel subplots. Laertes, having heard about Polonius's death, raises an army on his return from Paris to seek revenge on Claudius. Laertes is wrong in thinking that Claudius directly killed his father, though indirectly he is responsible, and he becomes, in Claudius's hands, a pliable tool for use against Hamlet. The ease with which Claudius manipulates Laertes contrasts sharply with the difficulty that Polonius, as well as Rosencranz and Guildenstem, finds in playing upon Hamlet's stops. "Call me what instrument you will," says Hamlet, "though you can fret me, you cannot play upon me" (3.2.369–71). Laertes's dedication to revenge, then, appears only to weaken his autonomy in contrast to Hamlet's ability to evade manipulation as he resists simple revenge.

David Leverenz reminds us the task of "[b]eing, not desiring or revenging," is Hamlet's most famous preoccupation (112).[25] It seems the evil Hamlet wants to confront extends beyond Claudius and the murder of his father. As Harry Keyishian points out, Hamlet struggles with the "general question of how to deal with suffering and wrongs that cannot be ascribed to some particular malicious enemy, but are caused by the general and intractable conditions of existence" (60).[26] While Hamlet's grief does not immediately inspire Hamlet to kill Claudius, it does lead him to confront one seemingly intractable condition of existence: what we take to be "known" about circumstances and people is always shaped by activities and personas that attempt to mask knowledge.

The first thing to note is how Hamlet's struggle is writ large in the play's overall action. Even though Hamlet does not appear in the first scene of the play, the atmosphere of foreboding and chill presages Hamlet's first scene and his struggle to know himself. The first words we hear in the play as the soldiers who keep watch encounter the Ghost are, "[w]ho's there?" (1.1.1), which establishes the confusion and uncertainty that complicates any easy knowledge of the self and others in the play. These words remain in the atmosphere as Bernardo and Marcellus first tell Horatio about the Ghost and then are horrified by its reappearance. The Ghost itself, being "invulnerable," and rendering their "vain blows malicious mockery" (1.1.151–2), establishes the idea that the known world contains figures who are incapable of being understood, whose opacity cannot be penetrated. This prepares for the introduction of the figure whose "inky" appearance, unpredictable manner, and conflicted motives will bring some of the darkness and mystery of the first scene into the colorful gaiety of Claudius's court.

Hamlet's first words establish in eight words his alienation from Claudius's court, along with his intelligence and wit. When Claudius seeks to use his marriage to Gertrude as a claim for intimacy with his nephew by addressing him as "my cousin Hamlet, and my son," Hamlet, in an aside, says wittily and bitterly, "[a] little more than kin, and less than kind" (1.2.64, 65), The remark "more than kin" turns Claudius's claim back on itself, for the doubled relationship, both father and cousin (a word used by the Elizabethans for a variety of close relationships), indicates, in Hamlet's view, the corruption of kinship that has occurred with his uncle's marriage to his mother, and the second clause extends that meaning in the phrase "less than kind." This utterance brings together four meanings that comment on each other. "Kind" is a variation of "kin," as in "kindred," so that Hamlet is saying that in marrying Gertrude Claudius has become less, rather than more, of a kinsman, because he has violated kin bonds by marrying his sister-in-law and by failing to grieve for his brother's death. In a second meaning "kind" has to do with natural kinds, as in "mankind," so that Hamlet is saying that Claudius's unnatural marriage violates natural law, and in a third meaning "kind" has to do with the kindness or affection that natural law demands of kin. In using the word "kind," Hamlet also indicates that Claudius is nothing like him. Hamlet here casts doubt on the seeming warmth of Claudius's address to him, and he implies that Claudius, even as he addresses Hamlet as his "cousin … and my son" perfectly well knows that his relation to Gertrude is incestuous, that he has "[p]opped in between th' election" (5.2.65) and Hamlet's hopes, and that Hamlet is, therefore, his enemy. Each of the three meanings contributes to the power of the other two, because the second clause asserts all the things that are wrong with Claudius being "more than kin."

Whatever we may come to believe about the issues raised by the play, this witty comment (or audible inner reflection) reveals Hamlet's sharp eye for hypocrisy and his ability to give biting expression to the bitterness of tragic circumstance. Hamlet's observation also reveals what is truly remarkable about his character's musings. In the act of demonstrating an insightful reading other people, he also acknowledges the limits of his knowledge. He has Claudius's measure here, but identifies him through the relative terms "more than" and "less than" – Claudius can only be known by his relation to and distance from values that are understood and considered unchanging. At the same time that Hamlet measures Claudius against these ideals (kinship and kind), he demonstrates they don't quite do enough to explain a person's actions or selfhood. He therefore brilliantly produces insight from an apparent deficit of knowledge. While in earlier and later plays Shakespeare leaves his audience to apprehend the emotional subtleties that derive from the mixture and juxtaposing of comic and tragic matter, in this play the comic and tragic sensibilities together compose the protagonist's character. As Hamlet plays the fool to himself, he savors all of the grim ironies that other plays leave to the audience. He is, as Snyder observes, "both inside his emotional conviction and outside it looking on" (93), a double position that makes his perceptions particularly compelling.[27]

Hamlet's character dominates the play to such an extent that the circumstances to which he reacts are often obscure. While Hamlet's eye is turned toward his world, our eye is focused on his responses rather than on that to which he responds. What is the nature of the world Hamlet confronts? First, there is the Ghost. Too often people talk about the play on the assumption that it goes without saying that a ghost should be obeyed. However, even without background material on the dubious status of and controversy about ghosts in the Elizabethan age,[28] the play makes clear that the status of the ghost is in question. The soldiers fear it, and Hamlet suggests that it might be a damned spirit using his father's likeness to ensnare his soul. It is a mistake to think that Hamlet's doubts about the Ghost are mere excuses for delay. Even if we assume that the Ghost is Hamlet's father, it does not necessarily follow that Hamlet should obey its demand to take vengeance on Claudius.

Even apart from these structural guides to how we are to view Hamlet, the combination of the dubious nature of the Ghost and the problematic nature of the revenge code would make it extremely foolish for Hamlet to "sweep to [his] revenge," "with wings as swift / As meditation or the thoughts of love" (1.5.31, 29–30). True, in the heat of the moment, when the Ghost confirms Hamlet's suspicions of his uncle and describes the manner of his father's death in gory detail, Hamlet promises that the Ghost's "commandment all alone shall live / Within the book and volume of [his] brain" (1.5.103–04). However, Hamlet's hesitations and his plan for the mousetrap play are the actions of a thoughtful person, even though he castigates himself for inaction. Hamlet is caught between values that seem to require immediate action and an awareness of the inadequacy of those values to offer knowledge of the self and others. On the one hand, he feels outraged by his father's murder and bound by his values, so that he sees and judges himself through his father's eyes. On the other hand, he recognizes that those values have been disconnected from real human emotion: he is in a situation in which obedience to his father, even assuming that he should obey, is difficult and frightening.

There is a further aspect of the Ghost to be considered. As our discussion of *A Midsummer Night's Dream* suggests, we can think about the supernatural characters in works of literature as figural expressions of aspects of the natural and social world. In *Dream,* the fairies embody the instability of intense human emotions. But what kind of human reality does the Ghost in *Hamlet* represent? By definition, a ghost is something from the past that continues a tenuous existence and that makes urgent claims upon the present. The conception of ghostliness is bound up with the idea of revenge, for revenge also disturbs the present by its demand that past wrongs be righted. To see the Ghost as representing this dimension of human life is to understand Hamlet as one who is haunted by the feeling that past, present, and future have become disordered, that his time is "out of joint" (1.5.197) and that his actions must somehow put the past to rest and restore time to its proper sequence.[29] This aspect of ghostliness is related to the two stories of the past that are associated with the Ghost. The first one is relevant to the play's socio-political events and concerns the story of the conflict between King Fortinbras and King Hamlet over a piece of land. That past action determines the present, for, as Horatio tells us, the young Fortinbras' desire to redeem his family honor by attacking Denmark explains the "sweaty haste" (1.1.81) in Elsinore to build ships and cannon. After Horatio gives a short history of the dispute and clarifies that it is the reason they have to be on a "watch," Bernardo concurs but adds that the conflict may also be the reason that the Ghost, a "portentous figure," has appeared (1.1.113). The sense of the past pressing into the present is then described horrifically when Horatio compares the appearance of the Ghost to the time before the "mightiest Julius fell" when the "sheeted dead / Did squeak and gibber in the Roman streets" (1.1.118–20), an act that was supposed to portend his assassination.

The forceful presence of the historical past parallels the second story that emerges when the Ghost, on his second appearance, tells Hamlet of Gertrude's presumed infidelity and of Claudius's brother-murder. These events from Hamlet's family past loom over his present in the same way as the public events loom over Denmark. Hamlet, of course, becomes aware of these events, but because they concern his parents they give the impression of reaching back into the deep past, which is to say, into childhood events. For this reason, and because of Hamlet's brooding mind and inquiry into his own motivations, Hamlet has an unusually dense psychological past, or unconscious. His reflectiveness causes him to suspect that the Ghost might be a devil who preys on his melancholy, who "[a]buses [him] to damn [him]" (2.2.604), or that the Ghost might be taking advantage of his imagination, which could be "as foul / As Vulcan's stithy" (3.2.82–3). The accumulating sense of mystery surrounding both historical and personal pastness and obscurities of the human soul culminates in the graveyard scene, in which Hamlet is confronted with the skull of his childhood playmate, the jester Yorick.

It is for all these reasons that the play lends itself so readily to psychoanalytic criticism, and makes Hamlet so available as a case study in the Oedipus complex. Whether or not one is disposed toward this kind of thinking, the important point is that, whatever we might think about the particular contents of his unconscious, Hamlet himself seems to understand that some of his motivations are hidden from him. His efforts to comprehend himself, along with all the ambiguities entailed in the past as represented by the Ghost, constitute a compelling internal drama.

The external drama that arises from the interior one consists of Hamlet's confrontation with a hostile court. The nature of that court is made abundantly clear in the political astuteness of Claudius's opening speech, in which he both establishes his authority as king and soothes whatever doubts his on-stage audience might secretly harbor. The situation with which Hamlet must cope emerges in the sharp contrast between Claudius's willingness to let Laertes go to France, and his refusal to have Hamlet return to Wittenburg. Claudius says that his reluctance stems from his concern for Gertrude's maternal feelings, but we can infer, given our knowledge of his guilt and his anxieties about Hamlet's strange behavior, that he wants to keep an eye on Hamlet. He may also be worried that Hamlet could raise an army in an effort to unseat him, which is what Laertes does later in the wake of his father's death.

The spying that marks so much of the play's action exacerbates the ambience of distrust. This motif first appears when, in his first act as king, Claudius dispatches Voltimand and Cornelius to Norway. In being shown in an act of diplomacy, he is immediately contrasted to his elder and more war-like brother. While diplomacy is not the same as spying, it too contrasts with a warrior code and does not win honor. Not too much later Polonius sends a messenger to spy on his own son, and later he throws himself eagerly into the task of prying into Hamlet's motivations. Polonius and Claudius make use of Ophelia to spy on Hamlet, and Claudius summons Rosencrantz and Guildenstern to spy on him as well. Finally, since Hamlet has set himself the task of discovering whether Claudius is guilty of regicide, he in turn spies on Claudius. The court of Denmark is a den of spies and counterspies in which no one, aside from the steady Horatio, can be trusted, not even Gertrude, not even Ophelia. Though Hamlet is involved in counter-spying, he sets himself apart from the calculating political world by expressing his true feelings, even in the process of concealing them by means of his "antic disposition" (1.5.181).

Hamlet's alienation from his mother and from Ophelia brings us to the third aspect of his world. Hamlet is revolted by the idea that his mother could desire a man as base as Claudius. The thought of his mother's sexuality disgusts him, and his repulsion is made worse by the Ghost's suggestion that Gertrude committed adultery with Claudius.[30] He says that his father is to Claudius as "Hyperion to a satyr" (1.2.140): Hyperion is the sun god; a satyr is a monster with a permanent erection. Even while with her first husband Gertrude showed her low taste by "hang[ing] on him / As if increase of appetite had grown / By what it fed on," while his father by contrast was so loving that "he might not beteem the winds of heaven / Visit her face too roughly" (1.2.144–5, 141–2). Gertrude's union with Claudius signifies a sexual appetite so repugnant to Hamlet that he compares their lovemaking to the evil attendant on the day of doom:

> Heaven's face does glow
> O'er this solidity and compound mass
> With tristful visage, as against the doom,
> Is thought-sick at the act. (3.4.49–52)

Here Hamlet describes his own emotional reaction to thinking about his mother's physical relationship with Claudius. He has turned to the abstracted ideas of heaven and hell to frame it, but in describing heaven as a body with a face that blushes, as a being capable of thinking and feeling sick about its thoughts, Hamlet describes what we can imagine is his own unmediated reaction, a reaction with which the audience cannot help but identify. His reference to Gertrude and Claudius's bodies as a "solidity and compound mass" is so horrifying, it calls up the disturbing nature of mortality itself – men and women are rendered into indeterminate material rather than individuals. Hamlet will eventually see this horrific materiality in *all* humans, even the most elevated of history, as he contemplates death in the graveyard scene.

In addition to rendering her sexually corrupt in Hamlet's eyes, his mother's union with Claudius makes her Hamlet's political enemy, apart from whatever personal feelings she has for him.[31] She does not seem to be fully cognizant of what Hamlet feels about Claudius, who, from Hamlet's point of view "killed my king and whored my mother, / Popp'd in between th' election and my hopes" (5.2.64–5), though she seems to have some inkling when she says that the cause of Hamlet's melancholy is no farther to seek than "[h]is father's death and our o'erhasty marriage" (2.2.57). When Hamlet in the closet scene first describes her copulation with Claudius "in the rank sweat of an enseamèd bed, / Stewed in corruption, honeying and making love / Over the nasty sty!," and then describes her present husband as "[a] cutpurse of the empire and the rule, / That from a shelf the precious diadem stole / And put it in his pocket—" (3.4.94–6, 102–04), political betrayal is added to sexual corruption. Hamlet's intense feeling about Gertrude's combined corruption and betrayal alienates him both from domestic affection and from power. Yet this alienation is not just a product of the act of betrayal itself. It is also a product of his fruitless effort to get to her feel the effects her actions have had on him. Kirsch observes that Gertrude is "essentially inert, oblivious to the whole realm of human experience through which her son travels" (28).[32] Her lack of feeling, of interiority, far from representing Shakespeare's failure to produce a three-dimensional character, can be understood as a depiction of the mourner's alienation from others (including those closest to him), being unable to convey an experience that transcends words and actions. When he confronts her in her private chamber, he asks her to remain still so that he can show her, through a mirror, her "inmost part" (3.4.21).[33] It turns out that Hamlet doesn't merely want to ruminate on what happened; he wants her to acknowledge and reveal the reasons for her actions, her emotions; he wants her to express an interiority she has so far withheld so that he can get to the heart of the matter that would explain her actions.

He says he will "wring" her "heart" but can only do so if it is made of "penetrable stuff" (3.4.36–7). Hamlet recognizes that he can only touch someone who allows the social mask to drop. For Gertrude to truly see herself and for Hamlet to connect to her, she must allow her emotions to be moved by Hamlet's distress and allow Hamlet to reach beneath the "brass" that "damnèd custom" has placed over her finer feelings (3.4.38–9). If Hamlet is enraged because she has violated what he considers natural and just by marrying his uncle, he is further estranged from her because "custom" has made her mask her feelings. Earlier he told Gertrude that his mourning clothes were "customary suits of solemn black" (1.2.78) and that they, along with all other outward signs of grief could not "denote" him "truly" (1.2.83). Hamlet's frustration derives from his sense that he is the only one who sees that a strict adherence to custom can be as – or even more – damaging than violating it.

From Hamlet's point of view, his relation to Ophelia is a mirror image of his relation to Gertrude. There are basically two ways to think about Ophelia. Most often she is viewed as an innocent victim, but that does not sit easily with the evidence of the play. Ophelia and Hamlet have known each other before Hamlet's sojourn in Wittenberg. Though Polonius tells her that she cannot expect Hamlet to marry her, Gertrude clearly expected Hamlet to marry Ophelia, as she implies when she says that she "thought thy bride-bed to have decked, sweet maid, / And not t' have strew'd thy grave" (5.1.245–6). Given Hamlet's isolation, his grief for his father, and his outrage at his murder and his mother's marriage to the murderer, it is not surprising that he should be angry when Ophelia, whom he presumably expected he could count on, refuses to see him. One should not assume that Ophelia had no choice but to obey her father, for we have seen in earlier plays and will see in later ones that fathers do not always exercise their authority rightfully, and that virtuous daughters often do not obey their fathers. Furthermore, one would have to imagine Ophelia as very stupid indeed if she were entirely unaware of the political implications of her brother's advice and Polonius's command that she see no more of Hamlet.

Much of Ophelia's story takes place behind the scenes, so that we have to piece it together. For example, we do not know exactly at what point in the action we are to imagine her returning Hamlet's letters to him or his coming to her room, but it is clear that when she allows Claudius and Polonius to use her as a decoy for their spying, she is betraying Hamlet. Even if Hamlet doesn't know that she is being so used, he has ample reason to be angry at her. He knows that she has rejected him, and he would know as well that she had run to Claudius and Polonius after he had rebuked her faithlessness by coming to her in the conventional garb of a distraught lover. The main brunt of his rage at her falls on Polonius, whom he blames for treating his daughter as a political pawn. When Polonius asks Hamlet if he knows him, and Hamlet responds, "[e]xcellent well. You are a fishmonger" (2.2.174), Hamlet accuses Polonius of being a bawd, for which "fishmonger" was a colloquial expression. When Polonius denies being a fishmonger, Hamlet replies, "[t]hen I would you were so honest a man" (2.2.176), meaning that an ordinary bawd who profits from woman's sex is honest in comparison to Polonius, who profits politically from denying Ophelia to him. That is why he tells Polonius that if he lets his daughter walk in the sun now, the way she will conceive will not be a blessing, but will show the fruits of corruption, as "the sun breed[s] maggots in a dead dog, / being a good kissing carrion" (2.2.181–82). Though Hamlet's reaction is intense, he is understandably furious at Ophelia, whom he had loved, and upon whom he had counted.

There is an implication that the story of Hamlet and Ophelia goes further. When Ophelia goes mad after Polonius's death, she speaks primarily in disjointed snippets of songs.[34] One of her songs describes a maid offering herself to a man. This maid knocks at his window in the early hours of the morning "to be [his] Valentine" (4.5.51), and the man "[l]et in the maid, that out a maid / Never departed more" (4.5.54–5). The maid laments then that the man will not marry her, and the man responds "[s]o would I ha' done, by yonder sun, / An thou hadst not come to my bed" (4.5.66–7). The song itself considers the nature of desire – revealing what Lacan tells us, that it is directed toward an Other and can never be satisfied fully. As we will see in *Troilus and Cressida*, Cressida will struggle with the gender politics that Ophelia's song describes. She will try to delay going to Troilus's bed, knowing that if she satisfies his desire, Troilus will no longer want her.[35]

If one takes Ophelia's mad songs as meaningful, and Shakespeare's other plays give ample warrant for thinking that they are, then we can infer that Ophelia feels utterly undone by the conflicted impulses of loving Hamlet, being forced to reject him, and being rejected by him.[36] The song lays blame equally on the man and the woman for the failure of the union to lead to something fruitful. One might even speculate that Ophelia offered herself to Hamlet in compensation for her betrayal and that he, perhaps, in order to punish her, treated her like a whore, as he had promised her father he would. To assume such a story makes her madness credible, for after her father's death and Hamlet's departure, she would be left utterly alone with her guilt and outrage. This would make her character much like that of Gertrude, "frail," without strong conviction and unreliable.[37]

Both the women in Hamlet's world are portrayed as inadequate, venal rather than as evil.[38] But this portrayal does not diminish the significance of the many images of sexual disgust and misogyny that appear in Hamlet's language. The misogyny is not only Hamlet's, for when Claudius and Polonius pose Ophelia with a prayer book as a decoy, they both comment on the image of hypocrisy they have thus created. Polonius's sententious comment that "with devotion's visage / And pious action we do sugar o'er / The devil himself" (3.1.47–9), stings Claudius, who says in an aside, "[t]he harlot's cheek, beautied with plastering art, / Is not more ugly to the thing that helps it / Than is my deed to my most painted word" (3.1.52–4). The image of female duplicity that Polonius and Claudius themselves have constructed becomes for the former an emblem of human depravity and for the latter an emblem of his own.

Though the circumstances that compose the world in which Hamlet has his being are themselves sufficient to constitute their own drama, in fact they function as the background for the drama of Hamlet's consciousness, which is opened to us in his many soliloquies and long speeches. These allow us to observe the inner drama of Hamlet's thoughts and feelings as he both deals with those around him and struggles to maintain a stoic sense of himself apart. Hamlet's self-awareness makes him stand out in literary history, especially when he confronts the implications for the private person of the possibility, advanced by Machiavelli among others, that what one exhibits to the world is not what is true of one's self, which opens up the possibility that others will not know who and what one really is. Hamlet addresses this issue in one of his most famous speeches:

> Seems, madam! Nay, it is. I know not 'seems.'
> 'Tis not alone my inky cloak, good Mother,
> Nor customary suits of solemn black,
> Nor windy suspiration of forced breath,
> No, nor the fruitful river in the eye,
> Nor the dejected havior of the visage,
> Together with all forms, moods, shapes of grief,
> That can denote me truly. These indeed seem,
> For they are actions that a man might play.
> But I have that within which passes show;
> These but the trappings and the suits of woe. (1.2.76–86)

With these words Hamlet defines the self as those feelings and that aware-ness that stand apart from social role. The real self cannot, therefore, be represented, for all action derives from social forms and roles, all of which can be imitated and therefore falsified; "these indeed seem." It is not that his clothing and behavior misrepresent him; he asserts that they represent him as truly as a self can be represented, but unlike the true self that can, in his conception, be known only to itself, all action can be imitated. In such a world, there is no way by which one can certainly know who enacts herself truly and who is out to deceive us for her own purposes. From this conception of a self flows Hamlet's preoccupation with the stage, his wonder that the actors can give fuller vent to feelings that have nothing to do with their lives than he can to those that are central to his, and to his reflections on the relation of the stage to life.

In the process of working out his destiny, Hamlet reflects upon major issues of his time, many of which are important for ours as well. The subject upon which he reflects most, and from which his other reflections emerge, is death. The "seems" speech above represents Hamlet's struggle to know and convey his identity as someone who grieves the death of a loved one, an event that leaves, as Kirsch reminds us, a "literally inexpressible wound whose immediate consequence is the dislocation, if not transvaluation, of our customary perceptions and feelings and attachments to life" (19).[39] When his friends wish to restrain him from following the Ghost, he says, "I do not set my life at a pin's fee" (1.4.65), and in his prolonged speech to Rosencrantz and Guildenstern, he expresses his weariness with the world, which, though wonderful and beautiful, seems to him "nothing ... but a foul and pestilent congregation of vapors" (2.2.303–04). However, when the players arrive, and he sees their passionate acting, he doesn't quite understand why he has lost his initial emotional impetus toward revenge. He castigates himself for being a coward, and hates himself for ranting rather than taking action. In the process of self-rebuke, however, he comes to realize that through the power of players, he can expose Claudius by stirring his guilt, by moving his emotions enough that he reveals the truth. He then produces a perfectly sensible plan for confirming Claudius's guilt.

Although his world weariness prompts thoughts of suicide, Hamlet fears death, and admits that he does – a most extraordinary thing for a tragic protagonist to do. In the "[t]o be, or not to be" (3.1.57–89) speech, he says that "conscience does make cowards of us all" (3.1.84). The word "conscience" in Shakespeare's time did double duty, having our sense of moral conscience, but also meaning consciousness. Therefore, it is his consciousness of death, as well as the Christian injunction against "self-slaughter," that makes him fear killing himself. Shakespeare is showing his audience that it is easy for people to promise to leap to their revenge, or to risk their lives in any other heroic way, but that the truth is that we fear death, especially when we have just experienced the loss of a loved one. Life is precious, and that the heroic gesture is not the whole truth, especially for the inner self. For the son of a warrior king to acknowledge that he feels himself a coward, to admit that he fears death, is a new kind of heroism, one based on self-understanding and a willingness to know the truth about oneself.

When he encounters Fortinbras' army, Hamlet's self-understanding leads him as close as he will come to question directly his father's values and the revenge ethos. In the soliloquy spoken on this occasion, Hamlet blindly struggles between his father's warrior values and those of a more questioning mind that values reason. He once again castigates himself, wondering that he still lives, and says, "'[t]his thing's to do,' / Sith I have cause, and will, and strength, and means / To do 't" (4.4.45–7). He compares himself in his inaction to a beast that merely sleeps and feeds, but the image of the beast brings to his mind the question of the role of "god-like" reason, which the Creator did not give us to "fust [grow mouldy] in us unused" (4.4.40). This conception of reason appeared earlier when he told Horatio that a beast would have mourned longer than did Gertrude. Reason, then, is not an opposite to feeling, but is that faculty that allows us to have proper and appropriate feelings. The same definition of reason appears when he admires Horatio as one in whom "blood and judgment are so well commeddled" (3.2.68) that he cannot be manipulated by fortune or by others. Reason grounds one in that selfhood that "passes show," and in doing so allows one to defeat those who, like Rosencrantz, Guildenstern, and Polonius, want to play upon one as upon a pipe. Hamlet begins this soliloquy by accusing himself of lacking reason, but he concludes that he has been using his reason to look "before and after," and that it is probably not "bestial oblivion" but rather the reverse, too much thinking, that has kept him from action. He once again berates himself for cowardice, for thinking instead of acting, but his mind swerves in a different direction when he sees Fortinbras' army:

> Led by a delicate and tender prince,
> Whose spirit with divine ambition puffed
> Makes mouths at the invisible event,
> Exposing what is mortal and unsure
> To all that fortune, death, and danger dare,
> Even for an eggshell. Rightly to be great
> Is not to stir without great argument,
> But greatly to find quarrel in a straw
> When honor's at the stake. (4.4.49–56)

He admires Fortinbras because he has been stirred to do something by recognizing its symbolic rather than literal value – a battle that emerges from something insignificant is meaningful when there are larger ideals "at the stake." All this time, Hamlet has been unable to find the use or power of abstract notions like honor, and the emptiness of those notions has rendered him incapable of acting on even the greatest of insults to his father and him. Hamlet's struggle, then, is to connect emotion (being moved) to an abstract principle, a connection that channels emotion into action (moving). What finally causes Hamlet to stir is not quite revenge, or a quest for honor. It seems to be propelled by his realization that the great sweep of mortality is more powerful and complete than abstract ideals, and it reveals a truth more basic than any others espoused in the play.

One of the play's puzzles is that we don't know exactly why he seems so world-weary and death-oriented even at the beginning of the play. It isn't that he doesn't have cause to be melancholy, with his father's death, his mother's marriage to a man he despises, and his loss of his own expectations to succeed his father as Denmark's king. But many people feel that there is some disproportion between the intensity of Hamlet's feelings and the circumstances that give rise to them. Lacan's observation that the death of another is the "one unbearable dimension of possible human experience" (37) offers one reason for this intensity.[40] Whatever the reasons, Hamlet seems to be preparing himself for death throughout the play. As we have seen, he does so by meditating on the value of life as well as by forcing his imagination to comprehend the realities of death. This effort underlies his earlier description of the process by which Polonius's dead body will decay, and the process by which "a king may go a progress through the guts of a beggar" (4.3.31–2). These literal truths become metaphors for the impermanence of human aspiration and ambition.

Hamlet's meditations on life and death come to a head in the carefully structured graveyard scene, which emerges as action from the rich imagery that has preceded it, beginning with Horatio's description of the Roman dead arising from their graves. Hamlet encounters his own double in the gravedigger, whose sardonic humor in "speak[ing] by the card" (5.1.137–8) as he tosses up the bones of the long dead resembles Hamlet's own. Here the grim humor of the gravedigger undermines the significance of life, as the earlier images of death become the actuality of open graves and moldering bones. Hamlet forces himself to look death in the face as he holds Yorick's skull close enough to feel nauseated. He directs Yorick's skull to "get you to my lady's chamber and tell her, let her paint an inch thick, to this favor she must come" (5.1.192–4). The death's head becomes the truth of our life, just as the naked skin is the truth beneath the cosmetics. Thus the "beautified Ophelia" comes to stand for all the strategies by which humanity seeks to avoid confronting death.

When he asks why imagination should not "trace the noble dust of Alexander till 'a find it stopping a bunghole" (5.1.203–04), Hamlet both questions the meaningfulness of the human enterprise and adopts a comic perspective on the human condition.[41] All this brings him closer to his own death. The little ditty that he sings about "Imperious Caesar, dead and turned to clay, / Might stop a hole to keep the wind away" (5.1.213–14) signals his rejection of his father's martial ambition, his own royal aspirations, and Claudius's appetite for crown and queen. It is only after Hamlet has completed this meditation on death that he announces himself as "Hamlet, the Dane" to the mourning party that assembles around Ophelia's grave. To announce himself in this way is a direct challenge to Claudius, for only the king can call himself the Dane. It is a challenge that has a suicidal aspect, for he also reminds Claudius that he has come back "naked" to the kingdom, that is, without the army he would need to unseat Claudius. Hamlet's struggle with Laertes at Ophelia's grave provides a visual prelude to the conclusion, in which Hamlet abandons himself to the drift of events that will bring him to join Ophelia in death.

It is fitting, however, that Hamlet should punctuate that journey with a final display of mental pyrotechnics when he mocks the foppish Osric, who calls him to the duel in which he will die. In this way, he maintains the comic distance from his own death even as he moves to embrace it. The combination of his wit, the drama of the final fencing match, and the melancholy beauty of his death when Horatio bids good night to his "sweet prince" (5.2.361) dramatically confirms the fundamental value of his stance in the world. The last scene provides a final irony that can be seen to wash back over the whole play. With his dying breath Hamlet gives his "election" to Fortinbras, but when Fortinbras arrives, he doesn't wait to be asked to take over the kingdom. The heroic King Hamlet fought Old King Fortinbras to reclaim a piece of Danish land, while Prince Hamlet gives the whole of Denmark to the young Norwegian warrior prince.

In submitting himself to Providence, Hamlet does succeed in killing Claudius, and, in a sense, leaves Gertrude to heaven, as the Ghost directed him to do. However, he does not exactly avenge his father's death, for when Hamlet finally does kill Claudius he does so in immediate reprisal for Claudius's attempt to kill him. Unlike revenge, immediate reprisal does not "taint" the mind and cause it to nurture rage and hatred over a prolonged period. In this Hamlet differs from the many other revenge heroes in plays of the time, which show the corrupting force of an obsessive concentration that renders the revenge hero indistinguishable from his enemies. By contrast, *Hamlet* rejects the revenge ethos, and a kind of submission triumphs.[42] He recognizes that "there is no action that can be commensurate with his grief, not even the killing of the guilty king" (35).[43] Mack writes that the "ambiguities of 'seem' coil and uncoil" (46) throughout the play.[44] Hamlet's question at the beginning of the play, which is "to be or not to be," thereby highlights what is unsettling and ambiguous about both life and death. As he prepares for his final confrontation with Laertes and Claudius, Hamlet addresses Horatio's worry that Hamlet is not ready to fight, that he has not practiced enough. He makes the famous assertion that "the readiness is all" (5.2.220) and, seeming to uncoil that earlier ambiguity, "to be or not to be," ends by advising Horatio to "let be" (5.2.222). A question about existence has been translated to his acceptance of existence as uncertainty, especially an unflinching acknowledgment that to exist is also to die. What makes Hamlet's study of grief and mortality so affecting is the detailed and psychologically powerful portrayal of a human consciousness that creates insight even as it ruminates on how little we know ourselves and those around us.

Notes

1 Marvin A. Carlson, *The Haunted Stage: The Theatre as Memory Machine*. Ann Arbor: The University of Michigan Press, 2003.
2 "The World of Hamlet." In *Hamlet: Critical Essays*. Ed. Joseph G. Price. London: Routledge, 1968.
3 Patricia Parker observes that "spying is everywhere in *Hamlet*, adding to the claustrophobia that pervades the world of the play" (257). She links this to the "political implications of surveillance" under Elizabeth I's reign (*Shakespeare from the Margins*, 270).
4 *The Comic Matrix of Shakespeare's Tragedies:* Romeo and Juliet, Hamlet, Othello *and* King Lear. Princeton: Princeton University Press, 1979.
5 *Hamlet in Purgatory*. Princeton: Princeton University Press, 2001.
6 Naomi Conn Liebler writes that the "violations that generate the play's action also engender a kind of mass separation and liminality for several of its principal characters" (182) and reads the play as an "essay in sustained liminality" (*Shakespeare's Festive Tragedy*, 182).
7 *Patterns of Knowledge*. Columbus: Ohio State University Press, 1972. For a useful discussion about the interiority of Hamlet and the question of whether this makes him "modern," see De Grazia, *Hamlet* without Hamlet, and Ann Thompson and Neil Taylor's introduction to the Arden *Hamlet*, 3rd series, 18–26. See also Richard van Oort, "Shakespeare and the Idea of Modern." *New Literary History* 37.2 (2006): 319–339.
8 For some, the play's aim is to depict not just a character but also a world filled with either mystery or disease. Maynard Mack identifies the "pervasive inscrutability" depicted in the play ("The World of *Hamlet*," 41). Phyllis Rackin argues that the "spiritual illness in Denmark does not originate with Hamlet, nor is it confined with the boundaries of his soul" (*Shakespeare's Tragedies*, 59). She says, rather that "imagery of poison and disease is associated with all of the characters, with the entire state and with nature itself" (59).
9 *Shakespeare's Tragedies*. For an example of a diagnosis of Hamlet's condition, see A.C. Bradley. He concludes that Hamlet was not melancholic but rather subject to "nervous instability, to rapid and perhaps extreme changes of feeling and mood" (*Shakespearean Tragedy: Lectures on* Hamlet, Othello, King Lear, *and* Macbeth. 1904. London: Penguin Books, 1991. 111). For other examples, see Soellner's discussion of theories of "underlying causes" of Hamlet's state of mind (*Patterns of Self-Knowledge*, 176–177).
10 Marjorie Garber recounts how Freud formulated his Oedipal theory, in *Shakespeare and Modern Culture* (pages 205–207).
11 New York: W.W. Norton & Company, 1976.
12 In *Suffocating Mothers*, Janet Adelman notes that Gertrude "becomes the carrier of a nightmare that is disjunct from her characterization as a specific figure," (16). In other words, Hamlet *feels* more about Gertrude than we are

able to account for in her words and actions. Lisa Jardine sees Gertrude as the "focus of guilt" because "she embodies the claims of kinship on women important to the line" (*Reading Shakespeare Historically*, London: Routledge, 1996. 47). In "Desire and the Interpretation of Desire," Jacques Lacan describes Ophelia as the "essential pivot in the hero's progress toward his mortal rendezvous with his act" because she is the "object" that "satisfies no need," the other that is sought but never available. (*Yale French Studies*, No. 55/56, *Literature and Psychoanalysis. The Question of Reading: Otherwise.* (1977): 11–52. 15)

13 Hamlet *Without Hamlet*. Cambridge: Cambridge University Press, 2007.
14 "Hamlet's Grief." *ELH* 48.1 (1981): 17–36.
15 "Hamlet's Grief."
16 "Shakespeare's Memorial Aesthetics" in *Shakespeare, Memory and Performance*. Ed. Peter Holland. Cambridge: Cambridge University Press, 2006. 43–62.
17 Steven Mullaney helpfully suggests that "Elizabethan England was not a revenge culture: it was an otherwise-preoccupied culture that found something it needed in stories borrowed from revenge societies on the continent. These were stories about social systems that were dysfunctional or broken […] societies in which the desire to put things right, the need for justice, has become inseparable from the need to violate what's right, the dictates of law and social order" (*The Reformation of Emotions in the Age of Shakespeare*. Chicago: The University of Chicago Press, 2015. 84–85).
18 For a description of the revenge plot in Shakespeare's source for the Hamlet story, see Greenblatt, *Hamlet in Purgatory*, 205–206).
19 *Comic Matrix*.
20 *Hamlet in Purgatory*.
21 *Hamlet in Purgatory*. Greenblatt's overall argument is that the play grapples with the difficulties of relating to the dead in the wake of the Protestant Reformation. The Reformation dispensed with the idea of purgatory, which had been a way for the living to maintain a connection with the dead.
22 "The World of Hamlet."
23 *A Theater of Envy*.
24 *A Theater of Envy*. Rackin argues that Hamlet wants revenge, but wants more than "simple revenge" (63). He wants, she says, "the purgation" of Claudius's evil (*Shakespeare's Tragedies*, 65).
25 "The Woman in Hamlet: An Interpersonal View." In *Representing Shakespeare: New Psychoanalytic Essays*. Eds. Murray M. Schwartz and Coppelia Kahn. Baltimore: The John Hopkins University Press, 1980. 110–128.
26 *The Shapes of Revenge: Victimization, Vengeance, and Vindictiveness in Shakespeare*. New Jersey: Humanities Press, 1995.
27 *The Comic Matrix*.
28 See Stephen Greenblatt, *Hamlet in Purgatory*, for more on ideas of ghosts at the time of the writing of the play.

29 Greenblatt says the Ghost represents "the unwilled, ghostly return and renewal of an old impression" (*Hamlet in Purgatory*, 214). Naomi Conn Liebler points out that Hamlet exhibits a "longing for old days and old ways, a nostalgia that would restore what was lost by the king's murder" (*The Comic Matrix*, 179).

30 Leverenz notes here that the Ghost's commands "exaggerate father's virtues, demean Hamlet's responses, and establish a confusing set of connections between nature, lust, feeling, and Gertrude" ("The Woman in Hamlet," 117).

31 John Dover Wilson emphasizes that we cannot underestimate how upsetting it is to Hamlet that Claudius has taken the throne from him: "brothers do not succeed brothers," he reminds us, "unless there is a failure in the direct line of succession" (*What Happens in Hamlet*. Cambridge: Cambridge University Press, 1951. 31). De Grazia concurs, explaining how important the premise of the play is, which is "at his father's death, just at the point when an only son in a patrilineal system stands to inherit, Hamlet is dispossessed" (Hamlet *Without Hamlet*, 1). She reminds us that such a dispossession would have been "unthinkable" in a "hereditary monarchy like England's" (1).

32 "Hamlet's Grief."

33 Chris Laoutaris describes Hamlet as performing a "vivisection of Gertrude's body" here (73), an act that is part of his "pornographic fantasy" of Gertrude's "concealed interior" (65). Laoutaris writes that more broadly, Hamlet tries to "secure authoritative knowledge through a mastery of the maternal body" (77), something that would "allow him to get to the heart of the 'matter'" (80). *Shakespearean Maternities: Crises of Conception in Early Modern England*. Edinburgh: Edinburgh University Press, 2008.

34 For more on Ophelia's songs, see Scott A. Trudell "The Mediation of Poesie: Ophelia's Orphic Song." *Shakespeare Quarterly* 63.1 (2012): 46–76; Gina Bloom, Anston Bosman and William N. West. "Ophelia's Intertheatricality, or, How Performance Is History." *Theatre Journal* 65.2 (2013): 165–82; Caralyn Bialo, "Popular Performance, the Broadside Ballad, and Ophelia's Madness." *SEL Studies in English Literature 1500–1900* 53.2 (2013): 293–309.

35 Maurice Charney observes that Hamlet shares with *Troilus and Cressida* a "discordant, satirical tone and its sense of great hopes and expectations that are lost or destroyed" (*Shakespeare on Love and Lust*. New York: Columbia University Press, 2000. 73).

36 For a useful discussion of the "rhetorical structure and dramatic function" of Ophelia's madness, see Carol Thomas Neely "'Documents in Madness': Reading Madness and Gender in Shakespeare's Tragedies and Early Modern Culture." In *Shakespearean Tragedy and Gender*. Eds. Shirley Nelson Garner and Madelon Sprengnether. Bloomington: Indiana University Press, 1996. 75–104.

37 For more on Ophelia, see Bicks, Caroline. "Instructional Performances: Ophelia and the Staging of History" in *Performing Pedagogy in Early Modern*

England: Gender, Instruction, and Performance. Eds. Moncrief, Kathryn M. and Kathryn R. McPherson. London: Routledge, 2011.

38 Charney describes Ophelia's "extraordinary passivity," which leaves her "devalued" and "disempowered" (*Shakespeare on Love and Lust*, 76). Conn Liebler writes that Ophelia is "hybridized" as evident in her mermaid-like death, and is "permanently indistinct" (*Festive Tragedy*, 184). Matthew A. Fike explains that Hamlet "sees whoredom everywhere [...] in Ophelia because he presumably fornicates with her [...] and in Gertrude because she incestuously weds Claudius" (112) because he has not "adequately integrated the shadow" (119), which is, according to Jung, "everything that the subject refuses to acknowledge about himself and yet is always thrusting itself upon him directly or indirectly" (qtd. in Fike, *A Jungian Study of Shakespeare: The Visionary Mode*. New York: Palgrave Macmillan, 2009. 119).

39 "Hamlet's Grief."

40 "The Interpretation of Desire."

41 Synder charts the "comic" interaction of the gravediggers in this scene, which suggests that "human choice seems no more than a bad joke" (*The Comic Matrix*, 127).

42 Rackin suggests that "the common fate of Hamlet and Laertes" may be "Shakespeare's implicit criticism of the revenge code itself" (66–67).

43 "Hamlet's Grief."

44 "The World of Hamlet."

7

Troilus and Cressida

Troilus and Cressida is doubly problematic. It shares with the other so-called "problem comedies" (*Measure for Measure* and *All's Well That Ends Well*) a jaded and cynical tone and an array of somewhat unlikeable characters, but it conforms to no one dramatic genre. The action comes to neither a tragic nor to a comic conclusion. There is no resolution, no satisfying sense of a narrative closure, or of things having worked themselves out according to some hidden sense of inevitability: things are just left hanging. At the end, Troilus does not die tragically, does not achieve happiness, and does not revenge the wrongs done him. *Troilus and Cressida* is more like a modern black comedy than like anything else written in its time. Allan Bloom describes it as "perhaps the bleakest of all Shakespeare's plays" (79).[1] Noting the play's "satiric detachment," R.A. Foakes observes that "no character is allowed to win sufficient prominence or sympathy to dominate the stage" (45).[2] While it may be difficult for an audience to identify and sympathize fully with any one character, Kott locates the brilliance of the play in its blending of comedy with a "most bitter philosophy and passionate poetry" (62).[3] And deeper meaning emerges when we realize this is one of Shakespeare's most self-reflexive plays. We are reminded in a variety of ways that we are an audience, and the characters themselves seem uncannily aware that they are actors in a play, that they are inheritors of Chaucer's version of the story in *Troilus and Criseyde*.[4]

While Troilus and Cressida are not exactly typical tragic figures, their desperation to achieve the kind of bond we see between Romeo and Juliet is tragic in that it is always overshadowed by their partial knowledge and our full knowledge that their relationship cannot achieve tragic completion. With Troilus and Cressida, Shakespeare depicts a young couple straining to create a bond of constant faith against a literary heritage that makes this impossible, and this becomes another way, though perhaps less satisfying than *Romeo and Juliet*, of charting the tragic susceptibility of people to forces, both internal and external, beyond their control. Shakespeare also makes it possible to locate the

Thinking About Shakespeare, First Edition. Kay Stockholder, revised and updated by Amy Scott.
© 2018 John Wiley & Sons Ltd. Published 2018 by John Wiley & Sons Ltd.

inevitable demise of a loving connection within the lovers themselves who sense that they are doomed to fail live up to the ideal of tragic love.

The play is difficult for various reasons. It contains many long, philosophical speeches, which, many have thought, represent Shakespeare's views (just because they are long and philosophical). It is better to pay attention to the particular motives of the speakers and to interpret their philosophizing in terms of the dramatic action. Many of the characters, in their own way, acknowledge or suffer from the unpredictable nature of desire and emotion, the violence done to bonds that hold lovers and factions together. In wooing Cressida, Troilus tries to allay her fears of committing to him. He says that there is no real outward monster in "Cupid's pageant" and explains to her that the only frightening thing is within lovers themselves: the gap between what the lover wants and what he or she is capable of enacting. "This is the monstrosity in love, lady" he explains, "that the will is infinite and the execution confined, that the desire is boundless and the act a slave to limit" (3.2.80–2). The play searches out these limits, looking at how characters contribute to the "montrosity" of a world in which action cannot do justice to feeling and in which love and war are equally violent and inextricably linked.

The usual critical questions about the play are whether Troilus is a kind of Romeo figure, who unfortunately does not meet a proper Juliet, and whether Hector is a heroic figure whose dedication to a medieval courtly mode of warfare puts him at a disadvantage in confrontation with the crude and pragmatic Greeks. There are several possible permutations here. If one sees Troilus as a tragic victim of a corrupt world, but Hector as merely posturing, then Troilus stands out alone as a bright spot on a dark field. The play then becomes a tragedy of unrequited love and disillusioned youth, with the disillusionment focused primarily on the faithlessness of women. If one sees both Troilus and Hector in a positive light, then it becomes a double tragedy of disillusionment, Troilus experiencing his romantic disillusionment, and the audience experiencing Hector as the victim of the sad failure of a dead ideal. If one sees the play in this way, then even heavier emphasis falls on the deficiencies of women, for the blame for Troilus's tragedy would fall totally on Cressida, and the blame for the debased martial values falls on the whorish Helen. In my view, these approaches to the play do not account either for the way the play is structured, for the language of jadedness and disgust that gives it its characteristic tone, or for the way the play reveals to us how meaningful connections between people can deteriorate so quickly when subject to the vagaries of time and the changeability of emotions.

The entire play takes place in the aftermath of an act of desire that is also an act of war: overcome by her beauty, the Trojan Paris has kidnapped Helen from the Greeks and her husband Menelaus and has caused a war between the Trojans and the Greeks. *Troilus and Cressida* is structured around a double contrast that initially encourages a kind of thinking that is appropriate for some of the plays, particularly *The Merchant of Venice*. First, it is divided between the worlds of the Greeks and the Trojans, and that invites one to see one of these worlds as providing a standard by which to judge the other. However, this expectation founders since neither world possesses any moral authority. Second, the play is divided between the realm of love and the realm of war, in a way that might seem reminiscent of *Romeo and Juliet*. Again, however, the contrast of values one expects to find in such a structure fails to materialize, and neither love nor martial valor is held up as an ideal; in fact, the two realms have been entangled from the beginning. The collapse of these contrasts, which commonly function to provide meaning, accounts in large measure for the emptiness that many people sense in the play.

And yet the collapse of the realms of love and war into each other also amplifies the question that Shakespeare seems to be asking: what kind of moral or emotional strength is required to commit to someone or something over time? Falling in love, or taking what is desired, is different from *keeping* that desired person or thing. In reflecting on the reality that Troy has still not been conquered by the Greeks after seven years, Agamemnon reasons that trials like this are Jove's way of finding "persistive constancy" in men (1.3.21). The ideal of devotion – of remaining committed to a person or a cause – is set against Agamemnon's acknowledgment that "[c]hecks and disasters" are like knots caused by the accumulation of sap in a tree, sap that "[i]nfects the sound pine and diverts his grain / Tortive and errant from his course of growth" (1.3.5–9). In Agamemnon's likening of constancy to straight growth, Shakespeare once again signals that time has the capacity to change someone's devotion to a cause. And being faithful or true requires the maintenance of the correct path over time, as one ages through the "course of growth." The difficulty of maintaining "persistive constancy" – when so many factors can lead to "errant" growth – will be a preoccupation of the play as it develops the love and war plots.

The best way to trace the intersection of the various components I have touched upon is to look at the two council scenes that organize the portrayal of the Trojan and Greek worlds and from which flow the major plot lines. The Greek council scene takes place after two scenes introduce the enmeshment of the realms of love and war, the ways in which the intensity of love bleeds into the violence of war. In the first we see Troilus, in the posture of a courtly lover, announce that his love for Cressida robs him of any heart for the wars; "[b]ut I am weaker than a woman's tear" (1.1.9), he says, as he complains to Pandarus of the long delay in his meeting Cressida. However, when Aeneas comes to ask why Troilus is "not afield" (1.1.108), Troilus accuses himself of being womanish in tarrying behind, and belies his courtly stance by quickly going off to the wars with Aeneas. Love and war, it seems, are not as distinct as Troilus's courtly posture would have the audience believe. In a second scene, we see Pandarus prepare Cressida to accept Troilus, unaware that she is entirely ready to do so. He tries to glorify Troilus by claiming that Helen herself loves Troilus, that she "praised his complexion above Paris'" (1.2.99) and that "smiling becomes him better than any man in all Phrygia" (1.2.122). This is indeed a strange way to try to knit Troilus and Cressida together. Girard makes the point that Pandarus does not here highlight "any genuine quality in Troilus that would make him intrinsically worthy of love" (122)[5]; Pandarus instead makes Helen the "true incentive" (122), counting on Cressida's envy of her, her desire to be like her. There is thick irony here – Helen, one half of the broken marriage that began the war, becomes instrumental in producing an *idea* of enduring love, one in which Troilus and Cressida both claim to believe. In fact, the presence of the go-between Pandarus illustrates how far we are from *Romeo and Juliet*. Although the nurse and Friar Laurence ostensibly help Romeo and Juliet, the young lovers' desire and bond seemed to spring naturally at their first meeting. There is a sense in *Troilus and Cressida* that love is strenuously manufactured even if it is also initially *felt*.

Girard's idea that the lovers are Pandarus's "customers" and that Pandarus makes of the experience of love a "market" (152) is particularly convincing in the context of Pandarus's praise. Love is therefore always complicated because outsiders set and manipulate its value. As Patricia Parker notes, the play as a whole "endlessly debates" the "question of value or price" (223). The Trojans will decide their future in the war with the Greeks by arguing about whether or not Helen is "worth" the fight, and Cressida, as Janet Adelman puts it, "identifies herself as a thing" that "gains its value not through any intrinsic merit but through its market value, determined by scarcity" (47). The overall suggestion is that ideals like love and honor have no fixed worth and are instead endlessly relative.[6] Pandarus encourages Cressida to love Troilus because Helen admires him *more* than Paris and because Troilus smiles *better* than any man in Phrygia. In this context, it would be impossible to know where to locate the "true" Troilus or then cultivate "true" love for him.

The bond between Troilus and Cressida is crafted in the context of the battle between the Greeks and the Trojans, a context that lessens any romance that might accumulate around the lovers and any broader heroic aura that might surround the warriors. These scenes provide the context for the meeting of the Greek council. The council scene itself is composed of lengthy speeches in which each self-inflated character tries to upstage his fellows. They preserve the outward forms of courtesy, but the underlying rivalry for status empties these rituals of meaning and reveal that even within presumably unified sides, there are divisions – factions created by personal feelings rather than political insight. The commander, Agamemnon, denies responsibility for the adversities the Greeks have suffered, by arguing that the gods are testing them. Nestor, who in Homer is a wise old warrior, here delivers a windy speech that adds nothing to what Agamemnon has just said.[7] The central drama of this rhetorical contest, however, takes place in relation to Ulysses, who traditionally is the most wily, intelligent, and civilized of the Greek heroes. He begins with an elaborate show of deference to his superiors, but the inner contradictions of his speech suggest that he is covertly mocking them. Having said that all men should be silent in the presence of the great Agamemnon, who is the "great commander, nerve and bone of Greece," he asserts that they should "hear what Ulysses speaks" (1.3.55, 58). And in case someone might have missed his subtle mockery, he repeats the ploy when he describes Nestor as "hatched in silver" (1.3.65) that is, either as one who was born with the wisdom that most men have only when old, or more simply as one whose silver hair ensures his wisdom and empowers him to "knit all Greeks' ears / To his experienced tongue" (1.3.67–8), but shows that he is anything but mesmerized when he repeats, "hear Ulysses speak" (1.3.69). As he proceeds to argue that both of them are totally wrong, the elaborate forms of deference again get emptied of their meaningfulness.

The content of Ulysses' speech repeats and amplifies these strategies. In his famous speech on degree, Ulysses argues that it is the Greeks' own fault, not that of the gods, that they have suffered losses, because in their camp, "[d]egree being vizarded, / Th' unworthiest shows as fairly in the mask" (1.3.83–4). That is, because the lower orders do not respect their superiors, the elements of the entire universe are out of joint, so that "appetite, an universal wolf, / So doubly seconded with will and power, / Must make perforce an universal prey, / And last eat up himself" (1.3.121–4). This speech is the most frequently quoted version of the "Elizabethan world picture," because it encapsulates in powerful images a conventional opinion of the time that social order is necessary to the healthy functioning of a nation. Furthermore, commentators on the play once argued that Shakespeare shares this conventional wisdom, and that it therefore follows that Ulysses should be seen as an admirable figure who presents the central message of the play.[8] There are several misconceptions here. The first is that all people at a given time subscribe to the orthodox worldview; the second is that all who speak conventional wisdom must be admirable characters.[9] Though other plays suggest that on the whole Shakespeare probably subscribes to this view, the scene itself does not reveal Shakespeare's view within Ulysses' vision. It does, however, show us how this presumed wisdom can be emptied of meaning by being pronounced in such a way and in such a context as to undermine the honor and dignity of Ulysses' superiors, whom he addresses. That is, in the very process of his powerfully resonant defense of the theory of hierarchy, Ulysses violates it in order to elevate his own position. He further elevates himself at the expense of his audience when he describes how Achilles and Patroclus mock their commanders, for in describing their mockery of Agamemnon and Nestor he subversively reproduces it.[10]

On another level, we can read the "universal wolf" speech not just as a defense of social order that Ulysses' own ridicule of his superiors in the scene renders hollow. It also displays the tendency of the mind to *want* to perceive the world as ordered by a series of fixed relationships – a network in which the qualities of a person can be known by of his or her place in the chain. Ulysses says that if degree is "vizarded," then "[e]ach thing meets / In mere oppugnancy" (1.3.110–11). Ulysses' argument is that order depends on the manner in which "things" or people "meet," that is, come together, interact with, and influence each other. While he claims that the "unity and calm of married states" (100) are fixed until disorder works to "[d]ivert and crack, rend and deracinate" (99) them, the idea that order derives from the manner of things "meeting" adds a dynamic and unpredictable element to the entire theory.

Ulysses' socio-political theory mirrors the love story, in which Pandarus functions as the place of "meeting" for Troilus and Cressida, and it is through him that they see each other's value fixed. As the Trojan warriors parade across the stage in 1.2, the scene just before Ulysses makes his speech about degree, Pandarus encourages Cressida to watch and tells her "I'll tell you them all by their names as they pass by, but mark Troilus above the rest" (1.2.183–4). And indeed, as the warriors pass, Pandarus acknowledges the present soldier but deviates from the order to ask, again and again, questions like "[w]hen comes Troilus? I'll show you Troilus anon," (194–5) and "I marvel where Troilus is" (1.3.220). When Troilus actually passes their view, Pandarus assesses his virtues in relation to Hector, finding Troilus's "helm more hacked than Hector's" (1.3.234–5). Cressida mocks Pandarus' comparison of Troilus to the others, seeing his assessment of the soldiers' worth as a fiction: when Pandarus makes the claim that Troilus smiles better than other men, Cressida, noting the absurdity of his praise, replies "O, he smiles valiantly" (1.2.125). And yet she falls in love, whether or not she endorses the kind of order paraded in front of her by Pandarus, which is a manipulation of order that itself signifies a fundamental disorder in human relations. It would be impossible to say how much Pandarus' deployment of relativity has contributed to Cressida's emotion, but she says "more in Troilus thousandfold I see / Than in the glass of Pandar's praise may be" (1.2.286–7). While she claims greater insight into Troilus's worth than Pandarus, she reveals she has absorbed his way of thinking, for she defines her own view of Troilus's worth *against* Pandarus' version.

When Pandarus judges the worth of the Trojan soldiers against each other, he does produce a fiction inasmuch as it places Troilus at the top of line, above the more celebrated and older soldier Hector. The relativity that Pandarus uses to tempt Cressida, while it seems a dangerous way to promote a lasting love bond, does reveal that no matter how strong the desire to view the world in terms of order, one cannot fully banish the threat of disorder. The point is not that the world actually does fit neatly into the "line of order" that Ulysses praises (1.3.88); rather, the "universal wolf" is always present, but it is kept at bay by the belief that the world does or can work as ideally as Ulysses says it should. The play as a whole shows us, in the moments when the illusion of an "authentic place" (1.3.108) wears thin, the everyday disorder of real life and relationships.

After Ulysses makes his speech about degree, the scene comes to a head when Ulysses, who prides himself on his wit, reveals that he feels personally slighted because Achilles and Patroclus "tax our policy and call it cowardice, / Count wisdom as no member of the war, / Forestall prescience, and esteem no act / But that of hand" (1.3.197–200). He uses the plural pronoun "our" to refer to the Greek policy, but all know that Ulysses is the prime strategist. Therefore, it is Ulysses' own "degree" that Achilles violates when he dismisses Ulysses' contribution as "bed work, mappery, closet war" (1.3.205). Ulysses in turn reduces Achilles' famed heroism to "the ram that batters down the wall," while equating himself with the reason that should "guide his execution" (1.3.206, 210). What is presented as impartial wisdom boils down to personal pique. The august Greek council scene thus degenerates into a squabble of contending egos, and its political significance is further diminished by the way in which it concludes. Aeneas arrives from the Trojan camp with a message that Hector, the leading Trojan warrior, challenges the Greeks to prove in single combat that their women are more beautiful than those of the Trojans. The action that constitutes the major plot of the play issues from this trivial challenge, as though to emphasize the utter meaninglessness of a war in which Greeks and Trojans alike die for the "contaminated carrion weight" (4.1.73) of a beautiful woman.

Ulysses' character is further undermined in the action that follows from the council scene in ways that confirm this reading of his role in it. He arranges for the Greeks to select Ajax, rather than Achilles, as their champion in single combat with Hector. His object is to pique Achilles, and later in the play he baits him by instructing the other warriors to ignore Achilles as they pass by, and to disparage him in his hearing. The entire effect here is to emphasize the factions within the Greek camp and to point out that after proclaiming the "calm of married states" to be essential to a healthy nation, Ulysses does nothing but disturb the calm. After his fellow Greeks have snubbed Achilles, Ulysses engages him in conversation about the nature of the self and about honor. Essentially the two vie to outdo each other in demonstrating their intelligence, just as the Greek leaders vied with each other. Ulysses tells Achilles that the "strange fellow" whose book he is reading argues that our attributes and virtues are ours only "by reflection" (3.3.96, 100), that is, we come to know them only as they are reflected back at us by others. Achilles, finding this wisdom to be common knowledge, extends the implications by adding that the reality of beauty depends upon an observer, and even the eye itself "turns not to itself / Till it hath traveled and is mirrored there / Where it may see itself. This is not strange at all" (3.3.110–12). Ulysses counters by elaborating his first comment:

> no man is the lord of anything,
> Though in and of him there be much consisting,
> Till he communicate his parts to others;
> Nor doth he of himself know them for aught

Till he behold them formed in the applause
Where they're extended; who, like an arch reverb'rate
The voice again, or, like a gate of steel
Fronting the sun, receives and renders back
His figure and his heat. (3.3.116–24)

Because this intellectual discourse is part of Ulysses' strategy to get Achilles back into the battle, as well as being part of the rivalry between the two men, its sincerity could be called into question. And yet, it offers another instance of the play being self-reflective. The "parts" that a man communicates to observers is like the parts, or roles, an actor may play, and the observer's reaction, in being termed "applause" is a reference to one of the few responses an audience can offer to a pleasing actor or play.

The truth of this reading – that the virtues of an actor and a play must be communicated to and recognized by and audience – is undeniable. And this entirely sincere expression of the actor–audience dynamic highlights yet another kind of bond, or unity, that is essential to produce meaning or achieve success. The play's political battles and Troilus's wooing of Cressida are versions of the playwright and actors' efforts to win the approval of the audience. In the end, Ulysses fails to make Achilles sufficiently worried about his reputation to return to battle; he returns only in grief and rage over the death of his lover, Patroclus. Finally, both men are shown to share a conception of the person in which the inwardness of a Hamlet must be shared with others to maintain and in some way make real the integrity of individual bodies and to knit them to other bodies.

Another feature of Ulysses' argument to Achilles is that honor can only exist as long as it is maintained over time. Past honor is quickly supplanted by more recent accomplishments, and thus the ideal itself is not a fixed place – a "fixture" – that is found once and lasts forever, but a tenuous state of being, a "course of growth," that must be actively sought over time. "Time hath," he explains to Achilles, "a wallet at his back, / Wherein he puts alms for oblivion, [...] Those scraps are good deeds past, which are devoured / As fast as they are made, forgot as soon / As done. Perseverance, dear my lord, / Keeps honor bright" (3.3.146–52). When he compares "good deeds" to "scraps" or garbage that are meaningless once over, Ulysses actually debases honor in itself, as it is in the moment it is earned, in order to encourage its continuance over time through consistent action. Ulysses finally boils down the long philosophical argument into a pithy statement that "things in motion sooner catch the eye / Than what not stirs" (3.3.184–5). Once again, the wisdom of Ulysses' speech is undermined by its calculating nature – he intends to lure Achilles back into the battle – and by his suggestion that deeds are only good if they "catch the eye," that goodness equates to brightness. He plays to Achilles' pride rather than to a sense that honor is desirable for its own sake. Yet his speech carries some of the play's overall message that to be true to an ideal, a person must embody it over time. Ulysses's philosophy reveals that honor, like so many other things in the play, is not fixed.

The Trojan council scene follows hard on that of the Greeks, separated only by a short scene in which we are exposed to the misanthropic Thersites' scurrilous abuse of the stupid Ajax. This council has been called by Priam to discuss Nestor's offer of peace. Though the argument in this scene is subtler and turns on more complex issues than did the Greek council, the brothers who participate in it are equally quick to inflate themselves and to insult and denigrate each other. Furthermore, these more philosophic arguments turn out either to have no bearing on the action that is finally proposed, or to be as much in the interests of those who speak them as are the cruder speeches of the Greeks.

Hector takes the lead in proposing to return Helen on the grounds that it is unreasonable to continue fighting in a wrong cause for an unworthy object. Troilus opposes him, not by arguing that their cause is just, but rather by questioning whether reason should be a guide to action. In doing so he carries forward the opposition between reason and honor that appeared in *Henry IV* and *Hamlet.* However, he brings a different spirit to the matter when he asks whether the great girth of Priam's dignity cannot be measured "[w]ith spans and inches so diminutive / As fears and reasons?" (2.2.31–2), thus making an equation between reason and cowardice – a connection with which we saw Hamlet grapple and with which he ultimately came to terms. In so doing, Troilus overturns the conventional hierarchy of human faculties in which reason should reign supreme over the will, which in turn should regulate the passions in accordance with reason's dictates. Helenus, the priest, quips that Troilus is opposed to reason because he is stupid, and Troilus returns the barb, accusing Helenus of self-indulgence.

Troilus then introduces a view of value that suggests it is not fixed but a product of people's perspectives. He counters Hector's assertion that Helen is not worth fighting for with the brief question, "[w]hat's aught, but as 'tis valued?" (2.2.52). Troilus's position is that there are no absolute standards, and that all value is relative. This profound question about the nature of value haunts the entire action. Troilus's arguments, like those of Ulysses, turn out to be unselfconsciously self-serving. In response to Hector's traditional view that it is idolatrous to value something more than its intrinsic worth, Troilus resorts to a devious argument in which he asserts that reason, far from being the superior faculty, should carry out the dictates of the senses:

> I take today a wife, and my election
> Is led on in the conduct of my will –
> My will enkindled by mine eyes and ears,
> Two traded pilots twixt the dangerous shores
> Of will and judgment. (2.2.61–65)

In asserting that his senses must function as mediators between his will, or what he wants, and his judgment, or his reason, he comes closest to honestly expressing what drives characters in the play to do and say what they do. That is, rather than endorsing the belief that reason must direct the will to control the passions as in conventional Platonic or Christian morality, in Troilus's version, the passions often mobilize people's energies and determine the judgments people make.

While Troilus encourages the Trojans to continue to value Helen as highly they did when Paris was first encouraged to take her, Troilus nonetheless undermines his own argument in the process of making it, for he describes Helen in ways that debase her. He says that Paris brought home a queen whose "youth and freshness / Wrinkles Apollo's and makes stale the morning" (2.2.78–9). Presumably he means that in comparison to her youth, Apollo, or the sun, seems old, and in comparison to her freshness the morning seems stale, but the line reads equally powerfully with the opposite meaning – that she is destroys the morning's freshness and the sun's brightness. This negative reading of Helen is further supported by fact that the term "stale" in Shakespeare's time was used to describe a prostitute. It is this second reading that accords with the images of Helen that permeate the play. Even Paris, who, as Priam says, "has the honey still" of Helen's capture, also uses ambiguous images when he says that he would have "the soil of her fair rape / Wiped off in honorable keeping" of the "ransacked queen" (2.2.148–50). The scene in which she appears shows her as trivial and venal in a way that reinforces Diomedes' passionate denunciation of her to Paris:

> For every false drop in her bawdy veins
> A Grecian's life hath sunk; for every scruple
> Of her contaminated carrion weight
> A Trojan hath been slain. Since she could speak,
> She hath not given so many good words breath
> As for her Greeks and Trojans suffered death. (4.1.71–6)

In the absence of any alternative view of her, when Troilus himself speaks of Helen in images that suggest her worthlessness, he belies his own argument that her value derives not from her, but from the value she acquires from those who fight for her. Therefore, though the question he raises has genuine philosophical import, his manner of argument undermines the seriousness of the question, the more so because the off-stage audience knows what his on-stage audience doesn't – that he is covertly defending his choice of Cressida as a lover.

Thus is Troilus's argument compromised (though his premise is not thereby invalidated), and one would expect that Hector's view would command greater respect. However, no sooner has Troilus finished than Hector sets himself up as a kind of Aristotle lecturing to neophytes. He adopts some of the self-inflating manner that we saw in the Greek camp, but he delivers a straightforward speech, based on what would be common sense for most people, to the effect that Helen was wrongly taken, and therefore should be returned to her people and her rightful husband. However, he undermines the status of reasonable argument as a basis for action when he unexpectedly does an about-face and comes down on the side of keeping Helen because, "'tis a cause that hath no mean dependence / Upon our joint and several dignities" (2.2.192–3). Hector thus disperses the meaningfulness of the entire debate, and further undermines its import when he announces that he has already sent the Greeks the challenge that we have previously heard them receive. The implication is that he assumed before this council ever took place that they would keep Helen, and that the rest has been a rhetorical exercise or show. That Hector chooses the word "dependence" to defend his decision to keep her is telling. It speaks to the idea of "meeting" or coming together that both upheld and threatened Ulysses' idea of order. If we were to make the mistake of thinking dependence of one person on another could be an intimate, valuable bond, the play here positions it as a negative state simply because it seems meaningless since Hector himself has already outlined valid and politically sound reasons for ending the war.

The play also stresses the prevalence and destructive power of trivial vanity. Vanity empties whatever it touches of stable meaning and fixed worth. This motif receives its culminating statement toward the end of the play when Hector, having refused to fight with Thersites as too base an adversary to give him honor, fights instead for the glittering armor of an unknown enemy. When he has defeated his adversary, he says, "[m]ost putrefièd core, so fair without, / Thy goodly armor thus hath cost thy life" (5.8.1–2). The image easily stands for the whole of the war, but takes on added irony when Achilles' Myrmidons attack and kill the now unarmed Hector, who himself becomes the "putrefièd core," who gave his life for glittering armor. The image of the glittering decay is a comment on the Trojans and Greeks alike. But one cannot conclude from this that Shakespeare thinks that inquiry into the basis of right action and the nature of honor is futile; we have already discussed how these questions are central both to *Henry IV* and *Hamlet*.

The challenge of adhering to "honorable keeping," a challenge that marks both the Greek and Trojan experience with war, also shapes the relationship between Troilus and Cressida. Troilus casts himself as courtly lover in the first scene, but his feeling for Cressida seems as violently sensual as are Paris' "hot deeds" with Helen. As Troilus anticipates his first tryst with Cressida, he emphasizes the extremity of passion that he espoused in the council scene. He says that his senses are so transported by the imagination of making love with Cressida that he fears that his dream of "[l]ove's thrice repurèd nectar" (3.2.21) will be too much to bear in reality and cannot really be fulfilled. Maurice Charney suggests that we can see the demise of Troilus's desire foretold in the "extravagant, overwrought, even grotesque" imagery Troilus's use to describe his passion for Cressida (71), that overworked, "thrice repuréd" nectar which is "too sharp in sweetness" (3.2.20, 22). David Koula notes the "self-obsessive nature of Troilus's passion" at this moment, "of its tendency to prolong and intensify the process of yearning rather than to seek consummation in active experience and the responsive love of another" (275).[11] The extremity underlying his "self-obsession" appears when, before their night together and in the face of Cressida's doubt about his sincerity, he declares himself, with dizzying wording, to be "as true as truth's simplicity, / And simpler than the infancy of truth" (3.2.168–9). He strains to express his sincerity, but in saying there is a form of truth "simpler" than others, he subjects the idea of truth, like so many other values in the play, to the force of relativism. Troilus uses the term "infancy" to describe his state of pure love. In drawing on the language of the stages of life, Troilus echoes *The Merchant of Venice*'s song, which said that fancy often dies in its "cradle," meaning that desire does not last long. This will certainly prove true of Troilus's desire for Cressida. In linking love, especially sensual love, to a state of childlike innocence, Shakespeare renders it ironic. This state of innocence cannot last. Time intervenes and children age, moving steadily away from what they might consider their purest selves. Under this perspective, there can be no absolute and fixed "right" and "wrong" on which to base one's actions. This is why the decision to continue to wage the war becomes so complex for both sides. Troilus's assertion is also self-contradictory, because were it true he could not say it. That is, a fully naive person cannot know himself or herself to be naive. Furthermore, this assertion concludes a cynical speech to Cressida in which he exclaims on how uplifted he would be if he could believe that "it could be in a woman" to equal him in "integrity and truth" (3.2.157, 164), hardly the view of someone who is himself "simpler than the infancy of truth." The cynicism of the characters, or the ultimate fate against which they work, reflects that of the play when Troilus, Cressida, and Pandarus each define themselves in terms of their literary forebears. With a great rhetorical flourish, Troilus says that "[a]s true as Troilus" will "sanctify the number" of all true lovers' verse, Cressida says that if she be false, then "[a]s false as Cressid" will express the essence of all falsehood, and Pandarus says that if they are false to each other, then all "goers-between" such as he will be called Pandars (3.2.181, 195, 200). This blurring of the line between the play and its sources emphasizes the already scripted nature of the action and the sense of inevitability that time, and the changeable emotions of people over time, will eventually compromise the "integrity and truth" of Troilus and Cressida's love.

Part of the play's brilliance is the manner by which it complicates the Troilus and Cressida story. Elizabethan audiences would have been familiar with the narrative that a false Cressida betrays a loyal Troilus. That scholars and stage directors can both follow this narrative *and* challenge it speaks to the play's subtle manipulation of the script that it also follows. The negative view of

Shakespeare's Cressida is tenacious. Allan Bloom reads the play within this narrative by arguing that Shakespeare's Cressida is a "perfect coquette" whose journey in the play is a "descent into wantonness" (83). He adds that by the end of the play, Troilus is the only "true person" in the play (95).[12] E. Talbot Donaldson, on the other hand, marvels at the endurance of this interpretation of Cressida, remarking that "[s]uch preoccupation with establishing Cressida's sluttishness seems to reflect a kind of emotional involvement with her that is less literary than personal." He says, "I can think of no literary characters who have been subjected to criticism less cool-headed than Criseyde and Cressida" (86) and reminds us that we must attend carefully to Cressida's words. She demonstrates "vitality," he says, with the "brevity of her comments," and "her questions establish her as someone unsure of herself, but alert and seeking answers" (87).[13] We are thus disposed to be sympathetic to her if we are alert to the vitality with which Shakespeare has imbued her. Moreover, the reading of the play that sees only Cressida's "sluttishness" fails to account for the psychological currents that are discernible both before and after the lovers consummate their union, currents that can render Troilus cruel or woefully naive and Cressida tragically vulnerable.

Early in the play, Pandarus and Cressida engage in verbal banter as Pandarus tries to "sell" Troilus as desirable. When Cressida appears to resist this product, Pandarus says "[y]ou are such another woman! One knows not at what ward you lie" (1.2.260). Cressida's response seizes the idea of "lying" that Pandarus brings up, and plays upon the word. She begins with the literal term, to be laying down, and gradually transforms "lie" to mean "rely": "[u]pon my back to defend my belly; upon my wit to defend my wiles, upon my secrecy to defend mine honesty; my mask to defend my beauty; and you to defend all these: and at all these wards I lie, at a thousand watches" (1.2.262–6). Donaldson writes that most editors interpret the speech as Cressida's bawdy description of "offering herself up to sexual attack" (89). Yet he instead argues that Cressida reveals herself as someone "who realizes how inadequate her defenses are against Pandarus and Troilus from the outside and against her love for Troilus on the inside" (89). Inevitably enfolded into these meanings of "lie" is another one that haunts the play: falsehood. While Cressida gradually seems "false" to Troilus in the play, this speech, in which she travels through the various meanings of the word, unfixes the idea of falsehood from any concrete and stable position. Her fluid language enacts this destabilization of our judgment.

Cressida's admission of fear that her worth depends only on keeping herself chaste gives her character complexity and realistic depth, leading many to "defend" Cressida against readings like Bloom's. While Cressida is always on the verge in the play of living up to the traditional script, Janet Adelman contends that at the start of the play, "we feel her presence not as a stereotype but as a whole character" whose "chief concern is with her vulnerability" (46, 47).[14] In his Arden edition of the play, David Bevington points out that "nowhere, despite what men will say of her, does Cressida reveal herself as driven by promiscuous sexual desire" (53).[15] Instead, he says, Cressida is trapped in a realistic emotional confusion: she experiences "the longing for trust and the opposite fear of loss of autonomy" (54). She reflects on and articulates this conflict beautifully in the moments before she will give herself to Troilus. "I have a kind of self resides with you," she says, "But an unkind self that itself will leave / To be another's fool" (3.2.147–9). In this complicated statement, Cressida admits to a growing division within her. We could read this as her awareness that part of her seeks the union with Troilus and part of her resists the thought of being made a "fool," or possession, of another. But the particularly convoluted wording – "an unkind self that itself will leave" – challenges understanding and leaves us wondering where to locate Cressida's true "self." At the very least, Cressida highlights two possible selves – the kind and unkind – and she seems to hover between them, recognizing that in giving herself to Troilus, she is losing a part of herself that cannot be recovered.

Just as Cressida has been afforded more sympathetic readings, Troilus has been subject to more critical ones. As Bevington and others note, Troilus seems preoccupied with having a sensual experience. Were this all that he wanted, he would pursue and achieve it as a sensualist. Yet he also seems to want something pure and innocent, which part of him understands cannot be achieved through bodily, worldly experience. Adelman says that his desire is for a "fusion with the beloved" so complete that it "annihilates boundaries, transforming identity itself" (39). Koula makes the point that the "real object of [Troilus's] aspiration is a generalized, bodiless image of perfection which completely excludes [...] all contingencies inherent in the relationship between person and person" (276). The play consistently demonstrates that a state of "bodiless perfection" is unattainable. In seeking out this impossible state, and in seeking it through physical intimacy, Troilus may be cheating himself and Cressida of an authentic, emotionally resonant connection. As Bevington observes, the sensual experience is subject to "disillusionment" (23) if one hopes to achieve a transcendent union through it, and it "leaves little room for more tender emotions of mutual sympathy and commitment" (41). These tender emotions are completely absent from the play.

Thus, the fantasy that Troilus seeks in fact becomes detrimental to any sustained connection between the two lovers because it serves only to remind Troilus and Cressida of what they may be lacking. Marianne Novy describes the bond between Troilus and Cressida as "unintegrated sexuality" (115),[16] so that once Troilus has had this sensual experience with Cressida, he has no further physical longing for her and seems anxious to leave her, telling her repeatedly to return "to bed" (4.2.4, 7) in a scene that darkly echoes the similar but much more tender scene in *Romeo and Juliet*. Novy observes that at this point Troilus seems "anxious to be off in the world of men who think about other things than love" (118) and describes his treatment of Cressida here as "condescending" (118). Similarly, Bevington says that Troilus speaks "patronizingly" here, "in the language of command" (43),[17] and Girard says that because at this point Troilus's "original 'desire' is completely dead" (128), he is insensitive to Cressida (128).[18]

While Troilus and Cressida's union is scripted to be destroyed from the beginning, there is psychological depth to its demise. Both lovers struggle with what they know about the reality of love, and these internal struggles begin to shape how they relate to each other. In addition to making Troilus seem to lose his desire for Cressida, as she has feared he would, Shakespeare also crafts a Troilus who is deeply afraid that Cressida will not remain faithful to him once she is sent to the Greeks in exchange for Antenor. At first he says "[b]e thou but true of heart," and when Cressida resents his doubt, he explains he expresses it not from "fearing" or doubting her, but simply as a reminder that he will try to visit her in the Greek camp (4.4.58, 62). And yet moments later, after exchanging tokens, Troilus repeats the plea, urging her "[b]ut yet, be true" (4.4.74). When Cressida objects again to his doubt, he reveals that he is indeed worried that the Greek youth, "full of quality," will tempt Cressida; this "godly jealousy," he admits, makes him "afeared" (4.4.76, 80, 82). Girard argues that Troilus's desire for Cressida is inflamed again only because Troilus has been reminded of "the Greek's erotic reputation" (130); she has become valuable again as an instrument by which Troilus measures himself against the Greeks and as a means of maintaining what he believes to be true about himself. He does not love her, but he needs her.

When Cressida boldly asks Troilus if he thinks she will be tempted, he replies that while he does not think she intends to be unfaithful, he points out that "something may be done that we will not; / And sometimes we are devils to ourselves / When we will tempt the frailty of our powers, / Presuming on their changeful potency" (4.4.94–7). Troilus's doubts about Cressida's ability to be faithful are in fact larger doubts about human constancy and the limits of the human will. He does not single Cressida out; in fact, he uses the pronoun "we" to include himself as subject to such vulnerabilities. He notes that the failure of will comes from within ("we are devils to ourselves"), and this is evidenced in their uncomfortable parting exchange. How can a union possibly last when every "self" carries within it another self, an unkind self, a devil?

The deterioration of love into uncertainty appears nowhere so graphically as in this scene of triple eavesdropping in which Thersites eavesdrops on Troilus and Ulysses as they eavesdrop on Cressida and Diomedes. The layers of observation, into which the play's audience must also be included, make it hard to pinpoint the "truth" or sincerity of Cressida's original bond with Troilus or her reasons for transferring her affection from Troilus to Diomedes. Cressida seems torn between fully offering herself to Diomedes and maintaining her vow to Troilus. Several times she resists Diomedes, only to draw him back into the scene as he is about to angrily leave. The audience is not privy to

Cressida's internal thoughts as they are to Troilus's when he observes and comments on the exchange; her reasons for calling Diomedes back are obscure even if we believe Thersites' cynical interpretation that she toys with Diomedes simply to increase his ardor. Diomedes himself, seeming to prove Thersites' view of her behavior, expresses impatience with Cressida's dithering and presses her even harder to confirm her "surety" (5.2.61). Earlier in the play, Cressida herself lamented giving herself too quickly to Troilus; we may feel that perhaps she is strategically toying with Diomedes because she has learned her lesson. But even if we admit that much, we must still recognize that she might be doing so because she is still driven by fear of being vulnerable to a powerful man. Her manipulation of Diomedes then could be her way of asserting her power over him in a context over which she has no control. Moreover, if we take her at her word that she must withhold herself to increase her lover's ardor, we must then acknowledge too her admission that she was unsuccessful at withholding her love from Troilus, a failure that bespeaks of her "real" attraction to him. Cressida's uncertainty reaches its pitch when she gives Diomedes the love token that Troilus gave her and then tries to retrieve it several times.

When Diomedes leaves, we are finally privy to Cressida's thoughts. But they are convoluted, and seem to dislocate responsibility for her betrayal of Troilus. Rather than her actions issuing from a unified person with a governable will, they issue from a divided body that cannot control itself:

> Troilus, farewell! One eye yet looks on thee,
> But with my heart the other eye doth see.
> Ah, poor our sex! This fault in us I find:
> The error of our eye directs our mind.
> What error leads must err. O, then conclude:
> Minds swayed by eyes are full of turpitude. (5.2.110–15)

Cressida's body is split in several ways. At first she explains that one eye remains on Troilus while the other, influenced by her heart, looks at Diomedes. Furthermore, she explains that women's heart-led eye, a mistake in itself, then "directs our mind" into making another mistake. There is a chain of mistakes, she indicates, that has led her from Troilus to Diomedes. Troilus revealed to us that there are degrees of truth in the play, and Cressida here reveals there are also degrees of error. And her reference to the steps her body has taken to break her faith with Troilus echoes her earlier reference to her "kind" and "unkind" selves – two halves within her that cannot be reconciled.

Sensing the division within Cressida and reluctant to believe her betrayal, Troilus exclaims afterward that "[t]his is and is not Cressid" (5.2.150). Troilus himself struggles to produce a narrative that would explain or excuse her betrayal, indicating the level of his anguish or the level of his own emotional confusion. At first he generously hopes that critics of women will not "square the general sex / By Cressid's rule." "Rather," he says, "think this not Cressid" (5.2.135–6). Then, revealing how much his love for Cressida is entangled with his competition with the Greeks, he proclaims that he hates Diomedes as much as he still loves Cressida. Finally, Troilus levels the blame entirely on Cressida, in an anguished lamentation: "O Cressid! O false Cressid! False, false, false! / Let all untruths stand by thy stainèd name" (5.2.182–3). Troilus's grief itself has gone through a transformation – first absolving women in general, then finally condemning Cressida and using her example to define future "untruths." Even as Troilus laments the loss of his love, we can hear his condemnation of her as "false, false, false" ringing in our ears and remember Cressida playing with the word "lie" to articulate her need for self-defense.

As Adelman notes, however, at this point in the play Cressida makes a "sudden move into opacity" (50),[19] with no further words and with a diminishing presence in the play. Adelman is right to say that because we do not know her thoughts and feelings as she gives herself to Diomedes, she "seems to betray us the same time as she betrays Troilus" (51).[20] If we have been attendant and sympathetic to her self-doubts, worries, and observations earlier in the play, we are not likely to simply dismiss her actions as wanton or opportunistic. But we have no evidence with which to fully absolve her of the guilt that she has always, from the beginning, carried.

Love's tantalizing nectar was once so refined in Troilus's mind ("thrice repurèd"), that he felt it would be "too subtle-potent" for his "ruder powers" (3.2.23–24). By the end of the play, the whole of the affair is returned to the images of garbage that characterized Helen when Troilus says of Cressida that "[t]he fragments, scraps, the bits and greasy relics / Of her o'ereaten faith, are bound to Diomed" (5.2.163–4). Where once Troilus imagined love with Cressida as an act of consuming a refined, sweet liquid, now he feels he has been consuming something gross and disgusting material, something that others have also consumed. Here there is nothing "subtle-potent" left for Troilus to believe in, and the play has never given to us an example of it. The reality of Cressida's faith, and the nature of love in general, likely falls somewhere between the nectar and the scraps that represent the extremity of Troilus's thinking. At the play's end, we are left with Troilus's promise to pursue Diomedes on the battlefield, and with Pandarus' epilogue, in which he wishes upon the audience the venereal diseases that have been a major source of images throughout the play. While Hamlet said that the world was "nothing ... but a foul and pestilent congregation of vapors" (2.2.303–04), he clearly felt that it was more complicated than that, and even that it afforded admirable examples of value and beauty. The characters in *Troilus and Cressida* seem never to get very far beyond an acknowledgment of the "frailty of our power."

Notes

1 *Shakespeare on Love and Friendship*. Chicago: University of Chicago Press, 2000.
2 *Shakespeare The Dark Comedies to the Last Plays: From Satire to Celebration*. London: Routledge, 1971.
3 *Shakespeare Our Contemporary.*
4 For a discussion of Shakespeare's use of Chaucer, see E. Talbot Donaldson, *The Swan at the Well: Shakespeare Reading Chaucer*. New Haven: Yale University Press, 1985. See also Kris Davis-Brown, "Shakespeare's Use of Chaucer in 'Troilus and Cressida': 'That the Will Is Infinite, and the Execution Confined.'" *South Central Review* 5.2 (1988): 15–34; Jill Mann, "Shakespeare and Chaucer: 'What is Criseyde worth?'" *The Cambridge Quarterly* 18.2 (1989): 109–128; David McInnis, "Repetition and Revision in Shakespeare's Tragic Love Plays." *Parergon* 25.3 (2008): 33–56; *Love, History and Emotion in Chaucer and Shakespeare:* Troilus and Criseyde *and* Troilus and Cressida. Eds. Andrew James Johnston, Russell West-Pavlov and Elisabeth Kempf. Manchester: Manchester University Press, 2016. See also Daniel M. Murtaugh, "Troilus And Cressida in the Light of Day: Shakespeare Reading Chaucer." *English* 65.250 (2016): 191–210.
5 *Theater of Envy.*
6 Ralph Soellner suggests Troilus himself sees people in terms of their commercial value and locates them in a "shifting and changing" system "in which pearls can be marked up and down according to the dictates of the will, an instrument very much subject to envious and calumniating time" (*Shakespeare's Patterns of Self-Knowledge*. Columbus: Ohio State University Press, 1972. 204–205).
7 For more on Nestor, see Maurice Charney, *Wrinkled Deep in Time: Aging in Shakespeare*. New York: Columbia University Press, 2009. 70–72.
8 For example, see E.M.W. Tillyard, *The Elizabethan World Picture*. London: Chatto & Windus, 1943.
9 For example, one of the more popular bits of wisdom to come from *Hamlet* is Polonius's advice to Laertes: "to thine own self be true" (1.3.78). While the phrase is undoubtedly touching and wise, Polonius would never be termed an admirable character, and since the play at large explores how difficult it is to know oneself, being true to oneself proves an almost impossible task.
10 In a starkly different interpretation, Allan Bloom describes Ulysses as "triumphant" in the play, as someone who "represents the consolation of philosophy in a dark world" (*Shakespeare on Love and Friendship*, Chicago: Chicago University Press, 1993. 81).
11 "Will and Reason in *Troilus and Cressida*." *Shakespeare Quarterly* 12.3 (1961): 271–283.
12 *Shakespeare on Love and Friendship.*

13 *The Swan at the Well: Shakespeare Reading Chaucer.*
14 *Suffocating Mothers.*
15 "Introduction." *Troilus and Cressida.* The Arden Shakespeare. Revised Ed. Ed. David Bevington. London: Bloomsbury, 2015.
16 *Love's Argument.*
17 "Introduction." *Troilus and Cressida.*
18 *Theater of Envy.*
19 *Suffocating Mothers.*
20 *Suffocating Mothers.*

8

Othello

Othello carries forward the motif of love-death romance that Shakespeare had not dealt with directly since *Romeo and Juliet*. Like the earlier play, *Othello* generates, from the very beginning, a sense of the inevitability of the lovers' demise. However, this play differs from the earlier one in that it links that sense of inevitability to the characters of the lovers themselves and to the nature of romantic love, rather than seeing it at work in external circumstance alone. It involves us in the complex mixture of social and personal imperatives and motivations that can make romantic love simultaneously momentous and fragile. Indeed, *Othello* depicts a kind of intimacy so powerful it renders the lovers vulnerable to internal doubts and external manipulation. What results is a harrowing account of the nature of love. A.C. Bradley identifies the "dark fatality" of the play, in which love is defined as a "tortured mixture of longing and loathing" (169).[1] In his nihilistic reading of the play, Girard says *Othello* is about "the darkest desire, a desire no longer tempted by anything but its own apocalyptic self-destruction" (295).[2] The term "apocalyptic self-destruction" suits the play; it may be a story about one man torn apart by his own doubts, but the play's harrowing tone and imagery makes it seem like the stakes are nothing less than humanity itself. Othello's inability to believe Desdemona, a woman so thoroughly good she refuses to denounce Othello even as she lay dying, feels like a triumph of evil over good.

Romeo and Juliet attributes its tragic inevitability to an ominous Fate that issues from the past of the lovers' families and turns their generative powers against themselves. This linking occurs first in the Prologue, and it is carried forward by means of the lovers' premonitions. In *Othello*, the sense of inevitability arises from the enmity of Iago, whose villainy is often seen as what drives the play, though Othello and Desdemona certainly contribute to their own destruction. References to hell and damnation from the most pervasive image pattern of the play, and it is clear that Shakespeare demonizes Iago. As the tempter, Iago plays on Othello's tendency to degrade and distrust women, while Desdemona, as a compassionate guardian angel, calls for Othello's act of faith.

Thinking About Shakespeare, First Edition. Kay Stockholder, revised and updated by Amy Scott.
© 2018 John Wiley & Sons Ltd. Published 2018 by John Wiley & Sons Ltd.

The prominent role of Iago and his manifest villainy is, however, liable to obscure aspects of Desdemona and Othello themselves that are necessary for the action to take the course it does. From the beginning, Othello is characterized as an outsider. In the first scene, Iago expresses his resentment of Othello for not nominating him his lieutenant. Iago's hatred plays on and stresses Othello's physical difference and spatial distance from the Venetians. When Iago and Roderigo maliciously inform Brabantio that his daughter Desdemona has run away with Othello, they call Othello "the thick-lips," and liken him to "an old black ram" and a "Barbary horse" (1.1.68, 90, 114). Further stressing Othello's difference from Venetians, Roderigo terms Othello an "extravagant and wheeling stranger" (1.1.139), Brabantio then follows suit when confronting Othello. He attacks Othello with emphasis on Othello's complexion, saying that because Othello is "[d]amned," he likely "enchanted" Desdomona to his "sooty bosom" (1.2.64, 71). Conversely, Desdemona is called a "white" ewe (1.1.88) and is insistently called "fair."[3] The implication is that because he has dark skin and because he is not Venetian, Othello is a malevolent outsider.

To see the lovers in the context of the opposition between light and dark skin is to confront an upsetting racial discourse. Celia R. Daileader explains that at the time of the writing of the play, those with a "dark complexion" were associated with the "unlovely and therefore lascivious" in opposition to an idea of "fair" which carried a sense of "beautiful" that also had a "moral resonance" (14). In *Othello*, Daileader argues, Shakespeare "pairs a black man and a white woman in such as a way as to render the former a vehicle for misogynist figurations of a woman's sexual sullying, with all the racist-voyeuristic titillation that such a spectacle provides" (15).[4] Thus, Desdemona is guilty "by association" with Othello (26) and even has "complicity in her own murder" (24).[5] Natasha Korda considers how the racial and gender discourses of the play reflect the cultural belief that "women and Africans" have a "skewed relations to material objects" (113). The distinction between primitive and civilized objects "accords personhood to those recognized as 'one of us'" and denies personhood to the other (113). Korda explains how Desdemona's handkerchief, a symbol of the civilized, is incorrectly overvalued by Othello, a mistake that leads to their downfall. It is not possible to absolve Shakespeare of being racist or misogynistic. Ultimately, we must remember that the play's exploration of the characters' motivations and actions is necessarily entangled with the discourses that frame and shape them.[6] As in *The Merchant of Venice*, in *Othello* Shakespeare plays with racial stereotypes. What is particularly difficult to come to terms with is that we are clearly not meant to identify with Iago, so we can view his slurs against Othello with disdain. And yet Othello himself is not an admirable character, and in some ways, the negative views of him are borne out over the course of the play. Thus, we must consider more closely some questions of characterization: who is Othello, and what causes him to lose faith with Desdemona so easily?

Though he is perceived as a stranger, Othello prides himself on his martial reputation, and on his importance to Venice. Shakespeare makes very clear the degree to which Othello's sense of identity rests on his self-definition as one who manifests the control and self-confidence that befits a general. This mastery appears when he says, "[m]y parts, my title, and my perfect soul / Shall manifest me rightly" (1.2.31–2), when Iago tells him that Brabantio is up on arms against him, and in his equanimity in the face of an incensed Brabantio and his officers who have drawn their swords: "Keep up your bright swords, for the dew will rust them" (1.2.60). It appears as well in the assured and measured tones with which he explains his marriage to the Senate. This same easy self-command, however, acquires an ironic edge when he takes charge after Iago has instigated a fight to disturb the peace of the night between Cassio and Montano. Here Othello acts in his accustomed manner as he cashiers Cassio, but the very trait that seemed his strength now appears as a weakness that makes him vulnerable to Iago's manipulations. Othello's sense of himself in these incidents is entirely congruent with the way in which the Venetians think about him, for the action confirms his confidence that the Turkish threat makes his services indispensable.

His absolute adherence to this martial self-image means that he has left the more tender parts of his character malnourished. Othello's sketch of his past to Desdemona makes clear that he not only thinks of himself as a military commander, but as *only* a military commander. He has suffered and endured a hard life, and with travail has earned the status he now enjoys. It would seem that he has never known his original family in a normal way, and he has never had a family of his own. His life has consisted of the soldier's camaraderie, and he does not think of himself in relation to women, wives, or female tenderness. Thus, however valued he is, he remains an outsider, a stranger, to the Venetian social world and domestic space. This sense of himself coheres with the Venetian view of him. Brabantio invited him to his house and was entertained by his tales, but he left Othello alone with Desdemona because it simply did not strike him that his daughter could love the Moor. Othello's awareness of the limits of the love that Brabantio bears him appears in the fact that he and Desdemona elope, without even thinking to seek Brabantio's consent.

It would seem, then, that Othello has internalized the Venetian view of him as a martial hero who is unsuited to the softer pleasures of love and marriage, and certainly unsuited to court the elegant daughter of a Venetian aristocrat. When Desdemona encourages him to tell his story and then weeps over his recollected sorrows, Othello opens his soul to her. Given such a psychological experience, it is not surprising that Othello's love should blossom in response to Desdemona's pity: "She loved me for the dangers I had passed, / And I loved her that she did pity them" (1.3.169–70). However, having thought of himself as without such ordinary human needs and having made do without their fulfillment, he now makes himself vulnerable.[7] He is like parched soil. If no rain falls, it does not appear to need watering, for nothing grows there. But if it is watered and if living things begin to sprout, then it no longer seems able to exist without rain. As Janet Adelman observes, in "[m]aking himself susceptible to Desdemona's pity, [...] Othello unmakes the basis for his martial identity, exchanging it for one dependent on her" (65). In allowing himself to feel immense love for Desdemona, he then makes himself vulnerable.

The awakening of this new and unfamiliar part of himself endangers Othello's sense of self. His sense of these dangers appears in the images he uses to persuade the Senators to allow Desdemona to accompany him to the wars. He quite properly assures them that he will not "your serious and great business scant" (1.3.270), but a more anxious emotional note enters when he adds:

> No, when light-winged toys
> Of feathered Cupid seel with wanton dullness
> My speculative and officed instruments,
> That my disports corrupt and taint my business,
> Let huswives make a skillet of my helm,
> And all indign and base adversities
> Make head against my estimation! (1.3.271–7)

The sense of ironic foreshadowing here is not just based on our knowledge of Iago's lurking hatred. It has to do with the fact that Othello here trivializes Desdemona and dismisses the significance of her love. He himself knows that his love for Desdemona is deeper than what he describes as "light-winged toys / Of feathered Cupid," and that Desdemona's love is fundamentally important to him. Because he here separates his public representation of himself from what both he and the audience know to be his inner life, the image of his warrior helm becoming a housewive's skillet lessens the connection he ostensibly means to preserve. As Othello sees things, the tender side of himself that has wakened in response to her love renders him vulnerable to humiliation and threatens to subvert his martial self-definition. But we already know that he is not accustomed to think of himself as lovable. We will also know shortly, from the scene in which Desdemona banters with Cassio and Iago while she awaits Othello's arrival in Cyprus, that she is a person accustomed to courtly and witty flirtatiousness. Later Othello will say that his jealousy cannot be aroused by the fact that his "wife is fair, feeds well, loves company, / Is free of speech, sings, plays, and dances well" (3.3.198–9), but it is easy to imagine that it would not take much provocation to rouse jealousy in an older man married to a young aristocrat, who thinks of himself as an outsider, as unattractive to women, and who has been accustomed to think of himself as unlovable. That he has a ready catalogue of her charms, charms inevitably enticing to other men because they are insistently social in nature, in itself speaks to his potential for jealousy, whether he will admit it or not.

Furthermore, jealousy once roused in a person such as Othello, whose self-definition depends, as we have seen, on having control of himself and of others, would be far more traumatic than usual. Whereas before being married to Desdemona the manliness that is so central to his self-esteem depended only on himself, as a married man his manliness now depends also on her, for she has it in her power to render him a cuckold. A man who has an unfaithful wife was imagined to gain horns on his head and was termed a "cuckold," an object of ridicule in the public eye. Othello would need "ocular" proof, one way or another, to rid himself of the agony of uncertainty when so much is at stake, but such certain proof can be had only for guilt, as innocence cannot be proved. That is, one might prove that one has not committed adultery, for example, on such and such a night and time, but one cannot prove that one is innocent of committing it at any night or at any time. We therefore have a portrait of a person whose social situation would incline him toward jealousy, and whose psychological proclivities would demand the certainty that can come only from a verdict of guilty. Such a verdict would in a single stroke utterly strip him of both self-esteem and love. It is as though Othello intuits his vulnerability and fears the fragility of his happiness when, upon his reunion with Desdemona, he says, "[i]f it were now to die, / 'Twere now to be most happy" (2.1.187–9). The death orientation of his love is emphasized by Desdemona's response, "[t]he heavens forbid / But that our loves and comforts should increase / Even as our days do grow!" (2.1.192–194). Like Romeo and Juliet, Othello and Desdemona rush to their "edge of doom," but in the case of the latter lovers, they themselves, with Iago's help, are death's agents.

There is another potentially disturbing aspect to the circumstances in which Othello and Desdemona fall in love. Othello gives no overt sign that he resents the Venetians who make use of his martial prowess, but scorn him as a man. Presumably, his having internalized their view of him protects him from such resentment, and enables him to take pride in his assigned role. However, one would suppose that a person in so demeaning a situation would harbor unconscious feelings of hatred and resentment toward those who benefit from his service. Furthermore, one would imagine that from the point of view of the Venetians, Othello in marrying Desdemona would be reaching beyond his station. He would be seen as trying to break the barriers to full acceptance into Venetian society. Some signs of Othello's buried resentment of the Venetians appear in his scorn for the "curlèd darlings" (1.2.69) out of whose ranks her father expected Desdemona to choose a husband. And a hint that Othello's unacknowledged aspiration gives him an uneasy conscience appears when he speaks to Iago while they await Brabantio's arrival. He first asserts his right to "as proud a fortune / As this that I have reached" (1.2.23–4) on the basis of the "men of royal siege" (1.2.22) who were his forebears. But then, as though answering an inner voice that suggests that the high fortune he expects from marrying Desdemona might have something to do with his love of her, he denies an accusation that has not been made:

> For know, Iago,
> But that I love the gentle Desdemona,
> I would not my unhousèd free condition
> Put into circumscription and confine
> For the sea's worth. (1.2.24–7)

This combination of aspiration and fear of seeming to love only as part of that aspiration can make for a psychologically uncomfortable stance even in the modern world, but unlike a modern person, Othello cannot admit to such aspirations without violating his own standards. Othello's investment in remaining unaware of aspirations that could hardly fail to be excited by his circumstances gives his character a brittleness upon which Iago can capitalize.

As long as Othello believes in Desdemona's love, even if his marriage does not give him the entrée into Venetian society for which he might secretly have hoped, he has the satisfaction of their love. Beneath the surface of consciousness, he has the additional satisfaction of having evened the score by taking her from those who demeaned him, and of proving himself worthier than the "curlèd darlings." But once he no longer believes in her love, then things are worse than before. For not only would he suffer the shame of cuckoldry that Iago claims is so common among the Venetians, and that is indeed a ubiquitous theme of comedy in Shakespeare's time,[8] but he would experience that ordinary mockery as the scorn of those into whose ranks he had sought entry. He would imagine himself the object of mockery not only for being cuckolded, but also for having aspired beyond his place. This double humiliation that doubly calls his manhood into question explains why Othello bids farewell to his occupation, to the "plumèd troops and the big wars / That makes ambition virtue!" (3.3.365–6). But, as he says, the mockery is not the worst of it. He could have borne to be "[a] fixèd figure for the time of scorn / To point his slow unmoving finger at!" (4.2.56–7). As long as he believes himself loved, he can manage whatever secret and shameful ambition lurks beneath the threshold of his consciousness. But once he thinks himself betrayed by Desdemona, he is left only with the self-loathing born of self-deception added to his initial sense of his own unfitness for the soft pleasures of love and marriage.

It is this kind of highly wrought psychological torment that Othello expresses when, in a convoluted passage, he says that if he is deprived of the "fountain from the which [his] current runs" (4.2.61) then one of two things can happen. Either he "dries up" (4.2.62), that is, returns to the parched emotional life that was his before he loved Desdemona, or, that not being possible, he can keep the fountain of his soul that flows from Desdemona, "as a cistern for foul toads / To knot and gender in!" (4.2.63–4). Prior to knowing Desdemona, his soul was parched. She was the fountain of clear water that brought him to life, and he cannot reverse the emotional road he has traveled. Therefore, if she no longer loves him, the ardor of romance cannot conceal the more knotted and dubious emotions that lay beneath consciousness. He is left with a murky but intense sense of himself, which he expresses in Hamlet-like images, as the foul and muddy source of a corrupt generation. In his suicide, Othello gives full expression to the division between the conscious sense of self with which Othello begins the play and his inner self-doubt. Before stabbing himself, he says:

> Set you down this;
> And say besides that in Aleppo once,
> Where a malignant and a turbaned Turk
> Beat a Venetian and traduced the state,
> I took by th' throat the circumcisèd dog,
> And smote him, thus. (5.2.361–6)

Othello as the Moor now identifies with the Turks, the enemies of Venice that brought Othello to Cyprus, at the same time as he defines himself as the warrior defender of the Venetians. He is both the "circumcisèd dog" who is the enemy of everything Venetian, and the hero.

As this account of Othello's situation and psychic predisposition makes clear, one does not need an Iago to account for the onset or the turbulent intensity of Othello's jealousy. Though Iago encourages Othello's tendency to doubt that Desdemona could love him, it is clear that Othello has within him all the capacities for doubt and for rage that Iago inflames. As Coppelia Kahn writes, "[i]n *Othello*, cuckoldry is a lie, but it convinces Othello because it confirms the fears he already has about women" (140), and then Iago uses the lie to "create a bond between himself and the Moor based on their mutual fantasy of women as betrayers and men as sexual rivals" (140).[9] Othello is a stranger, a Moor, an older man, and a soldier, and he is an outsider to the elegant Venetian world from which Desdemona comes. His soul has been parched for the love that is suddenly his, but the difficulty is not only that he cannot quite believe that someone like Desdemona could find him lovable, it is also that the role of a lover and husband is difficult to square with that of warrior and outsider. His self-definition as commanding, martial, and brave crumbles in the face of Iago's version of him as a cuckold. He is left at the mercy of his self-doubts, his jealousy, and his rage at the Venetian aristocracy. As a member of that class, a presumably unfaithful Desdemona cannot fail to symbolize the Venetian view of him, and her murder is thus his effort to rid himself of a hated self-image.

But what about Iago? He brilliantly manipulates Othello, a man whose rigidly role-bound self-definition renders him open to manipulation. Iago plays on Othello's sexual insecurity, his need for certainty, and his hidden distrust of Venetians. Iago becomes an externalized form of Othello's inner doubts, an incarnation of all the difficulties that beset a romantic relationship that attempts to bridge so huge a social divide. However, Iago is also fascinating in his own right, so much so that he can take over the play. Just what kind of person is he?[10] To answer this, we must first ask a question Iago himself tries to explain: why does he hate Othello? Initially, he cites Othello's nomination of Cassio as his lieutenant as the source of his anger. Later in a soliloquy, he gives another reason: "I hate the Moor; / And it is thought abroad that twixt my sheets / He's done my office" (1.3.387–9). As Robert B. Heilman points out, the "and" in this passage is quite telling; it shows, he says, "[t]he charge against Othello is an afterthought," that the "hate is prior, and a motive is then discovered and happily pounced upon" (31).[11] Though Iago later repeats his suspicion about Othello and his wife, neither that nor Cassio's lieutenancy seems to account for the intensely obsessive and intimate quality of his hatred for Othello. Coleridge's oft-quoted comment is that Iago exemplifies "motiveless Malignity,"[12] a phrase that captures the sense of mystery about him. Noting Iago's "proliferation of motives," Rackin suggests that he is "groping for explanations of an enmity he feels but cannot himself understand" (70), a state that implies we can be mysterious to ourselves, that there are some realities that we will not allow to surface. Kott similarly says that "Iago hates first, and only then seems to invent reasons for his hate" (85). Indeed, no ordinary motivation explains the way in which he thinks about himself. Through Iago's shifting motivations, the play at large explores the mysteriousness of human emotion and inclination, outlining but never making definitive the reasons for the way people feel and act as they do. There is something truly terrifying in the notion that Iago's hate cannot be fully explained, and this contributes to the sense that, as Kott says, *all* characters are "more and more deeply submerged" in the "landscape of darkness" (90–1) that will consume even the brightest of lights.

The sense of hateful intimacy comes into play from the very beginning when we see Iago's imagination fully engaged in Othello's lovemaking as he describes it to Brabantio, as Othello "covering" Desdemona like a horse covers a mare, and Othello and Desdemona "making the beast with two backs" (1.1.114, 118–9). Iago's dark obsession with Othello develops as his mind tracks Othello's every thought and feeling, so that he can toy with Othello's agonies like a fisherman with a fish. It culminates when Othello and Iago, in a chilling version of a marriage vow, kneel, and commit themselves in a "sacred vow" to Desdemona's murder. Othello says, "[n]ow art thou my lieutenant," and Iago answers, "I am your own for ever" (3.3.494, 495). There is an excess of erotic pleasure in Iago's intensity that calls any straightforward revenge motivation into question. Rackin remarks on Iago's "moral and psychological dependence on Othello" (85) that seems to exceed the circumstances that ostensibly give rise to it.[13] As in *Troilus in Cressida*, in *Othello*, dependence is a force that drags both parties downward and constitutes a perversion of intimacy.

The other quality that sets Iago apart from Shakespeare's less complicated villains is his pleasure in thinking about himself as evil. In this he comes closest to Richard III, for, like Richard, he enjoys his own stratagems, and he enjoys being able to rely on his powers of improvisation. To some extent Richard also enjoys being a villain, but there are differences. Richard espouses the alienation from ordinary pleasures that his misshapen body has thrust upon him. It may be a bit excessive to imagine someone being "determinèd to prove a villain" (*Richard III* 1.1.30), but his pleasure in his wit makes him something of a con man, and there is nothing odd in itself about Richard's desire. Like Claudius, and many of Shakespeare's characters, he wants to be a king. Iago is like Richard in his con-man pleasure in his own wit, but he differs from Richard in that his only other pleasure derives from watching Othello's agony. The combination of Iago's lack of interest in ordinary human goods (he shows no pleasure when Othello makes him his lieutenant) and the intimate pleasure he takes in tormenting Othello, as well as his cleverness in doing it, produce an image of a thorough-going sadist.

One source of Iago's intense bitterness is his superior intelligence, which makes him resentful of his low social status. This resentment appears in the pleasure he takes in duping Roderigo, and it shows as well in the scene in which he, along with Desdemona and Cassio, await Othello's arrival in Cyprus. Here Iago presents his crudely misogynistic wit as plain speaking, but reveals his bitter resentment when he observes the more courtly Cassio with Desdemona and reflects, "[v]ery good; well-kissed! An excellent courtesy! 'Tis so, indeed. Yet again your fingers to your lips? Would they were clytser-pipes [enema tubes] for your sake!" (2.1.174–7). Such a man would choose the soldier's life because it to some measure softens social distinctions, and it provides male camaraderie as a substitute for intimacy with women, whom he dislikes and disparages. It also provides an outlet for his tendency to divert erotic desire into aggressive activity. As he is an outsider to elegant Venetian ways, he has taken refuge in the pride and camaraderie of soldiering.

These attributes, with the exception of his manipulating intelligence, give him much in common with Othello. The play suggests that he shared this camaraderie with Othello despite their formally unequal status, and the intense intimacy of his hatred suggests that for Iago camaraderie is also erotic. His "love" for the General adds a certain romantic anguish to what he views as Othello's double betrayal of their comradeship, traduced by both Othello's marriage into the Venetian aristocracy and his choice of Cassio over Iago for the position of lieutenant. Since Iago either doesn't grasp or is unwilling to admit the nature of his own feelings, he explains himself in diabolic terms. He says of his plan, "[i]t is engendered. Hell and night / Must bring this monstrous birth to the world's light" (1.3.403–04), he calls upon the "[d]ivinity of hell!" and he boasts, "[w]hen devils will the blackest sins put on, / They do suggest at first with heavenly shows, / As I do now" (2.3.344–7). By embracing the diabolic, he succeeds in concealing his real motives even from himself.

Girard suggests that Iago and Othello become each other's "mirror image," and Shakespeare "deflects" to Iago the "ugliness that should belong to Othello, a whole landscape of infernal jealousy and envy" (291). Shakespeare develops this "infernal landscape" as a metaphor for both men's internal struggles. The subterranean darkness is where they see themselves and others, and it also more broadly serves as a metaphor for the psyche itself. When Iago repeats his claim that Othello has cuckolded him, he says that the thought "[d]oth, like a poisonous mineral, gnaw" his "innards" (2.1.298). The motif of the "poisonous mineral" and the innermost self as a subterranean space is sustained throughout the play in relation to how Iago feels about his own hatred, how he enacts his revenge on Othello, and finally how Othello's jealousy warps his view of Desdemona. When Emilia admits she has in her possession the handkerchief that will falsely implicate Desdemona, Iago notes that while the handkerchief will be helpful to make Othello jealous, "[t]he Moor already changes with my poison. / Dangerous conceits are in their natures poisons, / Which at the first are scarce found to distaste / But with a little act upon the blood / Burn like mines of sulfur" (3.3.341–5). Just as Iago spoke of the nature of his own hatred – as a poisonous mineral – in the same way he imagines this same kind of poison working on Othello. Iago imagines the poison working deep within Othello, the "mine of sulfur" standing both for Othello's interiority and as an image of hell – sulfur was also known as brimstone, and its unpleasant qualities were fitting symbols for the landscape of hell. Later in the play, when Desdemona expresses her innocent affection for Cassio, Othello responds with the curse "[f]ire and brimstone!" (4.1.232), a phrase that comes directly from the Bible (in Genesis and Revelation) and that describes the punishment for sin.

The play consistently shows that this image – of the place deep within the earth that seems to stand for the human psyche and also a symbol of hell – is not Iago's alone. It returns when Othello accuses Desdemona of adultery. When she asks what she has done to arouse his anger, Othello doesn't explicitly answer, but instead says that she has committed "deeds" that are so terrible, that "[t]he bawdy wind, that kisses all it meets, / Is hushed within the hollow mine of earth / And will not hear 't" (4.2.80–1). On the surface, Othello's metaphor suggests that Desdemona's crimes are so terrible, they cannot be named. However, the comparison between the wind and the mine also fits the relationship between Desdemona and Othello. In Othello's jealousy, he views Desdemona as the "bawdy wind" – flirtatious and freely giving of her charms. Then Othello's own psyche, whether he admits it or not, is the "hollow mine," where the poison of doubt and jealousy have burned away all valuable materials. Desdemona, like that flirtatious wind, is swallowed up entirely in the abyss of Othello's jealousy, and she is silenced finally when he smothers her.

After he has killed her, Othello seems to realize that Desdemona was not the wind at all but rather essential to him and his sense of self, a deeply precious part of his interiority – in doubting and killing Desdemona, Othello has hollowed out his own mine. He tells Emilia that "[i]f heaven would make me such another world / Of one entire and perfect chrysolite, / I'd not have sold her for it" (5.2.149–51). He in effect claims that Desdemona now is more valuable to him than the best possible world, idealized and materialized as a gem. It is a painfully poignant moment because it is not possible to make "another world" out of the one that Othello has destroyed; his realization has come too late. His sentiment should also strike us in that it imagines Desdemona as a possession. Even though he vows that he would not sell her, his turn to the language of trade or commerce shadows the insight he aims to articulate.

Even though Desdemona is undoubtedly innocent of the charges Othello makes against her, critics have vastly different ways of viewing her as a character. We have already seen that Daileader sees her as a product of misogyny, polluted by her association with Othello. Like Iago, some of Desdemona's feelings and actions could also be accounted for in terms of naturalistic psychology. She is a sheltered young woman with a taste for the exotic. She is truly loving and compassionate; she enjoys being flirtatious and enjoys the prospect of having some influence with her powerful and impressive husband. Having no idea, however, of the stormy passions of the man she married, she becomes paralyzed by fear in the face of his anger. In her terror, she behaves in ways that might as well have been calculated to increase it.

Lena Cowen Orlin, however, writes that she warns her students against "overhumanizing" Desdemona, who, she says, is not a consistent or unified character. She urges them instead to see her as an "artfully created embodiment of female behavior and feminine responses, in all the variety and ambiguity perceived by men" (181).[14] Orlin says that "while Desdemona's innocence is necessary, so too are the elements in her that raise doubts, that exonerate Othello of comic credulity, that enable her to exemplify all the tragic confusions about women that men hold" (182–3). Kott's reading of Desdemona suggests that the very qualities that foster complete intimacy are those that threaten that closeness. Kott contends that while "Desdemona is faithful," she is "sexually obsessed with Othello," and the violence of her obsession is the very reason Othello views her as unfaithful (90–1).[15] Girard, going even further than Kott, argues that Desdemona fell in love with the hyperbolically martial Othello in the first place because she "yearns for spectacles of violence," a yearning, he suggests, that causes her to in effect seek her own death (293).[16] On the other hand, Janet Adelman says that even though "she pays for Othello's fantasy with her life, Desdemona remains largely independent of it, innocent not only of the crime Othello imagines but also of the fantasies that infect him" (64).[17] Even if we see, as Adelman does, Desdemona's innocence, the extremity of her goodness, as Shakespeare writes it, seems impossible or unnatural. Langis calls it her "hypervirtue" (51). This virtue, out of place in a world that refuses to believe in it, only inflames Othello's jealousy and has the effect of making Othello seem to us even less sympathetic and more monstrous than he might otherwise be. If Desdemona is the incarnation of ideal love, then Othello shows us that an imperfect and petty world cannot possibly accommodate it.

Thus, Desdemona's portrait is overladen with imagery that associates her with the divine and angelic. Some of it comes from Othello, who, even as he prepares to murder her, compares Desdemona's fairness to the illumination offered by candlelight, a "flaming minister" (5.2.8), and as symbolic of the light of day. Were it only Othello who so represents her, we might see him as one who sees women as either angelic or whorish. In that case, the play would be about the dangers of this kind of dehumanizing idealization, but much of the imagery comes from other characters, who seem to endorse her excessive virtue. Cassio demurs from Iago's somewhat titillating comments on Desdemona with, "[s]he is indeed perfection" (2.3.25), and Emilia compares her now dead mistress to an angel who was "heavenly true" (5.2.140).

This idealizing tendency also appears in the bedroom scene where Desdemona seems incapable of believing that a woman could cuckold her husband, that she could behave "[i]n such gross kind" (4.3.65). She asks Emilia, "[w]ouldst thou do such a deed for all the world?" (4.3.67). Emilia answers with a series of ironic and playful yesses, and then goes on to make a strong feminist point in asserting that men who mistreat their wives ought to know that, "[t]he ills we do, their ills instruct us so" (4.3.106). Desdemona's response is the opposite. "Beshrew me," she says, "if I would do such a wrong / For the whole world" (4.3.81–2). We have seen that Othello will echo this idea after killing Desdemona, when he vows that he would not exchange for Desdemona for the "entire and perfect" world should he be blessed with her again. Othello, like so many of us, makes this declaration of loving sacrifice after the fact, when it is too late. Desdemona, however, does not need the wisdom offered by time of make a willing sacrifice of herself for him. The contrast between Emilia's nurse-like common sense, attractive as it is, and Desdemona's unwillingness to wrong a husband, even if he should wrong her, raises the latter above the ordinarily and sensibly good. Her vow "by this heavenly light" (4.3.69) that nothing could make her false coheres with her earlier statement to the Senate that her "heart's subdued / Even to the very quality of my lord" (1.3.253–4). For her, the perfection of her love manifests itself in the perfection of her submission. The naturalistic representation of Desdemona fully translates to the idealistic when she briefly regains consciousness after Othello smothers her. At first, she cries out that she has been "falsely, falsely murdered," but then she says "[a] guiltless death I die," and when Emilia asks her who has done this to her, Desdemona replies "[n]obody; I myself." (5.2.120, 126, 128). Desdemona displaces blame from Othello to herself, a loving submission that takes on a more than human radiance when, with her last words, she asks Emilia to "[c]ommend me to my kind lord" (5.2.129). As Langis and others point out, "[m]arriage for the early moderns was fraught with anxiety far more acute than what we today might experience as wedding jitters" (52).[18] Desdemona's submission to her marriage should make us uncomfortable; however much we might admire her devotion, we cannot forget the end to which it moves.

It is my view that to some measure the strong symbolizing tendency of the play tends to pull away from, rather than reinforce, the psychological naturalism that gives the characters their force. It also tends to overshadow the play's exploration of the way in which romantic love can encourage a dangerous idealization of the beloved. That heavy symbolism, in concert with the troubling race and gender discourses that are woven together, accounts for why audiences, and students like those mentioned by Orlin, are left in Michael Neill's words, "disturbed" by "perhaps the most shocking" ending in Shakespearean tragedy (384, 383).[19] Shakespeare was to make a more powerful fusion of the symbolic and the naturalistic in *King Lear,* with its own shocking ending, and a more fully naturalistic exploration of romantic love in *Antony and Cleopatra.*

Notes

1 *Shakespearean Tragedy: Lectures on* Hamlet, Othello, King Lear, *and* Macbeth. 1904. London: Penguin Books, 1991.
2 *A Theater of Envy.*
3 For example, 1.1.20, 1.2.66
4 *Racism, Misogyny and the* Othello *Myth: Inter-racial Couples From Shakespeare to Spike Lee.* Cambridge: Cambridge University Press, 2005.
5 The play's "pervasive tropes of magic and demonic incorporate references," she says, apply to both Othello and Desdemona, just as the words nested inside their names reveal: "hell" and "demon" (*Racism, Misogyny*, 24).
6 For more on *Othello* and race, see Emily C. Bartels "Making More of the Moor: Aaron, Othello, and Renaissance Refashionings of Race." *Shakespeare Quarterly* 41.4 (1990): 433–454; Rudolph A. Shaw, "'Othello' and Race Relations in Elizabethan England." *Journal of African American Men* 1.2 (1995): 83–91; Dympna Callaghan. *Shakespeare Without Women: Representing Gender and Race on the Renaissance Stage.* New York: Routledge, 2000; Ania Loomba, *Shakespeare, Race, and Colonialism.* Oxford: Oxford University Press, 2002; Debra Johanyak, "'Turning Turk,' Early Modern English Orientalism, and Shakespeare's *Othello.*" In *The English Renaissance, Orientalism and the Idea of Asia.* Eds. Debra Johanyak and Walter S.H. Lim. New York: Palgrave Macmillan, 2010. 77–96; Viviana Comensoli, "Identifying Othello: Race and the Colonial (non)Subject." Early Theatre 7.2 (2004): 92–96; Joyce Green McDonald, "Black Ram, White Ewe: Shakespeare, Race and Women." In *A Feminist Companion to Shakespeare.* Ed. Dympna Callaghan. Oxford: Wiley Blackwell, 2016. 206–225; Ian Smith, "We Are Othello: Speaking of Race in Early Modern Studies." *Shakespeare Quarterly* 67.1 (2016): 104–175.
7 Snyder suggests that this speech is "disturbing" because it show us that for Othello, love has a "proxy quality" in which the "dangers" he recounted to Desdemona "have served as a counter between them, a substitute for direct engagement, or, at best, a preliminary to something not yet achieved" (*The Comic Matrix*, 75).

8 See Katherine Eisaman Maus, "Horns of Dilemma: Jealousy, Gender, and Spectatorship in English Renaissance Drama." *ELH* 54.3 (1987): 561–583.

9 *Man's Estate: Masculine Identity in Shakespeare.* Berkeley: University of California Press, 1981.

10 Rolf Soellner says that Iago is "too small a man to be the devil incarnate" and is a "man of multiple and petty resentments, a malcontent who sets himself apart form the social order and delights in the disorder he creates" (*Shakespeare's Patterns of Self Knowledge*, 262).

11 *Magic in the Web: Action and Language in Othello.* Lexington: University of Kentucky Press, 1956.

12 Colderidge, Samuel Taylor. *Lectures 1808–1819 On Literature.* Ed. R.A. Foakes. Volume 2. Princeton, New Jersey: Princeton University Press, 1987. 2: 315.

13 Soellner writes of their "peculiar closeness, almost a melting of the one into the other" (*Patterns of Self Knowledge*, 275).

14 "Desdemona's Disposition."

15 *Shakespeare Our Contemporary.*

16 *A Theater of Envy.*

17 *Suffocating Mothers.*

18 See Maus, *Being and Having,* and Mary Beth Rose, "The Heroics of Marriage in *Othello* and the Du*chess of Malfi.*" In *Shakespearean Tragedy and Gender.* Eds. Shirley Nelson Garner and Madelon Sprengnether. Bloomington: Indiana University Press, 1996. 210–238. Marianne Novy argues that Iago disrupts the "mutuality" of marriage and replaces it with the "patriarchal imagery of possession" (*Love's Argument*, 139).

19 "Unproper Beds: Race, Adultery, and the Hideous in *Othello.*" *Shakespeare Quarterly* 40 (1989): 383–412.

9

Macbeth

As we have seen, *Othello* dramatizes the psychological complexity of romantic love, which Shakespeare externalized as Fate in *Romeo and Juliet*, and to which he would return, with great discernment, in *Antony and Cleopatra*. In *Macbeth*, he includes a love relationship of a peculiar kind, one that at first glance appears as a mere adjunct to the horrors that follow upon the protagonist's murderous ambition. The focus on the lust for power, dread, and self-loathing in *Macbeth* makes it a version of *Hamlet* turned inside out, as if Shakespeare wrote the Scottish play by re-imagining *Hamlet* as a play centered on the villain Claudius.

Macbeth is one of Shakespeare's most simple and straightforward plays, but it is also the most puzzling. It is simple in several ways. It is unusual among Shakespeare's plays in that it has only a single line of action. It is sparser even than *Othello*, which concentrates on Iago, Desdemona, and Othello, but includes the subsidiary stories of Roderigo and Cassio. Here there is no double-plotting to complicate things. In line with the sparse action, *Macbeth* has the most limited cast of characters of any play, and the two main characters are completely dominant. That is overstating things a bit, for Duncan's gentleness contributes to the theme of violated nurturing, Banquo's self-restraint posits the possibility of resisting the witches' blandishment, and Macduff's love of his children and moral uprightness function as a foil to Macbeth. However, they are relatively simple and uncontroversial figures, and the only figures who are commandingly interesting are Macbeth and Lady Macbeth, and of those two, the greatest emphasis falls on him.

The play is simple in yet another sense; there is no way to disagree about the moral of the story. One may disagree about the degree to which Macbeth is responsible. Some argue that it is really all Lady Macbeth's fault, and some that it is the fault of the witches. But no one argues that Macbeth's deed was a good one, or that he was right to have killed Duncan, Banquo, Lady Macduff, and her children, and to have turned his country into a realm of nightmare. That very simplicity, however, constitutes a problem. For if one asks what the play is "about," the answer that it is about the evil of regicide or the horrors of undue

Thinking About Shakespeare, First Edition. Kay Stockholder, revised and updated by Amy Scott.
© 2018 John Wiley & Sons Ltd. Published 2018 by John Wiley & Sons Ltd.

ambition seems inadequate. The play may well be interested in creating an atmosphere and experience of horror rather than strictly imparting a moral lesson.

The atmosphere of horror is due partly to the play's association of Duncan's murder with disturbing images of "procreation" and sexuality (203).[1] Macbeth and Lady Macbeth cultivate a nightmare version of romantic, married love. They are in accord throughout much of the play, but their version of unity is one that destroys more conventional relationships that usually create and preserve romantic love, fertility, and kinship. If the killing of the king represents the full consummation of the Macbeths' nightmare union, it reveals too that they cannot sustain their intense connection without the mutual drive to destroy. After Duncan's death, they are suddenly no longer speaking the same language, and Lady Macbeth slips away from the play's action as she descends into madness. *Macbeth* dramatizes a desire that seeks violence and violence that is borne of desire, in ways that echo *Troilus and Cressida*.

Macbeth launches us into a world that challenges easy categorizations in the first scene when we meet, before anyone else, the three witches. We first hear Macbeth's name from their lips, and their frequent, unusual intrusions into the story make them a kind of gruesome chorus. Naomi Conn Liebler points out that the bearded witches "subvert standard social definitions of the 'feminine'" (218),[2] as does Lady Macbeth, who acts with traditionally masculine initiative and derides traditionally feminine qualities. As the witches have power to manipulate Macbeth, so does Lady Macbeth. As we encounter them planning to seduce Macbeth into his crime, so we encounter Lady Macbeth planning to steady his will. As they arise from a barren heath, so Lady Macbeth calls on spirits to render herself barren. All of these correspondences suggest that the witches function for Macbeth as an extension of the ways in which he sees Lady Macbeth, and perhaps women in general. They are violent and destructive women, but as "Bellona's bridegroom" (1.2.56), as Ross calls him, he is drawn to them.[3]

Adelman calls the sphere of the witches and Lady Macbeth the "perverse nursery" (135).[4] Indeed, Lady Macbeth takes a rather extraordinary stance against feminine softness and motherly tenderness, the "milk of human kindness" (1.5.16) that she worries is excessive in Macbeth's character. She calls for "spirits" to "unsex" her, "[m]ake thick" her blood and change the milk in her "woman's breasts" to "gall" (1.5.40, 42, 46–7). She invites us to consider her female body and its biological workings with respect to childbearing and rearing – menstruating, procreating, breastfeeding – in nightmarish ways that seem designed to shock us. Though it is only in her imagination that these assaults on the female body take place, the violence of her thoughts is a deliberate attempt to further bolster her own burgeoning lust for Duncan's murder, a lust that will galvanize Macbeth to overcome his own misgivings about violence. For example, Lady Macbeth, upset at Macbeth's misgivings about murder, says that she has known "how tender 'tis to love" her nursing baby, but horrifically adds, "I would, while it was smiling in my face, / Have plucked my nipple from his boneless gums / And dashed the brains out, had I so sworn as you / Have done to this" (1.7.56–9). For good reason, this is one of Lady Macbeth's most chillingly famous declarations.

As Lady Macbeth's reference to killing her child makes clear, the play does not simply portray a world without loving bonds; it shows us a world that relies on establishing a feeling of love and trust in order to destroy the beloved. The only way the Macbeths can kill Duncan is to establish intimacy with him – to lure him to their home and envelop him with the tantalizing warmth of kinship, just as Lady Macbeth imagines killing her baby precisely in the moment that it is *smiling in her face*. With his reference to the nursing baby smiling at his mother, Shakespeare captures the beauty of one of the most intense bonds possible, that of the mother and child, at its closest possible moment – so that Lady Macbeth can betray it in excruciatingly vivid terms. It matters little what has "really" happened to that baby she says she did tenderly nurse. We might well feel devastated for this imagined child, so well does Shakespeare convey in so few words its absolute trust in its mother and her destruction of it. The idea of violence done to a baby is echoed later in the play when one of the witches horrifically calls for a "[f]inger of a birth-strangled babe" to throw in their cauldron (4.1.30). The play's tragic force seems to issue from these unnatural images; its compulsion is to highlight "destruction not creation" (173) at those moments that it calls attention to the reproductive capacities of women and their roles as mothers.[5]

The intimation that women pollute the nursery are part of the play's wider exploration of the limits of kinship bonds and the vulnerability of lines of succession to threats both near and far. Women would not have to be as horrific and destructive as Lady Macbeth to be threatening to the political and familial relationships that structure the kingdom. Mere infidelity could, as Stephanie Chamberlain observes, "undermine patrilineal outcomes," and produce a "generalized cultural anxiety about women's roles in the transmission of patrilineage" (73).[6] When Lady Macbeth urges Macbeth to murder Duncan, she must poison feelings that are supposed to underpin kinship bonds and act as security for lines of succession, feelings like loyalty, duty, and love.[7]

Duncan broaches the matter of succession early in the play, just after Macbeth has been named Thane of Cawdor and just after Malcolm describes the execution of the previous Thane of Cawdor for treason. With that man's betrayal of what Duncan calls his "absolute trust" (1.4.13) in mind, he announces who will be king after him. "Sons, kinsmen, thanes," he says, "[a]nd you whose places are the nearest, know / We will establish our estate upon / Our eldest, Malcolm, whom we name hereafter / The Prince of Cumberland" (1.4.35–40). In the process of nominating his son as successor, Duncan in fact calls attention to several kinds of relationships, people of varying intimacy that orbit the king. The bonds represented with each category require "absolute trust," if the king is to remain safe.

Duncan's reference to "those whose places are the nearest," though, is strangely vague. To whom does he refer? He has already listed "sons, kinsmen and thanes," so it may be part of an anxious recognition that there are some who regard the throne as theirs to inherit, some who might exceed or escape the category of son, kinsman, or thane. Duncan's announcement tries to quell ambitious hopes, but as we see in Macbeth's response in an aside, Duncan is not able to rule others' hidden passions, and Macbeth's darker feelings are roused by this announcement.[8] He feels even more compelled to indulge what he calls his "black and deep desires" (1.4.51) even while he acknowledges that success is not guaranteed. "The Prince of Cumberland," he muses, "[t]hat is a step / On which I must fall down or else o'erleap, / For in my way it lies" (1.4.48–50). As if to fully cement Duncan's failure to read the tenuous nature of his kinship bond with Macbeth, Duncan, full of admiration, tells Banquo that Macbeth is a "peerless kinsman" (1.4.59). Brett Gamboa points out that this phrase is one paradox among many in the play, creating an otherworldly atmosphere and "cancelling out the meaning they express in the very moments of its expression" (41).[9] Duncan means to say that Macbeth is the best kinsman of all, but by using the remarkably fraught word "peerless" to stand in for "best," Duncan's statement vibrates with prescient irony. But Macbeth, who on his own is sensible of the possibility that he might "fall," will require the influence of the witches and the stimulus of Lady Macbeth to "o'er-leap" the steps in succession that keep him from the crown.

When Lady Macbeth hears of Macbeth's promotion to Thane of Cawdor, she lists the reasons why Macbeth will not be able, on his own, to take the crown. She thus compels him, though he is absent, "[h]ie thee hither, / That I may pour my spirits in thine ear" (1.5.24–5). In the wake of *Hamlet*, in which the ghost recounts being murdered when poison is poured in his ear, we are right to think of Lady Macbeth's spirits being figured as poison. Lady Macbeth's counsel and courage are imagined as destructive, external agents that invade a person and change him from within. Adelman makes a point that Shakespeare deals with his culture's "primitive fears" of women, fears evoked so clearly in the suggestion that Lady Macbeth's energy is like poison, through the "ruthless excision of all female presence" (131); this helps explain Lady Macbeth's gradual disappearance from the play.[10] I think a general anxiety about subversive female power must factor in to Lady Macbeth's portrayal, but Shakespeare also shows us a Macbeth in a crisis of "kindness" that enfolds but is not limited to his relationship with Lady Macbeth. He is confronted with the broader ideal of the "natural," a crisis that challenges the possibility that there are stable and unchangeable categories of "natural" and "unnatural" and structures the play's investigations into traditional gender roles, political ambition, and succession.[11]

At the beginning of the play, the witches say "[f]air is foul, and foul is fair" (1.1.11), meaning that evil is their good, or that the foul weather is fair to them. The witches share with us a perspective of inversion that turns everything in the play inside out and empties ideals of their meaning and power. These images resonate through and epitomize the entire action in which Macbeth struggles to keep the categories of "fair" and "foul," "good" and "evil" separate. Macbeth echoes their inversion when he enters onto the blasted heath and comments, "[s]o foul and fair a day I have not seen" (1.3.38), either meaning that the result of the battle was fair but the weather is foul, or that the consequences of the battle are foul for the loser and fair for the victor. The meaning is different, but the echoing words link Macbeth to the moral inversion of the witches.

Macbeth extends this inversion to the witches' prophecy that he will become king, a prophecy he says that "[c]annot be ill, cannot be good" (1.3.132). His statement distorts natural order and meaning in two ways. First, it duplicates the witches' paradox that something can be its opposite – both good and bad. Second, he says that the prophecy is good without actually saying it is good, by saying it "cannot be ill." He then says that it is bad by saying "it cannot be good." Macbeth's language evades the very meaning it conveys, circling around what it is saying by saying what it is not. His hesitation, his desire to do what is unimaginable, plays out at the level of his language, as something that is also inexpressible. Macbeth then laments that "nothing is / But what is not" (1.3.143), and indeed, his words have borne this out. Desire, a force that operates independent of reason, seems to be the force that loosens language's ability to convey fixed, stable meanings.

That Macbeth is struggling with his "black and deep desires" is evident in his further reflection on why exactly the prophecy is "ill." He thinks it is good because it has promised him he will be king, which constitutes a political achievement, a "success" in his mind (1.3.133). But, after recognizing what is bad about the prophecy, he wonders "why do I yield to that suggestion / Whose horrid image doth unfix my hair / And make my seated heart knock at my ribs, / Against the use of nature?" (1.3.135–8). This complex question speaks to Macbeth's moral dilemma and the play's broader exploration of human nature and natural law. He wonders why he "yields" to something that makes his body respond in what he calls unnatural ways, "[a]gainst the use of nature," something that unfixes his hair and unseats his heart. Yet, Macbeth, confused, knows himself to be *yielding* to the violent act in spite of his body's rejection of it as unkind and wonders why. We have here Macbeth at the tipping point, at, as H.W. Faulkner terms it, "the brink of the unthinkable" (24).[12] He will not say he wants to commit murder here, but in his tentative equivocation about the "good" or "ill" of the prophecy, his desire seeps through.[13]

Macbeth considers a pounding heart and raised hairs as actions "against the use of nature." Yet they are a natural, instinctive response to a terrifying thought. He is still trying to maintain a distinction between the categories of natural and unnatural, but this speech records the collapse of these distinctions. What can be called "fair" or "foul" then, may be little more than illusions, categories in which we group much less definitive feelings, actions, reactions, and interactions; we try to believe in them to keep the nightmare at bay. What is natural about men and women, instead, might undermine or destroy "human kindness" just as often as it protects it.

Shakespeare sheds light on the darkest desires of men and women, so terrifying and base, so corrosive to all bonds, that we want to separate them from ourselves. In this way, we preserve the myth that men and women are fundamentally decent and those who go astray are accurately judged by natural law. When Macbeth references his pounding heart and raised hairs, members of the audience might recognize that their hearts have pounded before, their hairs have been raised. Indeed, the play itself will likely produce those reactions if *it* is successful; the play seems to *want* to produce these reactions. We are implicated in the experience of horror at what we would also call unnatural. The play's revelation is that the horror is not simply the witches, ghosts, or acts of murder; the real horror is that all humans, like Macbeth, might have the capacity to "yield" to acts that are morally repugnant. In this way, the horror might be embedded within natural human experience.[14]

What we see when Macbeth contemplates the good and the ill of the witches' prophecy is the beginning of his own unusual moral condemnation of himself.[15] Like Macbeth, Richard III is a self-confessed evil man, but up until the end of the play he enjoys his own evil, and does not condemn himself. In *Richard II*, Bolingbroke unseats Richard and arranges for his disposal. Before his death, he admits that the "crooked ways" by which he achieved the crown make him uneasy, but he has managed a quite normal life, and, though Claudius suffers from a pang of conscience, his victim's ghost haunts Hamlet rather than him. The same is true of Iago, who enjoys indulging his hatred and envy and takes delight in his stratagems. To the very end Iago gives no sign of the self-revulsion that would testify to the operation of a natural law at work in his soul. In contrast, Macbeth sees himself as violating his own nature from the play's beginning, and a rather odd moment in the play illuminates this aspect of his character.

When Banquo's ghost appears for a second time at the banquet table, Macbeth reflects that both before and after "humane statute purged the gentle weal" people have murdered men who did not "rise again / With twenty mortal murders [wounds] on their crowns, / And push us from our stools. This is more strange / Than such a murder is" (3.4.77, 81–4). Macbeth's question as to why he is singled out shows how much the play relies on Macbeth's awareness of the morals that should guide him, and this awareness in turn becomes our guide in judging him. This gives him a deep interiority and an extraordinary power to invite us into his psychic world in a way that can engage our sympathy even as we shudder with him as he contemplates his own actions and feelings. It is for this reason that so many viewers want to exonerate Macbeth by blaming Lady Macbeth or the witches.

The play is also intensely like a dream. *Macbeth* makes the dream-like component of literature itself very obvious by the way the language and images work. The protagonists anticipate their crime in language that recalls that of other figures in the play, both that of the dream-like witches and that of Duncan and minor characters. As a consequence, these figures start to seem like aspects of the protagonists' inner landscape, while they also remain independent identities. The characters become images writ large; they merge with other images, as well as with the dense network of forebodings and foreshadowings that resonate from one voice to another throughout the text.

Thus, the poetry of the play reproduces the dream-likeness of the protagonists' experience. Macbeth's encounter with the witches leaves him feeling that "nothing is but what is not" (1.3.143); he half-hallucinates a dagger and fully hallucinates Banquo's ghost, while Lady Macbeth enters fully into a dream world when she sleepwalks. The fluidity with which images of evil transform into action and characters, and actions and characters in turn generate images, creates patterns that heighten the sense of aesthetic inevitability. All tragedy gives us this sense that things could not be other than they are, that the end is in some way contained in the beginning, and in this way too art resembles dream, for the significance of a dream's beginning can be known only by the end toward which it leads. Tragic impact depends on a sense that neither the beginning nor the end has come about by accident, and that nothing is arbitrary. The end may not be just, but it has to feel fitting in some way. The strong sense of inevitability generated by the poetic fabric and the dream-like occurrences of *Macbeth* becomes a metaphorical expression of the fact that the external events are being shaped by desires of the protagonists that have eluded their awareness and thus escaped their wills. The force of the desire from which events arise is at once so compelling to the protagonists and so inimical, not only to others' well-being but to any ordinary conception of their own, that it tends to displace the moral response that their actions arouse.

In *Macbeth*, the desire that moves the text is peculiarly intense because it also defines the love relationship between its protagonists. This relationship is not generally attended to as such because the play connects it with murder and violence. People do not like to think about such things in conjunction with love. However, the love relationship between the protagonists in fact centrally structures both the action and the images. *Macbeth* places at the center of our vision a morally forceful story of untoward ambition, regicide, tyranny, and the slaughter of children, but the text is structured around the story of the relation between Macbeth and his wife. The combination of their collusive intimacy and their violent action binds them together by a perverse love, one that joins erotic passion to aggression and terror rather than to tenderness. The sexual overtones of the language surrounding the murder express the lovers' erotically perverse passions. As in dreams, the accompanying terror signifies the distance between their desires and those that generate ordinary well-being. That distance defines their love within an alternative reality, as if dream-like (or nightmarish) marriage could challenge the reality of our waking lives and our conventional unions.

Macbeth and Lady Macbeth are, oddly, the most intimate of Shakespeare's lovers. They sense each other's deepest feelings; each is fully known by the other; they have a common enterprise; and they rely on one another. They share the same figural language, including an eroticized language of violence. They collude in the actual murder of Duncan, and they talk about it in the same terms. Indeed, the murder arises from their relationship rather than from either of them as individuals. Neither alone seems capable of it; rather, they excite each other into the act of regicide, a deed Macbeth seems able to do only at the height of erotic arousal.

Their intense relation is suggested when we see first see Lady Macbeth; she is reading Macbeth's letter that describes his encounter with the witches and in which he reveals he has been made the Thane of Cawdor. We do not know when the letter was written, but realistically it can only have been written immediately after the witches' appearance, and it is Macbeth's first act toward fulfilling the dark desires stirred in him by their prophecies. His haste to inform his wife of the events reveals how important it is to him that she know about them. In so doing, he both defines his project as jointly hers and reveals that he instinctively relies on her to advance a plan, for he seems to assume that his wife will continue what the witches began. In fact, he calls her his "dearest partner of greatness" (1.5.11). The letter's brevity suggests a deep understanding between them, and there is a kind of generosity implied when he says that he wrote to her before arriving home because he did not wish her to "lose the dues of rejoicing by being ignorant of what greatness is promised thee" (1.5.12–13). She instantly intuits Macbeth's excited fear, and assumes, like him, that they will not rely on circumstances to fulfill the prophecy. Their shared mentality appears in the similar images in which they express their fearsome desires. When, a scene earlier, Macbeth learns he has become Thane of Cawdor and reveals his ambition to acquire a greater title, he says:

> Stars, hide your fires;
> Let not light see my black and deep desires.
> The eye wink at the hand; yet let that be
> Which the eye fears, when it is done, to see. (1.4.50–3)

Similarly, when Lady Macbeth learns of his new title and hopes to encourage him to seize the "golden round" (1.5.28), or crown, she says:

> Come, thick night,
> And pall thee in the dunnest smoke of hell,
> That my keen knife see not the wound it makes,
> Nor heaven peep through the blanket of the dark
> To cry, "Hold, hold!" (1.5.50–4)

Both invoke the night, both shudder with horror at the projected deed, and both create an inner division in wanting to hide the murder from themselves. This imagistic echo emphasizes their accord, in which his estimate of her is as accurate as is hers of him. Their mutual knowledge and, even more, their acknowledgments that each is known to the other give their relation such intimacy that it propels them to transform their horrendous fantasies into reality.

Lady Macbeth anticipates Macbeth's vacillation, and prepares herself for the active role his letter assigns her. When she asks the spirits to unsex her, and to "[c]ome to my woman's breasts, / And take my milk for gall" (1.5.47–8), she draws the images of violence that we first encountered on the battlefield into the familial and the sexual realms. She denies her ordinary sexuality, but invokes a new and perverse sexuality when she calls the spirits "murdering ministers," sucking her milk, now turned to gall. In imagining the murder as occurring beneath the blanketed darkness, as Macbeth had done, she adds erotic resonance to her violation of familial and sensuous tenderness: the contemplation of violence arouses her.

Macbeth enters into that aura of that perverse sexuality, and she greets him by saying that she feels "[t]he future in the instant" (1.5.58). With these words she echoes Macbeth's earlier feeling that "nothing is but what is not" (1.3.143). The present instant contains for Lady Macbeth the generative power that she denied in the previous passage. As she says, "[t]his night's great business" will give birth to "solely sovereign sway and masterdom" (1.5.68–70), to power, rather than to a sucking infant. Macbeth enters into his wife's unspoken thought and defines their love within it when he responds, "[m]y dearest love, / Duncan comes here tonight" (1.5.58–59). This terse exchange so emphasizes their deep mutual understanding that it drains the impact from Macbeth's vacillating "[w]e will speak further" (1.5.70).

The rhythm by which each excites the other to the point of action structures the scenes that lead to the murder. The first movement consists in Macbeth's sending the letter, Lady Macbeth's response, and his collusive reaction to her. The second begins when Macbeth, momentarily free of the rush of desire, enters a Hamlet-like meditation on the "bank and shoal of time" (1.7.6) between life and death. He acknowledges Duncan's merits, a king who has been "[s]o clear in his great office, that his virtues / Will plead like angels, trumpet-tongued against / The deep damnation of his taking-off" (1.7.18–20). But Macbeth also understands that he is connected to Duncan with a "double-trust" as a kinsman/subject and as a host of a guest (1.7.12–14).[16] He fears the consequences that he knows will follow if he violates this double-trust that preserves the affection and loyalty of both of these relationships and keeps the king safe. And as though intuiting the twisted nature of his desire, Macbeth imagines the retributive force of pity in the image of a child, a "naked newborn babe / Striding the blast" that will "blow the horrid deed in every eye" (1.7.21–4). This image of a baby as an agent of reprisal suggests that Macbeth has a dim awareness that his desire violates not only his obligations as Duncan's kinsman, subject, and host, but is also somehow entangled with and threatening to fertility embedded in love, sexuality, and family.

After contemplating these consequence of his plan, the flood of desire abates. He says he has "no spur / To prick the sides" of his "intent," and he is left only with "[v]aulting ambition," which, without the spur of desire, "o'erleaps itself / And falls on th' other—" (1.7.25–8). Just as previously Macbeth came, as though called, after Lady Macbeth's soliloquy, so she now comes, as though called, to do what both she and Macbeth anticipated she would. In this scene, she does what she promised she would do earlier – chastise "with the valor of [her] tongue / All that impedes [him] from the golden round" (1.5.27–8). "Art thou afeard," she asks him now, "[t]o be the same in thine own act and valor / As thou art in desire?" (1.7.40–2). By explicitly referencing the desire that gave rise to their plan, she functions to bring his enraptured vision, initially so separate from his ordinary reality and daily life, into the "[t]ime and the hour [that] runs through the roughest day" (1.3.149). It is worth considering in further detail her famous vision of infanticide. She overcomes the impeding pity that Macbeth associated with fertility in his image of the "new born babe," by equating pity with cowardice, by equating murder with manliness, and by imagistically annihilating the babe:

> What beast was 't, then,
> That made you break this enterprise to me?
> When you durst do it, then you were a man;
> And, to be more than what you were, you would
> Be so much more the man. Nor time nor place
> Did then adhere, and yet you would make both.
> They have made themselves, and that their fitness now
> Does unmake you. I have given suck, and know
> How tender 'tis to love the babe that milks me;
> I would, while it was smiling in my face,
> Have plucked my nipple from his boneless gums
> And dashed the brains out, had I so sworn as you
> Have done to this. (1.7.48–59)

In killing her infant in imagination, she responds to and works to destroy the feeling that underlay Macbeth's earlier image of an avenging infant striding the blast, the child that makes him reluctant to kill. She assumes that their love will be consummated in the murder, but this consummation is not generative in the conventional sense – it represents an alternative reality, intrinsically opposed to fertility, family, and society, which are all combined in the image of children.

Given the strong analogy throughout the play between the kingdom and a family, her argument that Macbeth's pledge to her is more binding than the pledge of a mother's love to a child opposes the love between herself and Macbeth to an encompassing shelter of creaturely accord that protects both infants and social harmony. Lady Macbeth defines their love in enmity toward king and country, tenderness and children. Her images, which resonate in the same ranges that his previously did, far from repelling him, bring him to the point where he can join the desire, first expressed in the horrifying images of the witches, to his own "act and valor" (1.7.41). When, at the end of the scene, Macbeth says that he will "bend up / Each corporal agent to this terrible feat" (1.7.80–1), it is clear that Lady Macbeth has succeeded in recovering Macbeth's desire (here with suggestively phallic force), and that she has become the "spur" to "prick" his intention.

The murder carries forward the erotic images of darkness and intimacy that characterize their relationship. Just as both Macbeth and Lady Macbeth characterize their desires as dark, so Duncan's bedroom is shrouded in darkness. That the hallucinatory dagger that points him toward Duncan fuses with the one he carries in his hand indicates a state of mind mid-way between dreaming and waking. In that fused state of consciousness, Macbeth makes explicit the previously subtle associations between sexuality and violence:

> Now o'er the one half world
> Nature seems dead, and wicked dreams abuse
> The curtained sleep. Witchcraft celebrates
> Pale Hecate's offerings, and withered Murder,
> Alarumed by his sentinel, the wolf,
> Whose howl's his watch, thus with his stealthy pace,
> With Tarquin's ravishing strides, towards his design
> Moves like a ghost. (2.1.50–7)

Having identified himself with "withered Murder," celebrated by witchcraft, the "stealthy pace" with which he approaches Duncan's bed suddenly becomes that of Tarquin about to rape Lucrece. It is not only that the murder carries sexual force, but also that the fused images of murder and of rape characterize the sexual feeling between Macbeth and Lady Macbeth. This fusion was suggested early in the play when Macbeth was referred to on the battlefield as "Bellona's bridegroom" (1.2.56), the husband-to-be of the goddess of war.[17]

When Macbeth emerges from the bedroom in which he has killed Duncan, Lady Macbeth greets him as "[m]y husband" (2.2.14). In this way, she reinforces the association between the murder and their love. Furthermore, Lady Macbeth participates in the murder that consummates their love as well as their joint enterprise. Though she castigates Macbeth for his fear of revisiting the bloody site of the murder, and feels as though he should finish the job, she enters the bedroom that Macbeth has just left and smears the swinish grooms with Duncan's blood. When she returns, she declares to Macbeth that "[m]y hands are of your color" (2.2.68), and the image of their equally bloodied hands confirms the bond that unites them.

The violence within which Macbeth and Lady Macbeth consummate their love generates both the story of their barren love and the images of children that pervade the text. Their violent love generates a barren scepter, while the normal fruition of love – children and parenthood – is denied them. They have made their world into a version of the wasteland that Titania, in *A Midsummer Night's Dream*, said was the product of marital dissension. The opposition between their barren love and a fertile world appears first in the contrast between the descriptions of the inside and the outside of their castle. Expecting Duncan's arrival early in the play, Lady Macbeth says, "[t]he raven himself is hoarse / That croaks the fatal entrance of Duncan / Under my battlements" (1.5.38–40), but as Duncan and Banquo approach the castle, Banquo observes that "[t]he temple-haunting martlet, does approve / By his loved mansionry that the heaven's breath / Smells wooingly here," and comments on the birds' "pendant bed and procreant cradle" (1.6.4–6,8). It is as though even the castle knows that "[f]alse face must hide what the false heart doth know" (1.7.83).

Before the murder, Macbeth saw "pity" as an avenging babe; after the murder, an image of a "bloody Child" (4.1.76 s.d.) assures him that he cannot be killed by man "of woman born" (4.1.80), and a crowned child tells him that he will live till Birnam wood comes to Dunsinane. Children have become his enemies, and as though knowing this, Macbeth turns against them. Having resolved to let the "very firstlings of [his] heart … be / The firstlings of [his] hand" (4.1.147–8), he determines to kill Lady Macduff and her children, though this is a gratuitous act because their murder cannot succeed in assuaging the terrible fears that afflict his nights. Furthermore, the very act that he says he takes to secure his throne in fact generates Macduff's outraged parenthood, which joins with the images of avenging children as Macbeth's nemesis. These images also unite with the more general images of Macbeth's loss of creature comforts such as sleeping, eating with others, and maintaining his membership in the human community. Instead of joining the festive table, Macbeth says he has "supped full of horrors" at the witches' cauldron (5.5.13); instead of having children, images of them represent inimical fates, and instead of experiencing the tenderness of parenthood, Macbeth is fated to be killed by one who represents the feelings he and his wife have denied in the name of their love and their ambition.

After the murder is accomplished, the relationship between the protagonists changes; their bond deteriorates as soon as their mutual desire has been fulfilled.[18] Macbeth begins to espouse his wife's definition of him as an unthinking man of action, and to redefine her in a more conventionally feminine role. In turn, she becomes more tentative with him. Macbeth keeps to himself his plans to murder Banquo; Lady Macbeth keeps from him her inner anxieties. We come upon her reflecting that, "['t]is safer to be that which we destroy / Than by destruction dwell in doubtful joy" (3.2.8–9). However, when Macbeth enters, lamenting the "restless ecstasy" of their nights and saying that he envies Duncan, who sleeps well "after life's fitful fever" (3.2.24–5), she denies her anguish by dismissing his, and he, in turn, conceals from her his plans to murder. Each withdraws from the other as they now "make [their] faces vizards to [their] hearts" (3.2.37). Macbeth indirectly broaches his plot against Banquo: "O, full of scorpions is my mind, dear wife! / Thou know'st that Banquo and his Fleance lives" (3.2.39–40). Lady Macbeth, no longer thinking of murder, tries to comfort him simply that "in them Nature's copy's not eterne" (3.2.41), but Macbeth takes this as approval of his plan for murder. Furthermore, in this scene, they use inappropriately tender terms to address each other, terms they had not used earlier: she addresses him as "[g]entle, my lord," and he calls her "love," and "dearest chuck" (3.2.30, 32, 48). Even more significant is Macbeth's desire to withhold his plans from her. When she asks "what's to be done?" he responds "[b]e innocent of the knowledge" (3.2.47–8). This directly reverses his earlier desire to keep her informed, expressed as a reluctance to deny her those "dues of rejoicing by being ignorant" (1.5.12–13). In recasting Lady Macbeth's lack of knowledge as "innocent" rather than "ignorant," he firmly denies their previous equality.

Having thus covertly gained her consent, Macbeth indulges in murderous anticipation in language filled with erotic suggestions:

> Then be thou jocund. Ere the bat hath flown
> His cloistered flight, ere to black Hecate's summons
> The shard-borne beetle with his drowsy hums
> Hath rung night's yawning peal, there shall be done
> A deed of dreadful note. (3.2.43–7)

"Hecate's summons," "drowsy hums," and "night's yawning peal" suggest the dark ease of seductive sleep that obscures the moral horror of what he is planning. He continues to savor the images in which he couches the murder: "Light thickens, / And the crow Makes wing to th' rooky wood; / Good things of day begin to droop and drowse, / Whiles night's black agents to their preys do rouse" (3.2.53–6). These words seem to affect Lady Macbeth, for Macbeth then notes "[t]hou marvel'st at my words" (3.2.57). Enjoying Lady Macbeth's silent response to his poetry, Macbeth anticipates the murder with a kind of swoon into an auto-erotic violence that now excludes his wife, for he urges her "hold thee still" (3.2.57). The process of the lovers' separation, begun after the first murder, will be completed after the second.

The banquet scene articulates the emotional dynamic of Macbeth and Lady Macbeth's alienation from each other. The scene begins with the guests assembling in decorous hierarchical order. Macbeth loses his place in that order to Banquo's ghost, who stubbornly occupies his seat at dinner. The discord between Macbeth and his wife reaches its height here, and the consequence for the nation is represented when Lady Macbeth dismisses her guests, telling them to "[s]tand not upon the order of your going" (3.4.120). This banquet at which no food is consumed represents the dissolution not only of social accord, but also the of the bond between Macbeth and his wife, for this is the last time that we see them together. Thus, the drama depicts their nightmare fulfillment of desire, their loss of intimacy, and the destruction of kinship bonds as joint consequences of their crime.

As Macbeth and his wife drift apart, they also change places. Macbeth becomes the man of action that Lady Macbeth wants him to be, a man who will enact the "[s]trange things [he has] in head" before they are "scanned" (3.4.140–1), while Lady Macbeth retreats into the inner world of imagination for which she previously had berated him. However, Macbeth's feelings about his wife remain a part of his sense of life's meaningfulness, and once having excluded her from his consciousness, he finds himself aging – "fall'n into the sere, the yellow leaf" (5.3.23) – but without the usual comforts of old age, such as "honor, love, obedience, troops of friends" (5.3.25). Their underlying bond appears when he prepares for his final battle outside the castle, while inside the castle she vainly washes her hands. His despair of her life mixes with his despair of the coming battle when he begs Lady Macbeth's doctor, with whom he has been consulting on her health, to then "find [Scotland's] disease, / And purge it to a sound and pristine health" and asks him, "[w]hat rhubarb, senna, or what purgative drug / Would scour these English hence?" (5.3.53–4, 57–8).

The last remnant of life's meaningfulness drains away with the news of her death, and Macbeth expresses this in a very famous soliloquy:

> She should have died hereafter;
> There would have been a time for such a word.
> Tomorrow, and tomorrow, and tomorrow
> Creeps in this petty pace from day to day
> To the last syllable of recorded time,
> And all our yesterdays have lighted fools
> The way to dusty death. Out, out, brief candle!
> Life's but a walking shadow, a poor player
> That struts and frets his hour upon the stage
> And then is heard no more. It is a tale
> Told by an idiot, full of sound and fury,
> Signifying nothing. (5.5.17–28)

At first, knowing himself to be in the midst of battle, Macbeth acknowledges he does not have time to fully mourn her death. But then, as his mind moves to the tomorrows of the future when there might be time to mourn, or tell a tale, he senses there will be no point. The future that stretches ahead – "To-morrow, and to-morrow, and to-morrow" – partakes of the present emptiness and "petty pace." He can take no joy in the prospect of escaping death or of everlasting life, when all recorded time is made up of the insignificant syllables of meaningless action that will still lead to death. On the phrase "creeps in this petty pace" his mind swings from the future to the past, and he associates the image of creeping at a petty pace with the earlier images of children. Like the future, the past also has been drained of meaningfulness. The desire that had lit all his "yesterdays" has drained away, and the days now lead only to the "dusty death" he projects onto the future. Therefore, he wants life's candle out, the light by which he can create any meaning of Lady Macbeth's death or by which he can testify to the meaningfulness of their bond. Finding no meaning in any of the narrative he has crafted or will craft, he sees life itself as a "walking shadow," and in that image he expresses his sense of himself as a bloodless husk, emptied of desire.[19]

The image of the moving shadow suggests the stage, but since the candle has been blown out, it is a darkened stage, a scene like Duncan's bedroom that Macbeth both wants and fears to see. As earlier the clamor at the porter's gate replaced Macbeth's vision of Duncan's gore, so now Macbeth in his mind's ear hears in the darkness the player who "struts and frets" upon the "bloody stage" he has made of his world. Rather than see an image of Duncan's bloody bedroom colored by his own desires and revulsion, guilt, and rage, he takes a further and final means to distance himself from that vision. He transforms the image of the stage to the less immediate one of a tale, but denies what the tale might reveal by attributing it to an idiot, an enlarged and grotesque version of a child. Macbeth thus eradicates the meaning of his past, present, and future because he fears that his bond with Lady Macbeth, the desire that gave rise to and fulfilled their mutual ambition, has amounted or will amount to nothing.

The attention I have given to the way in which the action of the play – the planning, execution, and consequences of the murder – become extended images expressive of the protagonists' emotions suggests that the play is a kind of poem come to life. In so far as we savor this aspect of the play, we get drawn into a kind of dream world imbued with the force of Macbeth's desire. If we pull away from the language, as the end of the play encourages us to do, we re-enter the ordinary world of moral judgment. The witches exist on the borderline of these two worlds. That they are seen by Banquo as well as Macbeth renders them part of Macbeth's waking world, but their supernatural attributes blend them into a dream realm, like the ghost in *Hamlet.*

Finally, a word about the porter scene, Act 2 Scene 3, which parallels the gravedigger scene in *Hamlet*, although it stands out more sharply than the latter because throughout the play Hamlet speaks with the same provocative literalness that characterizes the gravedigger, whereas in this play there are no other jokes or light moments. Nonetheless, just as the gravediggers bring out the preoccupation with death that has haunted the language throughout, so the Porter scene adds to rather than detracts from the sense of horror. First, far from bringing relief, the sound of Macduff and Lennox's knocking, which the porter ruminates on, intensifies the nightmarish interior of the castle where it strikes terror into the hearts of Macbeth and Lady Macbeth. It links the bloody bedroom to the outside world which will soon be infected by the events that have occurred within. Second, the detail of the porter's speech adds to the erotic suggestiveness of the previous scene, and it foreshadows both the couple's future and that of the country.

The porter associates Macbeth's castle with hell by referring to himself as the porter of hell-gate, and then imagines spirits who might be knocking on the door – the spirit of a farmer who hanged himself and a treasonous equivocator. When Macduff and Lennox enter the room, the porter tells them he has been drinking, an admission that inspires him then to think about drinking and lechery. He seizes on the idea of the equivocator and links moral equivocation to sexuality when he says that in provoking desire but inhibiting performance, drink, "may be said to be an equivocator with lechery: it makes him and it mars him; it sets him on, and it takes him off; it persuades him and disheartens him, makes him stand to, and not stand to; in conclusion, equivocates him in a sleep and, giving him the lie, leaves him" (2.3.30–5). He is a comic version of the witches' world in which "[f]air is foul and foul is fair," and he foreshadows the social chaos that will radiate from and express the hell of perverse sexuality within the castle. The porter's jokes on the morally equivocal are associated later with the diabolic witches when Macbeth blames his impending defeat on "th' equivocation of the fiend / That lies like truth" (5.5.43–4).[20]

Earlier when Macbeth's determination wavered, Lady Macbeth asked, "[w]as the hope drunk / Wherein you dressed yourself?" (1.7.36–7). Like the porter, she associates drunkenness with being unable "[t]o be the same in thine own act and valor / As thou art in desire?" (1.7.41–2). A few lines later she plans to ply Duncan's chamberlains with "wine and wassail" (1.7.65) and with little justice (especially since it later appears that she has also drugged their drink) but much imagistic force, she describes the "swinish sleep" of the "spongy officers" (1.7.68, 72). The image of the swinish and drunken chamberlains acquires sexual suggestiveness when the porter associates drunkenness with impotence, and the entire cluster of images adds a sexual dimension to Lady Macbeth's contempt of what she sees as Macbeth's unmanly vacillation.

Within the same cluster we also find the peaceful sleep that Macbeth foregoes associated with the drunken grooms who "mock their charge with snores" (2.2.6) are the object of Lady Macbeth's contempt. Therefore, her eagerness to "chastise with the valor of [her] tongue / All that impedes [him] from the golden round" (1.5.27–8) implies her scorn for and impatience with swinish impotence. The impotence she scorns is also associated with Duncan when he is in the bedroom surrounded by the sleeping grooms, who later also are gilded with his golden blood. But the character of Duncan, who said that he had "begun to plant [Macbeth], and will labor/ To make [him] full of growing" (1.4.28–9), also embodies the images of soft nurturing that she despises in Macbeth and represses in herself in order to rouse him to manly action. Manliness in both its social and sexual aspects is realized in murder, while the Macbeths associate quiet sleep, nurture, and social harmony with sexual and social impotence. The text therefore leaves no middle ground for ordinary, loving sexuality between the polarized images of impotence and the "restless ecstasy" of erotic violence. The porter scene not only extends the theme of equivocation from the witches into the social fabric of the play's world; its portentous grotesquerie reaches into the deepest recesses of the characters' psyches in the way, as Freud described it, jokes reveal what seriousness conceals.

Notes

1 Gloria Olchowy, "Murder as Birth in Macbeth." In *Performing Maternity in Early Modern England*. Eds. Kathryn M. Moncrief and Kathryn R. Mcpherson. Aldershot, England: Ashgate, 2007. 197–209.

2 *Shakespeare's Festive Tragedy*.

3 For more on the witches, see Peter Stallybrass, "Macbeth and Witchcraft." In *Focus on Macbeth*. Ed. John Russell Brown. London: Routledge, 1982. 189–209; Chapter 4 of Frederick Kiefer's *Shakespeare's Visual Theatre: Staging Personified Characters*. Cambridge: Cambridge University Press, 2003; David L. Kranz, "The Sounds of Supernatural Soliciting in 'Macbeth'." *Studies in Philology* 100.3 (2003): 346–383; Laura Shamas, *We Three: The Mythology of Shakespeare's Weird Sisters*. New York: Peter Lang, 2007; and E.S. Mallin, "The Charm in Macbeth." In *Enchantment and Dis-enchantment in Shakespeare and Early Modern Drama: Wonder, the Sacred, and the Supernatural*. New York: Routledge, 2017. 55–71.

4 *Suffocating Mothers*. According to Chris Laoutaris, the witches are threatening because they introduce "a nightmare scenario in which women could control, for their own maleficent purposes, the natural agents of procreation through the mediation of the domestic articles they had most ready access to." (*Shakespearean Maternities: Crises of Conception in Early Modern England*. Edinburgh: Edinburgh University Press, 2008. 187).

5 Coppélia Kahn, *Man's Estate: Masculine Identity in Shakespeare*. Berkeley: University of California Press, 1981. For a discussion of witchcraft, hysteria, and female agency, see Joanna Levin, "Lady Macbeth and the Daemonologie of Hysteria." *ELH* 69.1 (2002): 21–55. Levin says that witches and hysterical women were viewed as "antimothers" (34). See also Chelsea Phillips, "'Unsex me here': Bodies,

Femininity in the Performance History of Lady Macbeth." Testi e Linguaggi 7(2013): 353–361. In Freud's speculative interpretation, Lady Macbeth's references to reproduction and children early in the play and her breakdown at the end of the play constitute a "reaction to her childlessness, by which she is convinced of her impotence against the decrees of nature, and at the same time reminded that it is through her own fault if her crime has been robbed of the better part of its fruits" ("Some Character-Types Met with in Psycho-Analytic Work." *The Standard Edition of the Complete Psychological Works of Sigmund Freud.* Volume XIV (1914–1916): On the History of the Psycho-Analytic Movement, Papers on Metapsychology and Other Works, Trans. James Strachey. The Hogarth Press and the Institute of Psychoanalysis, London. 1974. 309–333. 320).

6 "Fantasized Infanticide: Lady Macbeth and the Murdering Mother in Early Modern England." *College Literature* 32.3 (2005): 72–91.

7 For more on *Macbeth* and kinship, see Rebecca Ann Bach, "The 'peerless' Macbeth: Friendship and Family in *Macbeth*." In *Macbeth: New Critical Essays*. New York: Routledge, 2008. 104–117.

8 Critics see Duncan here as straining to protect his throne and succession against threats of usurpation. Harry Berger Jr. writes that Duncan is "apprehensive," and his announcement of succession "is a way of insulating himself against the elevation of Macbeth to Cawdor," but "as he strives to bind them [his thanes] further to himself, his bondage to them increases" (*Making Trifles of Terrors: Redistributing Complicities in Shakespeare.* Stanford: Stanford University Press, 1997, 89). Deirdre Levinson writes that at this point, Duncan is "walking on eggs" ("Politics as Psychology as Politics." In *Ideas Matter: Essays in Honour of Conor Cruise O'Brien*. Eds. Richard English, Joseph Morrison Skelly. Lanham: University Press of America, 2000. 186).

9 "Dwelling 'in doubtful joy': *Macbeth* and the Aesthetics of Disappointment." In Macbeth: *The State of Play*. Ed. Ann Thompson. London: Bloomsbury, 2014.

10 Adelman says that the play indulges a "fantasy of absolute escape" from "maternal power" (*Suffocating Mothers*, 131).

11 Lady Macbeth's idea of "human kindness" is vital to the play. As we saw in Hamlet, "kind" is a remarkably elastic term, interchangeable with the term "kin." It also carries the sense of "natural," and, as Lady Macbeth uses it, the adjective "generous."

12 *Deconstructing Macbeth: The Hyperontological View.* Rutherford: Fairleigh Dickinson University Press, 1990.

13 Abraham Stoll describes how conscience in Macbeth is a "tragically equivocal moral guide" ("Macbeth's Equivocal Conscience." In *Macbeth: New Critical Essays*, 134). For a summary of performance and critical history that sees a clear distinction between good and evil in Macbeth and a history that sees ambiguity instead, see Nick Moschovakis's introduction to *Macbeth: New Critical Essays*.

14 In "Like a Poor Player: Audience Emotional Response, Nonrepresentational Performance and the Staging of Macbeth," Michael David Fox suggests another way in which the audience is folded into the play experience. He argues that the audience has an "empathetic response" to Macbeth and Lady Macbeth despite their crimes. He attributes this to the way in which the play metatheatrically highlights the bodies of the actors and shows the "thin line between reality and illusion" (*Macbeth: Critical Essays*, 218). So the audience, in feeling for Macbeth in some way, will not be in a position to judge him as unnatural or inhuman.

15 In *Shakespeare's Big Men: Tragedy and the Problem of Resentment*, Richard van Oort calls Macbeth's self-condemnation "bouts of internal reverie" and suggests that they derive from his "poetic imagination" (Toronto: Toronto University Press, 2016. 142. 145). But it is not just "self-condemnation that fires Macbeth's imagination. Paul A. Jorgensen examines the idea of the "sensible" at the time of the writing of the play and suggests that Macbeth's "downfall and suffering is due to his yielding directly to the imaginative faculty rather than to the reason and conscience that should control it" (*Our Naked Frailties: Sensational Art and Meaning in* Macbeth. Berkeley: University of California Press, 1971. 17). So too, Lady Macbeth's desire to pour "spirits" in Macbeth's ear suggests that she stirs his imagination negatively.

16 For more on the guest/host dynamic in the play, see James A.W. Heffernan, *Hospitality and Treachery in Western Literature*. New Haven: Yale University Press, 2014. Jeffrey Knapp writes that violence is a "*response* to civility, a dreamlike release from the social pressures of the 'gentle weal.'" "Shakespeare's Pains to Please." In *Forms of Association: Making Publics in Early Modern Europe*. Eds. Paul Yachnin and Marlene Eberhart. Amherst: University of Massachusetts Press, 2015.

17 For more on Macbeth's reference to Tarquin, see Arthur Kirsch, "Macbeth's Suicide." *ELH* 51.2 (1984): 269–296. See also, Bennett Simon, *Tragic Drama and the Family: Psychoanalytic Studies from Aeschylus to Beckett*. New Haven: Yale University Press, 1988.

18 Kirsch notes that the murder "seems to give new life to their marriage at the same time that it empties it" ("Macbeth's Suicide," 274).

19 Fox argues that this speech, in its reference to the strutting player, halts the "forward movement of the plot" to "connect the audience to the representing actor within the represented role" ("Nonrepresentational Performance in *Macbeth*," 220). See also Horst Breuer, "Disintegration of Time in Macbeth's Soliloquy 'Tomorrow, and Tomorrow, and Tomorrow'." *The Modern Language Review* 71.2 (1976): 256–271; and Howard Marchitello "Speed and the Problem of Real Time in Macbeth." *Shakespeare Quarterly* 64.4 (2013): 425–448.

20 Kirsch emphasizes the importance of the Porter scene, linking the porter's equivocations to the "garments of ambition that clothe Macbeth" (273).

10

King Lear

Most scholars place *King Lear* before *Macbeth*, though the evidence makes the reverse order possible. I have always felt more comfortable thinking about *King Lear* as coming after *Macbeth* because of its inclusiveness and range. However, in whatever order they were written, the two plays form a pair by way of opposition. Of Shakespeare's plays, *Macbeth* has the narrowest focus, the smallest number of significant characters, and the simplest plot line. Conversely, *King Lear* has a large number of significant characters, overlapping and intertwining plot lines, and is comprehensive in its dramatic concerns. Shakespeare achieves this enormous and complex canvas by bringing together and dovetailing two different stories from two different sources. The Lear story derives from Raphael Holinshed's *Chronicles of England*, perhaps the most important historical work of the period, and from an older play called *King Leir*, while the Gloucester sub-plot is taken from Sir Philip Sidney's prose romance, *Arcadia*.

King Lear not only draws from different sources, but it also comes to us in two texts: the 1608 Quarto and the 1623 First Folio. Each text contains passages that the other does not, passages that make the versions "interlock" (x).[1] According to Stanley Wells, "of all the Shakespeare plays surviving in two authoritative texts," *Lear* "is the one in which the differences are the greatest" (8).[2] Thus, editors have had to grapple with how to bring the play to an "ideal" state. Stanley Wells summarizes the editorial possibilities for the play:

> Each text could be reprinted independently, though a conscientious editor who knew both would inevitably draw on one in the attempt to correct manifest corruption in the other. It was also possible to conflate the two, introducing into one text some or all of the passages found only in the other. (7)[3]

These possibilities have been fraught with insurmountable questions: who is responsible for the additions to and subtractions from the folio text? Is there a way to create a definitive version of the play? Scholars have vehemently defended each side of the debate. The intricacies of the arguments for or against a conflated, or

Thinking About Shakespeare, First Edition. Kay Stockholder, revised and updated by Amy Scott.
© 2018 John Wiley & Sons Ltd. Published 2018 by John Wiley & Sons Ltd.

"one text" *King Lear* cannot be addressed here.[4] It is important to say, though, that *Lear* serves as a particularly complex example of the levels of mediation that all the plays undergo, the process by which Shakespeare's words come to us – from his pen in manuscripts now lost, through performances, promptbooks, memories, quartos, and folios, and finally to our book pages or computer screens.

Questions of the *Lear* text aside, many scholars view it, rather than *Hamlet*, as Shakespeare's "finest literary achievement"(1).[5] In its comprehensiveness, this play draws on nearly all of Shakespeare's previous dramatic experience. Not only does it have links to the histories and tragedies, but also, perhaps surprisingly, to the comedies. *King Lear* has been compared to Beethoven's Ninth Symphony. There is something apt about this, for in this enormous play Shakespeare brings together and orchestrates amplified variations of almost all of the themes and dramatic techniques that he has introduced in other plays. *Lear* gives new dimensions to the lines of connection between life and the stage, to the relations of comedy and tragedy, as well as to the, familial, social, and political bonds and existential concerns that have been our central focus.

In *King Lear*, these concerns reach a fever pitch for characters within the play world and for audiences watching the drama unfold. Samuel Johnson lamented that the play creates a "perpetual tumult of indignation, pity, and hope" in the mind (490).[6] The culmination of this tumult – the deaths of Lear and Cordelia – are, as J. Stamper describes it, a "raw, fresh wound where our every instinct calls for healing and reconciliation" (77).[7] Scholars have had different views on whether or not the play allows for the possibility of healing the wound. Some, reading Cordelia as a "figure of Christ" (449),[8] see her death as a kind of Christian sacrifice that offers Lear redemption, thereby satisfying our yearning for hope. Proponents of this so-called "Christian optimistic" view, William R. Elton explains, believe "the protagonist, among other characters, is, consequent to his sufferings, 'regenerated,' 'redeemed,' or 'saved'" (3).[9] They see, too, that "[n]atural law, in the traditional sense, presides over the tragedy" (5); that is, the bad are punished, and the good are rewarded. R.V. Young describes the opposing viewpoint, which insists the play "subverts a Christian or even enlightenment world view and anticipates the absurd universe of existentialism or postmodern materialism" (253).[10] Young himself articulates a middle road between the two, arguing that natural law is not absent but in "crisis" (259) because the characters who profess to believe in its operation in the world fail to fully comprehend it and indulge in "reprehensibly foolish vanity" (269). Young's overall argument is that while certainly not optimistic, the play's Christian resonances reveal a "religion of hope in a future life founded on grace" (273). We can agree with Young that there is certainly a spiritual element to Lear's journey, with references to divine grace and with Cordelia's tears described as "holy water" from "heavenly eyes" (4.3.31). But it is not so easy to chart Lear's spiritual trajectory or to assimilate Christian and pagan references under a coherent representation of faith.

On the heath, Lear asks the gods, whose anger he views as manifested in the storm, to keep the storm "o'er our heads" because its force will be able to "[r]ive [crack open], and "shake" the "concealing continents" of injustice, guilt, hypocrisy, and villainy; he then urges sinners to "cry" for "grace" from "dreadful summoners" (3.2.58–9). The term "grace" seems out of place in the violence of Lear's vision of divine retribution. The violence of his vision implies that he would like sinners to "cry" for grace and be refused it, especially since he is here still obsessed with his "two pernicious daughters" and their cruelty to him, a man "old and white" (22, 24). The culmination of his address to the gods and the storm here is his self-description as a "man / More sinned against than sinning" (59–60). The thought is a magnificent evasion of self-blame and accountability – he seems to absolve himself because others are worse than he. Lear seems unable to fully crack open his own "concealing continent" at this moment, a tendency he has shown from the start of the play. At the end of the play, he affords only dead Cordelia's living breath the ability to "redeem all sorrows" (5.3.271), but Cordelia has no more breath. It remains with the audience to ponder whether Lear has been redeemed despite her death and to consider how much Cordelia's death is a sacrifice for Lear's sins and of our peace of mind.

Lear's journey is psychological as well as spiritual. Though the play begins in the political realm, it rapidly plummets into the private realms of family and psyche. Lear thought he wanted to rest his head on Cordelia's kind nursery when he decided to abdicate, but by setting up the love test he created a situation in which empty rhetoric stood for love, and love was left almost without words. The same reliance on empty forms that led him to his other errors also makes Lear deaf to Cordelia's declaration that she loves him "[a]ccording to [her] bond, no more nor less" (1.1.93). Cordelia's bond is secured in natural law, but being unable to comprehend that, Lear makes his evil daughters his mothers, and under their cruel pedagogy suffers a child's humiliation as he travels backward in psychic time.[11]

We will see that his flawed perspective of the world in the beginning of the play will be to compare Cordelia to her sisters rather than value her worth on its own terms. To judge a person's worth in this way is to endorse and create inequitable relationships – Cordelia is powerful to him because she is better than her sisters rather than because she is intrinsically good. This line of thinking leads to the disastrous love test and his alienation from Cordelia. Lear's journey on the heath and through the storm recalibrates his way of thinking and makes his reunion with Cordelia possible, but the tragedy to which the play moves seems to make the cost of Lear's enlightenment too great.

Lear's love test of the play's first scene is designed to discover which daughter will "say doth love us most" (1.1.51); that daughter, he reveals, will receive the largest share of his kingdom. This leads to a competition in which Goneril and Regan use an insistent language of comparison and relation to convey their love. Lear to Goneril is "[d]earer than eyesight, space, and liberty, / Beyond what can be valued" and is "[n]o less than life, with grace, health, beauty, honor" (56–8). At the end of the speech, we are right to be skeptical of Goneril. She says that love makes her speech "unable" (1.1.60), but her verbosity belies this and makes her entire speech ring all the more hollow. When Regan must take her turn, she must find a way to outdo Goneril's language of excess, to make her expression more powerful than her sister's. She says that Goneril "comes too short" in her expression. Using the language of competition or war, she claims that she is "enemy to all other joys" when it comes to her love for her father (1.1.72–3). Yet Lear gives away his kingdom to Regan and Goneril based on this almost violent hyperbole, seemingly in equal measure, telling Regan that she will receive "[n]o less in space, validity, and pleasure / Than that conferred on Goneril" (81–2). He can afford to adopt an air of gracious equity here because, as we will see, he does not value Goneril and Regan as highly as he values Cordelia.

Lear asks Cordelia what she will say to "win a third more opulent / Than your sisters?" (86). The competition has always been weighted in Cordelia's favor, and as Lear disowns Cordelia, he will lament to Kent that he "loved her most" (123). All Lear really wanted was to have Cordelia confirm the value he had already placed on her and to hear her value him as highly as he expected. Because Lear's conception of love is competitive and relative, planned rather than spontaneous, her response is all the more devastating to him. Paradoxically, he does not esteem Regan and Goneril as highly as he does Cordelia, but he values their excessive flattery, which itself is possible only because they do not truly love him. This disjunction creates the conditions for the tragedy that ensues.

Cordelia neatly, without flowery language, expresses her love for her father in terms that remove her from the competition. "I love your Majesty," she says, "[a]ccording to my bond, no more nor less" (1.1.92–3). The language of excess and comparison used by her sisters gives way: when Cordelia says she loves "no more nor less" than her bond, we can see her rejecting the idea of credit and debit that has marked her sisters' speeches. Lear, of course, reacts badly to her measured declaration, and this impels Cordelia to further describe the nature of her bond to her father and question the logic of her sisters' statements:

> Good my lord,
> You have begot me, bred me, loved me. I
> Return those duties back as are right fit,
> Obey you, love you, and most honor you.
> Why have my sisters husbands if they say
> They love you all? Haply, when I shall wed,
> That lord whose hand must take my plight shall carry
> Half my love with him, half my care and duty.
> Sure I shall never marry like my sisters,
> To love my father all. (1.1.95–104)

While Lear seems barely to listen to Goneril and Regan's words, Cordelia has listened to them and pointed out that they do not make sense. Furthermore, love, for Cordelia, if it is felt deeply, will be linked with *acts*, of "care and duty." Such acts do not concern just familial relationships; they express the crucial components of a strong bond between the king and his subject, as Kent's loyalty to Lear so beautifully demonstrates. The great suffering of the play flows from Lear's and others' inability to recognize what Cordelia sees: that a sincere bond is something that must be acted upon rather than simply described.

Cordelia also recognizes something that Lear eventually understands – sincere, virtuous love requires the equality of both parties. Cordelia says that she loves her father because he "begot," "bred," and "loved" her. She emphasizes that her love is a "return" of his acts – they are the same – and that her love is a "right fit" for his. A sincere and lasting emotional connection cannot be sustained when one of those in bondage has less power or feeling than the other. Likewise, true justice cannot be obtained when a few powerful people have access to the means of authority and materials for living at the expense of those who have none. Lear, as with Othello, discovers the value of his real bond and Cordelia's wisdom too late. This is why the play is so harrowing, desolate, and affecting.

The basic structure of *King Lear* resembles the early comedies: the action begins in the world of the court and then moves to a wild heath before returning to the world of politics and social struggle. The scenes on the heath parallel those in the forest of *A Midsummer Night's Dream.* Like the pastoral setting of that play, the heath is a place that exposes a reality deeper than that found in the ordinary world, and it is a place of reformation. The reformation is more fully explored, and the self-understanding gained there is deeper than anything in the comedies, but an even greater difference distinguishes the heath from the pastoral settings of the early plays. In the court world of *Lear*, people play roles that have grown rigid and empty because those who play them have lost sight of their true feelings. By mistaking his kingly role for his personal reality, Lear collapses the stage that is the basis for life's meaningfulness and order. To be cast out onto the heath is to be made to face the primal chaos. The division is marked by the imagery of clothing that contrasts the gorgeous court raiment of Goneril and Regan to the nakedness of Poor Tom. Part of Lear's education consists in confronting the naked body that lies beneath the pretensions and inflated self-importance of the court. Lear must confront his own naked body and the naked needs that have always lurked beneath his royal grandeur. Only in this confrontation can he in himself find the springs of love and compassion that are represented by Cordelia's virtue. The alternative world of the heath forces upon Lear a glimpse of what he has lost, but the bonds between the world's stage and the body's reality have become attenuated. Lear undergoes spiritual reformation, but doing so does not entail a reformation of the court world and of his fortunes, as it does in the comedies. The good die along with the evil, for in the tragic world change comes too little and too late.[12]

With all its horrors, this play also has affinities with fairy tales. Like many fairy tales of the Cinderella type, the play opens with three sisters, the two elder being evil and inwardly ugly, and the youngest being beautiful and good. As in fairy tales, the evil sisters deceive their father with flattery and force the good sister into exile. Also as in a fairy tale, the good sister in *Lear* is denuded of both her father's "folds of favor" (1.1.221) and her dowry, but finds her Prince Charming, here the King of France, in whose eyes she is an "unprized precious maid" (1.1.263). Cordelia, like her counterparts, is utterly virtuous so that no mistreatment can tarnish the radiance of her love and compassion by evoking harsh feelings.[13] The injustice that she suffers is unable to diminish her love, and she loses her life in the effort to save her father from her wicked sisters.

Although it is possible to see her as offering her father spiritual redemption, the play remains a fairy tale gone wrong, for here such redemption does not reverse the flow of events, in which we see France lose the battle and Cordelia die. This evocation of the fairy-tale aura through Cordelia renders the tragedy all the darker, for the fairy tale suggests the promise of fulfillment of the heart's delight. It evokes the dream of restoration, of the return of a lost golden world in which evil can have no irrevocable consequence, and for which the child in us can still yearn. That is probably why many adults enjoy reading fairy tales to children, but do not read them otherwise; that is why they are fairy tales, and that is why they regularly begin: "A long time ago, in a land far away." The evocation of the fairy-tale world in a drama in which action has irrevocable consequences adds to the tragedy the poignancy of a lost dream.

The depiction of the irrevocable consequences of misconceived and misused authority relates *King Lear* to the history plays. Like them, it concerns issues of right and wrong rule, the legitimacy of authority, the evil of bad counselors, wars, and the fragile bond between rulers and subjects. When Lear decides to abdicate his throne, he violates political wisdom, the ideology of kingship as divinely ordained, and natural law as it was presumed to operate within a family. In assuming that the kingship is his to abdicate, he ignores its God-given nature, in which he otherwise believes. He also mistakes it for personal property by dividing it among his three daughters. This is a practical error, for to divide kingdoms was to invite civil war, but it is also a conceptual error as well. Here Lear, like Richard II, fails to distinguish between the country's land as the source of wealth, and the country as a spiritual entity under God. In asking his daughters to say how much they love him in return for their portions, he shows himself unable to distinguish between love and material reward on the personal level, just as on a political level he cannot distinguish between the country and its land. Lear's misunderstanding of his prerogatives as king brings him close to defining himself as a tyrant, as we see when Kent, a wise and unflattering counselor, advises Lear to revoke his sentence on Cordelia, and Lear silences him by saying "[c]ome not between the dragon and his wrath" (1.1.122). Finally, Lear also misunderstands his prerogatives as a father. He thinks he can disown paternity when he disclaims "[p]ropinquity, and property of blood" (1.1.114) in Cordelia, but the play emphasizes that family bonds cannot be erased – they are the most fundamental human expression of natural law. Natural law cannot be repealed; it can only be violated, and Lear's transgression of it unleashes the world-shaking fury of the storm on the heath.[14]

Like Richard before him, Lear leaves the political arena for a descent, or a journey of discovery, into himself and the sources of selfhood. Where Richard leaves the political arena late in his play, Lear's precipitous act occurs at the beginning. The political consequences of Lear's mistake are various. Well in the background, there are rumors of war brewing between the now separate entities, even as Goneril and Regan cooperate in humiliating their father. Kent says, "[t]here is division / Although as yet the face of it is covered / With mutual cunning, twixt Albany and Cornwall" (3.1.19–21). More visible is Edmund's manipulative use of Goneril and Regan's sexual rivalry over him. He serves as the play's Bolingbroke, though his strategies are more obvious. Most important is Lear's struggle to cling to the royal identity that he himself has emptied of meaning. He has precipitated a torturous journey that strips him of the roles and rituals of royalty, and so he must come to terms with the "bare, forked animal" (3.4.106) of the body natural beneath the royal robes.

In the second scene in which we see Lear, his royal bluster has noticeably lessened as he calls impatiently for his dinner and praises the now disguised Kent for tripping Oswald. Lear makes himself vulnerable to Goneril, who in any case wants an excuse to undermine his dignity by reducing his troupe of retainers. Later she and Regan collude in order to halve and then halve again, and then again, his retinue of a hundred knights. In the face of this un-daughterly assault, Lear begins to lose his hold on the manly self-esteem that previously defined his role as father and king. He wants to show "noble anger," but in fact "women's weapons, water-drops, / Stain [his] man's cheeks" (2.4.278–80). He is reduced to empty threats and almost comic impotent rage: "I will do such things – / What they are yet I know not, but they shall be / The terrors of the earth!" (2.4.282–4). This psychologically regressive journey culminates after the fury of the storm has stripped him of all pretensions, and his imagination returns to the moment of birth, the "first time that we smell the air" and "wawl and cry" (4.6.179–80). The regression underlies his political education, for being reduced to the body's infantile needs teaches him that his body natural is not his body politic. Thus, when the blinded Gloucester meets Lear on the heath and offers to kiss his kingly hand, Lear says "[l]et me wipe it first; it smells of mortality" (4.6.133). He acknowledges, though still indirectly, his own failure rightly to perform the role of king, describing his world as a place in which the "great image of authority" has been corrupted, as when the "creature run[s] from the cur" (4.6.157–8). These realizations are the precondition for his reunion with Cordelia, for her medicinal tears and kisses, and for the fresh garments that symbolize his readiness to partake in reciprocal love.

The psychic journey that is represented in Lear's literal journey to Dover and the spiritual and psychological journey to Cordelia articulate the play's multiple themes. One of these themes concerns the social injustice that follows upon the abuse of authority, a focus for Shakespeare in earlier plays. In *King Lear* it comes up first when Goneril and Regan reduce Lear's retinue, finally questioning his need for even one retainer. Lear objects that even the poorest person must have some belongings, things he calls "superfluous" (2.4.267) and then points out that Regan's hypocrisy, that her luxurious clothes are not serving her base needs at all, crying out, "[i]f only to go warm were gorgeous, / Why, nature needs not what thou gorgeous wear'st, / Which scarcely keeps thee warm" (2.4.270–2). The entire exchange reveals that what one needs is different from what one desires or wants, and it laments that those who have excessive resources operate at the expense of those who have few. After defending his desire for retainers, who embody the idea of superfluity, Lear undergoes a change that follows on his journey away from the world of the court. He notices the "looped and windowed raggedness" (3.4.31) of people like Poor Tom, and feels pity for "[p]oor naked wretches" (3.4.28) who, like the shivering figure of Poor Tom, have nothing to protect themselves from the elements:

> I have ta'en
> Too little care of this! Take physic, pomp;
> Expose thyself to feel what wretches feel,
> That thou mayst shake the superflux to them
> And show the heavens more just. (3.4.32–6)

And as though to be sure his point is not missed, Shakespeare has it repeated when suffering also awakens the blinded Gloucester to social inequity. Directing that his purse be given to a person he takes to be a beggar, he reflects:

> That I am wretched
> Makes thee the happier. Heavens, deal so still!
> Let the superfluous and lust-dieted man,
> That slaves your ordinance, that will not see
> Because he does not feel, feel your pow'r quickly!
> So distribution should undo excess
> And each man have enough. (4.1.64–70)

Both Lear's and Gloucester's perceptions of the need for distributive justice mark a stage of their self-discovery. They in effect search to reconnect with the people they alienated when they mistook excess – of flattering words, materials, servants, wealth – with necessity.[15] The key to reshaping connections with people and to discovering oneself, the key to "seeing," is "feeling," Gloucester suggests. In this way, the play might indeed offer a form of healing – we are given insight because we feel, with Lear, a kind of suffering that has the potential to shift our way of thinking about what makes a person valuable.

The explorations of the psychological analogues of political and social issues are amplified by the mythic quality of the play, which comes in part from a sense of timelessness and placelessness that renders its characters and its action larger than life. The play contains no strong time markers. We do not know how much time has passed between Lear's abdication and his reappearance in Goneril's house. We do not know how long it takes for him to travel from there to Regan's castle, or from there to Gloucester's. We do not know how long he spends on the heath in the terrible storm or how long is the journey to Dover. Everything seems to happen outside of ordinary time. Furthermore, the setting is like an impressionistic painting, atmospheric and indistinct. There are some castles, a hovel, and Dover, but we have no idea where they are in relation to each other. There is a barren heath whipped by winds and rains of supernatural force on which characters appear and disappear. Of course, there are places in the play, but they too remain open and undefined. This timeless and placeless quality in combination with action and issues that are comparable to those in the history plays lends to historical matters a cosmic significance.[16]

This quality is further enhanced by the sense of great antiquity introduced into the play by the frequent invocations of the ancient gods. Associated with aspects of nature as they were, the gods lend a supernatural cast to the forces that both dominate and elevate human affairs. The vast powers that appear to move behind the scenes are further heightened by the doubled stories of Lear and Gloucester. Gloucester's story parallels that of Lear in that his bastard son Edmund, the counterpart of Goneril and Regan, seeks to displace his legitimate brother Edgar, the counterpart of Cordelia, as Gloucester's heir. Edmund dupes Gloucester into believing that Edgar plots against his life, because he is impatient to come into his inheritance, whereas it is Edmund himself who exults that "[t]he younger rises when the old doth fall" (3.3.25). This use of double plotting to create parallel rather than contrasting stories increases the sense of a tragic inevitability; it makes the polarity between good and bad children seem like a universal pattern rather than a peculiarity of one family.

If the play does acquire a Christian character, it does so by virtue of its moral polarity and structural simplicity. At the center of the play are Lear and Gloucester, neither greatly good nor greatly evil. Gloucester trivializes life, for instance, reducing Edmund's conception to the "good sport" (1.1.23) he had at his making, and Lear trivializes his authority by using it for ego gratification. The rest operate as good or bad influences on the souls of the two fathers. Cordelia, Kent, and Edgar's compassion and loyalty cannot be shaken by the injustice they endure, and they remain the good angels of the play. Balancing them are Goneril, Regan, Edmund, and Oswald, whose vices are cruelty and self-gratification. Kent represents the ideal servant. He serves for love rather than reward, his fidelity is unshakable, and he will risk his life and living rather than pour the corrupting poison of flattery into the king's ear. He is a type that first appears in Shakespeare's plays as old Adam in *As You Like It*, and he represents the standard by which York in *Richard II* judges himself. His opposite number is Oswald, who serves for reward only and has no moral scruple. Kent calls him a "cowardly rascal" and says "nature disclaims in thee. / A tailor made thee" (2.2.55), implying that Oswald is not a "real" man or loyal servant. The animosity between Kent and Oswald represents the divide between a feudal conception of service in which loyalty surpasses individual concerns, and a more modem one of profit and self-interest. Moving slowly from a neutral position to the good side is morally outraged Albany, who is balanced by the cruel Cornwall.

Lear's Fool, in offering continual reminders of the error of banishing Cordelia and believing Goneril and Regan's expressions of love to be superfluous, works to reknit the fractured bond between Lear and Cordelia. He is mentioned first when Lear is told about his pining for the banished Cordelia, and she is his dominant theme as he plagues Lear with sharp reminders of his stupidity, telling him "[t]hou hadst little wit in thy bald crown when thou gav'st thy golden one away" (1.4.160–1). He disappears from the play without explanation as Lear starts his journey to Dover. Finally, when Edmund's servants murder Cordelia in prison, Lear laments, "[a]nd my poor fool is hanged!" (5.3.311). It is as though the Fool in his choric function speaks for, when speaking about, the banished Cordelia, just as Poor Tom in his choric function allows Edgar to speak his own truth.

The stark polarity between good and evil relates to another aspect of the play's structure. More than any other play that Shakespeare wrote, *Lear* develops a multi-layered conception of the world, from the personal, to the socio-political and cosmic. By having images from one level resonate on all the others, Shakespeare keeps the various levels of significance constantly in our awareness, and because of this multi-layeredness, themes that in other plays are like chamber music here have the force of an unstopped cathedral organ. For example, on the personal level we see both Lear and Gloucester commit acts of personal injustice toward their children. Lear feels himself "more sinned against than sinning" (3.2.60), and on the whole, partly because of the brazen hatefulness of Goneril and Regan, we tend to agree with him, despite having seen him bring his suffering upon himself. Injustice reappears on the social and economic level, and it also appears on the political level in the climactic scene that brings Lear and Gloucester together on the heath. Here Lear denounces the debased image of authority, the "dog" that is "obeyed in office," and the "rascal beadle" who "hotly lusts" to use the prostitute for the same act for which he orders her to be whipped (4.6.158–62).

The play amplifies all of these themes by adding a cosmic level, which appears in the language at the very beginning when Lear forswears his paternity "by the sacred radiance of the sun, / The mysteries of Hecate and the night, / By all the operation of the orbs / From whom we do exist and cease to be" (1.1.109–12), and when he calls upon Apollo and Jupiter to silence Kent. This level becomes more active when we hear thunder in the background as Lear vows that he would rather suffer the fury of the elements than remain with Goneril and Regan: it is as though the actual storm emerges from his thoughts. In this way, his figure at its most diminished also acquires a larger-than-life power, as he invokes the very storm that torments him. He is both vulnerable and commanding, directing the tempest that soaks him to the skin to "[c]rack nature's molds, all germens spill at once / That makes ingrateful man!" (3.2.8–9). Though it is hubris in Lear to align his cause with the seeds of creation, the wind and rain he summons nevertheless overcomes the old world and leaves its inhabitants bereft.

The cosmic dimension elevates the play's concern with justice and also sharpens the moral polarity. Gloucester's image of suffering people, "[a]s flies to wanton boys are we to th' gods; / They kill us for their sport" (4.1.36–7), is set against Edgar's view, one so rigorously just that it borders on cruelty, where even the blinding of his father can be an example of divine justice: "[t]he gods are just, and of our pleasant vices / Make instruments to plague us. / The dark and vicious place where thee he got / Cost him his eyes" (5.3.173–6). While Lear's daughters function as naturalistic figures with the ordinary psychology of sibling rivalry, they at the same time become opposing principles of creation. Cordelia is described as one "[w]ho redeems nature from the general curse / Which twain have brought her to" (4.6.206–07). Goneril and Regan's sexuality, on the other hand, is likened to the "riotous appetite" of Centaurs, and Lear says that beneath their waist is "all the fiends'. / There's hell, there's darkness, there is the sulfurous pit" (4.6.123, 127–8). While Cordelia is so generative, so powerful that she presides over and restores a decaying natural world, Goneril and Regan are so unnatural that they consume and punish.[17] Lear's tendency to compare his daughters has reached cosmic, mythic proportions, ready to break him apart and change the way he experiences love.

To these conceptions of nature, Shakespeare adds another: the natural wish for power. Congratulating himself on his success in deceiving his father, Edmund says:

> Thou, Nature, art my goddess; to thy law
> My services are bound. Wherefore should I
> Stand in the plague of custom, and permit
> The curiosity of nations to deprive me,
> For that I am some twelve or fourteen moonshines
> Lag of a brother? (1.2.1–6)

In opposing custom and the curiosity, or the traditions, of nations to the law of nature, Edmund denies the theory of natural law, and aligns himself with a Machiavellian understanding of power. Cordelia's "natural" bond, one which demonstrates sincere love by caring for others with reciprocal acts, and Edmund's "nature," which rejects custom and seizes power from others, constitute the two abstract poles that, in the drama played out between them, pull the human figures toward the moral extremities of absolute good and evil.

These cosmic forces circle back into human actions in Lear's comment on the lack of distributive justice. In the passage quoted above, he says that the superflux should be shaken – distributed – to the poor "to *show* the heavens more just" (my italics). Whether or not there is justice in the heavens, it cannot be manifested in society without just kings, and it cannot be manifested in the family without just fathers. Finally, these personal, social and cosmic layers resonate on the interpsychic level. Both fathers in the play see their children's faults as an extension of theirs or those faults are at least intimately entangled with their own sense of self. Lear suggests such a reading, probably more than he intends, when he says that Goneril and Regan are,

> my flesh, my blood, my daughter–
> Or rather a disease that's in my flesh,
> Which I must needs call mine. Thou art a boil,
> A plague-sore, or embossèd carbuncle
> In my corrupted blood. (2.4.222–6)

Gloucester says, "[o]ur flesh and blood, my lord, is grown so vile / That it doth hate what gets it" (3.4.143–4), and the principle of natural law that inscribes the consequence of its violation in the human psyche is invoked in the many references to the unnaturalness, the monstrosity, of Edmund, Goneril, and Regan.

One would think that all these elements taken together would guarantee that this play, perhaps more than any other, should have unalloyed tragic impact. Oddly enough, however, this vast orchestration, this Gothic cathedral of meaningfulness, includes within itself a more deeply embedded comic challenge than any other of Shakespeare's tragedies, a challenge to the meaningfulness and depth of the characters' sufferings. Earlier on I referred to the Fool and to Edgar in his guise as Poor Tom as choric figures because they comment on the moral implications of the action and thus guide the judgment of the audience. Most choric commentary, such as that in *Macbeth*, adds to the gravity of the action and to the magnitude of major characters. Here, however, the choric commentary draws out the implications of the action in a comic light. The Fool shows what is ridiculous in Lear by reducing his monumental error to a ditty about the King changing places with the Fool, and he both foreshadows and abridges the monumental cruelty of the evil sisters when he says, "[f]or you know, nuncle, / 'The hedge sparrow fed the cuckoo so long / That it had its head bit off by it young.' / So, out went the candle, and we were left darkling" (1.4.212–16). He reduces Lear's humiliation to a form of castration, always subject to uncomfortable humor. The same effect appears when Lear's heart rises in rage as he waits outside of Regan and Cornwall's castle. The Fool says, "[c]ry to it, nuncle, as the cockney did to the eels when she put 'em i' th' paste alive. She knapped 'em o' the coxcombs with a stick and cried, 'Down, wantons, down!'" (2.4.120–3). In this analogy, Lear's enraged heart is like the eels, and the cockney who beats them down stands for Regan. The fool not only mocks the impotence of Lear's rage, but also figures that rage as a phallus in the image of the eel and by the cockney's reference to them as "wantons." The Fool's homely humor based on the old saws of folk wisdom both punishes Lear for his stupidity and unrelentingly reminds him of his folly. The Fool's wit, which, in ridiculing the King, brings Lear to a lower social level, subverting the values to which Lear initially subscribed.

A similar quality pervades Poor Tom's invocation of the little devils that delight in tormenting people. When Lear and Kent first encounter Edgar disguised as Poor Tom, Edgar urges them to stay away because the "foul fiend" follows him (3.4.45). When Lear sees Poor Tom's distress, he reads his own distress into it and asks "[d]idst thou give all to thy daughters? And art thou come to this?" (3.4.48–9). Edgar's response, again focused on the "foul fiend," seems to make fun of Lear's predicament; he asks, "[w]ho gives anything to Poor Tom? Whom the foul fiend hath led through the fire and through flame, through ford and whirlpool, o'er bog and quagmire; that hath laid knives under his pillow, and halters in his pew, set ratsbane by his porridge" (3.4.50–4). The devils serve to mock the grand evil epitomized by the sisters and Edmund. The same reduction of sin occurs when, moments later, Poor Tom takes upon himself vices seen in the rest of the play. He has been:

> A servingman! proud in heart and mind, that curled my hair, wore gloves in my cap, served the lust of my mistress' heart, and did the act of darkness with her; swore as many oaths as I spake words, and broke them in the sweet face of heaven. One that slept in the contriving of lust and waked to do it. Wine loved I deeply, dice dearly, and in woman out-paramoured the Turk. False of heart, light of ear, bloody of hand; hog in sloth, fox in stealth, wolf in greediness, dog in madness, lion in prey. Let not the creaking of shoes nor the rustling of silks betray thy poor heart to woman. Keep thy foot out of brothels, thy hand out of plackets, thy pen from lenders' books, and defy the foul fiend. Still through the hawthorn blows the cold wind; says suum, mun, nonny. Dolphin my boy, boy, sessa! Let him trot by. (3.4.84–99)

This catalogue enumerates all the vices that comprise the central action; even the animals are those evoked in serious contexts, but here the corrupt sexuality, those "dark and vicious places" (5.3.175) that Edgar believes have caused Gloucester's fate, and that Lear sees around him in the lecherous flies and the hypocritical judge, becomes the most fundamental evil. Edgar sees sexual desire and the women who inspire it as aspects of the "foul fiend," the same foul fiend of the previous passage that "blows the cold wind." In this vision, the play's grand evil is reduced to devilish pranks. At the same time, evil itself is not chosen by human beings, but rather is something inflicted upon them. Poor Tom's exuberance in multiplying these images stands out all the more for going beyond any requirement of the plot. His language introduces into the play a grotesque world in which sin is not so much a moral category as a cruel joke. It is the world of Hieronimus Bosch, where there is no distinction between the pleasures of sin and the pleasures of its punishment.

A different kind of comedy enters the play when Lear comes upon Kent in the stocks. For one thing, the stocks are conventionally a punishment for lowly persons accused of trivial crimes, and as such were conventional props for a comic stage. Cornwall also insults the King, for as both Kent and Lear point out, the King's messenger stands in for the King himself. Lear feels the affront keenly, but tries to hold it off by refusing to believe that his daughter and Cornwall are responsible for Kent's bondage. He comes close to being as much comic victim as tragic hero when he comes upon Kent in the stocks, and Kent informs Lear that Cornwall and Regan are responsible; the conversation that follows descends into a comic routine that breaks all the rules of tragic decorum:

> Lear: No.
> Kent: Yes.
> Lear: No, I say.
> Kent: I say yea.
> Lear: No, no, they would not.
> Kent: Yes, they have
> Lear: By Jupiter, I swear no.
> Kent: By Juno, I swear ay. (2.4.14–21)

The exchange reveals a sort of humor that while not witty exactly, has the effect of comically highlighting Lear's lack of awareness, which then blends into his refusal to accept reality when it is revealed to him.

These winds of comedy that drain the significance of suffering blow nowhere so chillingly as in the scenes that follow upon Gloucester's blinding. When Edmund turns his father over to Regan and Cornwall for having violated their decree that no one help Lear, the evil sisters' and Cornwall's cruelty and Edmund's Machiavellian indifference reach their apex. Regan plucks his beard, and then Cornwall pulls out his eyes. This is probably the most horrendously violent action ever staged.[18] The scene calls upon visceral response to underwrite all the major themes and values of the play, and the meaningfulness of the Lear world depends upon this audience reaction. When Albany hears about the blinding, he says that unless the gods intervene directly, "[h]umanity must perforce prey on itself, / Like monsters of the deep" (4.2.49–50), and he draws what is perhaps too optimistic a conclusion when he hears that a nameless servant rose from what ought, on a tragic stage, to be his proper dramatic obscurity to give Cornwall his mortal wound. This action, Albany says, "shows you are above, / You justicers, that these our nether crimes / So speedily can venge!" (4.2.79–81).

Odd turns are taken in the aftermath of the blinding. When the sightless Gloucester asks that Poor Tom be his guide, Edgar comes to his mind, and he says, "O dear son Edgar, … / Might I but live to see thee in my touch, / I'd say I had eyes again!" (4.1.21–4). Edgar keeps his silence, but at his suicidal father's wish pretends to lead him to the edge of a high cliff. Gloucester thinks that he throws himself from a great height, but what we see is a pratfall on a flat stage. In performance, the comedy of this scene cannot be overcome, nor should it be. Edgar says, "[w]hy I do trifle thus with his despair / Is done to cure it" (4.6.33–4), but his declared moral purpose does not cancel the grotesque humor. He now takes on a different persona for his blind father, whom he directs to look up at the non-existent cliff from which he had fallen to see "some fiend," whose "eyes / Were two full moons; he had a thousand noses, / Horns whelked and waved like the enridgèd sea" (4.6.69–72). In describing his own previous persona as a fiend, he merges his previous identity as Poor Tom with that of the foul fiend who, as he previously stated, "hurts the poor creature of earth" (3.4.117). The comedy of the scene gives way to Gloucester's sad resignation, only to be followed by Lear's entry *"mad, fantastically dressed with wild flowers"* (4.6.79 s.d.) and the climactic meeting of Gloucester and Lear. By the end of the play, it is as though Poor Tom has taken on a parodic life of his own when Edgar in his own person says that he does not know why he did not reveal his identity to Gloucester. Touches of comedy continue to the end, for Albany says "[g]reat thing of us forgot!" (5.3.240) when Edmund in the process of repenting mentions that he has ordered Lear's and Cordelia's execution. Tragic momentum momentarily breaks down into a comic scuffle.[19]

I have touched here on disturbing aspects of the play, aspects that cannot, I think, be dismissed. The net result of these comic intrusions is to raise a question about tragedy itself. Tragedy creates a meaningful world from human suffering. It generates figures whose fates matter, and who encourage us to take seriously our own suffering. However painful the events one witnesses in watching tragedy, in this sense at least tragedy is life-affirming. To bring to bear on events that are normally the stuff of tragedy the reverse telescope of the comic perspective is to drain the well-springs of human significance and to further question the strength of bonds that people make with each other. It is to reveal that the tragic and comic views of life are not built into experience, but are arbitrary. Anything that occurs can be taken seriously or not, though when we violate the social consensus about what ought to be mocked the coloring of the comedy changes. This black comedy in *King Lear* carries on from *Troilus and Cressida*. Though here it remains in tension with a tragic view, it shows Lear in his opening act allowing the cold wind of farce to blow across the tragic stage, undermining the conditions that make it possible to see life as more meaningful than the lives of flies appear to laughing boys or human affairs to the gods.

Notes

1 Sir Brian Vickers, *The One King Lear*. Cambridge, Massachusetts: Harvard University Press, 2016.
2 *King Lear*. The Oxford Shakespeare. Oxford: Oxford University Press, 2000. Richard Knowles observes that "the play of Lear has always been in constant flux" (124) because of these variations, he describes the drawbacks of each text: the Quarto is "full of error and nonsense" and the Folio is longer than a reasonable acting text would be (129, 127). ("The Evolution of the Texts of Lear." In *King Lear: New Critical Essays*. Ed. Jeffrey Kahan. New York: Routledge, 2008. 124–154).
3 "The Once and Future King Lear." In *The Division of the Two Kingdoms: Shakespeare's Two Version of King Lear*. Eds. Gary Taylor and Michael Warren. Oxford: Clarendon Press, 1983.
4 For more on the texts of King Lear, see Steven Urkowitz, *Shakespeare's Revision of King Lear*. Princeton, 1980; Peter M. Blayney, *The Texts of King Lear and their Origins*. Vols 1–2. London: Cambridge University Press, 1982; Robert Clare, "'Who is it that can tell me who I am?': The Theory of Authorial Revision Between the Quarto and Folio Texts of 'King Lear.'" *The Library* 17.1 (1995): 34–59; R.A. Foakes, "The Reshaping of King Lear," in King Lear: *New Critical Essays*. 104–123.
5 Stanley Wells, "Introduction," *King Lear*. The Oxford Shakespeare. Oxford: Oxford University Press, 2000. For more on the nature of *King Lear*'s popularity, see Marjorie Garber's chapter on *Lear* in *Shakespeare and the Moderns*. New York: Anchor, 2008.
6 *The Works of Samuel Johnson*. Vol. II. New York: Alexander V. Blake, 1838.
7 "The Catharsis of *King Lear*." In *Aspects of* King Lear. Eds. Kenneth Muir and Stanley Wells. Cambridge: Cambridge University Press, 1982. 77–86.
8 Peter Milward. "The Religious Dimension of *King Lear*." In *Shakespeare's Christian Dimension: An Anthology of Commentary*. Bloomington: University of Indiana Press, 1994. 448–452.
9 King Lear *and the Gods*. Lexington: University of Kentucky, 1988. Elton goes on to summarize notable arguments for and against the Christian "optimistic" view of the play. The Christian dimensions of the play are discussed in Rosalie L. Colie, "The Energies of Endurance: Biblical echo in *King Lear*," in *Some Facets of* King Lear: *Essays in Prismatic Criticism*. Eds. Rosalie L. Colie and F.T. Flahiff. Toronto: Toronto University Press, 1974. 117–144; Cherrell Guilfoyle "The Redemption of King Lear." *Comparative Drama* 23.1 (1989): 50–69.

10 "Hope and Despair in *King Lear*: The Gospel and the Crisis of Natural Law."
In King Lear: *New Critical Essays*. 253–77. For more on King Lear and the
absurd, see Kott on the similarities between *Lear* and Beckett's *Endgame* in
Shakespeare Our Contemporary and R.A. Foakes's discussion of Kott's theory
in "King Lear and *Endgame*" in *Shakespeare Survey 55: King Lear and Its
Afterlife*. Cambridge: Cambridge University Press, 2002. 153–158. Garber
discusses Lear and Endgame in *Shakespeare and Modern Culture*.

11 Janet Adelman sees in Lear's struggles a "terrifying dependence on female
forces" that render him infantile and encompass the "intensity and fragility of
the hope for a saving maternal presence that can undo pain" (*Suffocating
Mothers*, 104). Lear's reversion to childishness is negative in Adelman's reading,
as she points out that fathers in *King Lear* are uncomfortable that they must
rely on female bodies to procreate and notes that the play consciously omits
"Queen Lear" from the anonymous source play (104). C.L. Barber and Richard
P. Wheeler suggest that the play carries Lear "back to the source of self in
earliest infancy, to a deeper, more archaic level of being where self and world,
child and parent interpenetrate" (69). *Bloom Reviews: William Shakespeare's*
King Lear. Ed. Harold Bloom. Broomall, PA: Cheslea House Publishers, 1999.

12 For Freud, the play dramatizes the process by which the old man must
"renounce love, choose death and make friends with the necessity of dying"
(301). Freud reads Cordelia as a symbol of death and says that in finally
recognizing Cordelia's value and embracing her at the end of the play, Lear
embraces his mortality. *The Standard Edition of the Complete Works of Sigmund
Freud*. Trans. James Strachey. Vol. XII. London: The Hogarth Press, 1958.

13 See Stanley Cavell's chapter on *King Lear*, "The Avoidance of Love," in
Disowning Knowledge: In Seven Plays of Shakespeare for a discussion of
Cordelia's words and actions. Cambridge: Cambridge University Press, 1987.

14 As Katherine Eisamann Maus explains, "the effect of *Lear*'s wholesale
disjointings is to complicate, almost to the extent of annihilating, the powerful
connections between property and power" (*Being and Having*, 112). She says
that the by the end of the play, no one seems to even want the kingship. For
more on the politics of *King Lear*, see Paul A. Cantor, "King Lear: The Tragic
Disjunction of Wisdom and Power" in *Shakespeare's Political Pageant: Essays
in Literature and Politics*. Ed. Joseph Alulis and Vicki Sullivan. Lanham:
Rowman and Littlefield, 1996. 189–207; Leon Harold Craig, *Of Philosopher and
Kings: Political Philosophy in Shakespeare's* Macbeth *and* King Lear. Toronto:
Toronto University Press, 2001; Mark A. McDonald, *Shakespeare's* King Lear
and The Tempest: *The Discovery of Nature and the Recovery of Classical
Natural Right*. Dallas: University Press of America, 2004.

15 Barber and Wheeler suggest that the play exposes the "destructive side of
human bonds." (*Bloom Reviews*) Similarly, Conn Liebler describes King Lear's
"focal concern" as the "vulnerability of identity at the margins, the boundaries
of bonds" (*Festive Tragedy*, 197). Identity is shaped, she suggests, through one

person's relationship to another, and the play challenges "virtually every kind of human interrelatedness and definition of identity: feudal, familial, spousal, national" (*Festive Tragedy*, 197).

16 Helen Gardner writes that because "both time and place are handled with extreme casualness" in the play, it isn't possible to "propose a time and place scheme for *King Lear*" ("from *King Lear*," *King Lear: Critical Essays*. Ed. Kenneth Muir. London: Routledge, 1984. 251–274. 255).

17 For more on *King Lear* and gender, see Dympna Callaghan, *Woman and Gender in Renaissance Tragedy: A Study of* King Lear, Othello, The Duchess of Malfi, *and* The White Devil. Atlantic Highlands, NJ : Humanities Press International, 1989; Ann Thompson, "Are There Any Women in King Lear?" *The Matter of Difference: Materialist Feminist Criticism of Shakespeare*. Ed. Valerie Wayne. New York: Harvester Wheatsheaf, 1991. 117–128; Catherine S. Cox, "'An Excellent Thing in Woman': Virgo and Viragos in 'King Lear'" *Modern Philology* 96.2 (1998): 143–157; Cristina León Alfar, *Fantasies of Female Evil: The Dynamics of Gender and Power in Shakespearean Tragedy*. Newark: University of Delaware Press, 2003; and Philippa Kelly, "See What Breeds about Her Heart: 'King Lear,' Feminism, and Performance" *Renaissance Drama* 33 (2004): 137–157.

18 See Stanley Cavell's chapter on *King Lear* ("The Avoidance of Love") in *Disowning Knowledge in Seven Plays of Shakespeare*. See especially pp. 46–48; Chapter 2 of R.A. Foakes' *Shakespeare and Violence*. Cambridge: Cambridge University Press, 2003; Chapter 4 of Richard Meek's *Narrating the Visual in Shakespeare*. Farnham: Ashgate, 2009; and David B. Goldstein, "Facing King Lear." In *Shakespeare and the Power of the Face*. Ed. James A. Knapp. London: Routledge, 2015. 75–92.

19 For more on *King Lear* and comedy, see G. Wilson Knight, *The Wheel of Fire: Interpretations of Shakespearian Tragedy*. London: Routledge, 1930, 2001. Knight calls the mixing of comedy in the tragedy a "sublime incongruity" (181). See also Frances Carole Speyer, *Anger Has Privilege: A Study of Comedy in Tragedy in* King Lear. Denver: University of Colorado Press, 1966; Russell A. Peck, "Edgar's Pilgrimage: High Comedy in *King Lear*." *Studies in English Literature, 1500-1900* 7.2 (1967): 219–237.

11

Antony and Cleopatra

After having fashioned the horrendous and polarized worlds of *Macbeth* and *King Lear,* Shakespeare created a very different environment in *Antony and Cleopatra.* The play continues the concern with romantic love from where Shakespeare left it in *Othello.* In that play, as in *Romeo and Juliet,* the lovers inhabit a charmed circle, affected by but resistant to intrusions from the social and political world around them. In *Romeo,* the external world breaks into the enchanted circle, while in *Othello* external factors join with pressures from within the relationship. In *Antony and Cleopatra,* external forces pressure but have no power to forbid love. There are other differences; Antony and Cleopatra have been lovers for a long time, and they are older than conventional lovers. However, the vicissitudes of their relationship show them held within the charmed circle. Like that of Romeo and Juliet, their love cannot exist within the ordinary world of marriage and family, and it draws inward, away from the public world of politics and war. As in *Macbeth,* the lovers' shared language conveys the deep bonds between them, and apparently supernatural occurrences reveal their inner states. Like *King Lear,* this play also tests its tragic impact against a comic challenge, but here the outcome depends upon the protagonists themselves. An important part of their drama consists in each of the lover's struggle to assert his and her *own* powers, even as the play gradually indicates that their individual strengths are in fact shared; though Antony and Cleopatra at times are at their weakest, politically and martially, they are ready to imbue each other with a potency that observers within the play, and the audience of the play, cannot help but acknowledge, even if they ridicule it.

Janet Adelman describes the play's "spaciousness and generosity" as a product of its characterization of Cleopatra, who is linked to images of Egyptian land and water and becomes a figure of "promiscuous generativity" (175).[1] A dominant image in the play is that of the river Nile, which, as the play reminds us, is a body of water that nourishes Egypt by overflowing its banks. Antony describes this process to the Romans: "[t]he higher Nilus swells / The more it promises; as it ebbs, the seedsman / Upon the slime and

Thinking About Shakespeare, First Edition. Kay Stockholder, revised and updated by Amy Scott.

ooze scatters his grain, / And shortly comes to harvest" (2.7.20–3). When the river breaches its banks, the finite line between water and land is obliterated, creating a hybrid zone of "slime and ooze." This wonderfully evocative emphasis on muddy places of reproduction stands too for the space the lovers seem to occupy. The more dramatically and emotionally Cleopatra expresses her connection to Antony, the more Antony is drawn to her and the more difficult it becomes for each lover to retain a sense of self separable from the other. The passion that each lover experiences gives them a sense that their identities are like elements, frighteningly changeable, or like a solid body or structure capable of being rendered liquid – as the references in the play to melting suggest. And even though that changeability and liquidity are threatening, moments when the lovers are distant, clinging to their autonomy, offer a sense that their investment in each other can never fully be withdrawn and that the blending of the self into the lover makes for a lasting connection. In the aftermath of Antony's disdain for Cleopatra while in Rome or when Cleopatra sails away from Antony at the Battle of Actium, the lover's connection only intensifies.

The first words in the play, Philo's lamentation over Antony's attraction to Cleopatra, initiate this connection between the Nile's overflowing to the lover's emotions. "[T]his dotage of our general's," Philo says, "O'erflows the measure" (1.1.1–2). Excessive, unmeasured desire was a poor foundation for a lasting union in *Troilus and Cressida*. In *Romeo and Juliet*, Friar Lawrence likens desire to the explosion of gunpowder: it is intense but brief. And while Romeo and Juliet are undoubtedly sincerely bonded, their union, because it is forbidden and because they take their own lives in their love's infancy, is never challenged by the course of time. In *Antony and Cleopatra*, however, the intensity of the attraction between the two lovers outlasts time's alterations and defies even their own – and the audience's – reservations.

The most startling thing about *Antony and Cleopatra*, especially in contrast to the other tragedies, is its lack of an obvious moral frame. *Macbeth* is replete with a sense of evil. *Othello* is built on the moral polarity between a diabolical Iago and a heavenly Desdemona, and the same moral polarity shapes the cast of characters in *King Lear*. *Antony and Cleopatra* is also built on a polarity, but it is not a moral one. It is built on the opposition between Rome and Egypt, which represent opposed ideas and values. This opposition appears in the multiplicity of short scenes that move incessantly between the two settings, just as Antony vacillates between the values they represent. Egypt is associated with women, love, sensuality, and feasting. Emotion overwhelms reason, relaxing the hard outlines of self into sensual pleasures. Cleopatra is a clearly individuated character, but she is also associated with the mysteries of the goddess Isis and the ever-flowing Nile. She has the aura of an archetype, a pre- or trans-historical serpentine power deeper than and threatening to the individual enterprise associated with crowns and coronets.

By contrast, Rome is associated with individual striving, great enterprise and achievement, calculating reason, power, and dynastic ambition. On the basis of this contrast, some critics judge the two protagonists harshly. The terse form of this view is that the play is about a middle-aged drunkard and a whore, older versions not of Romeo and Juliet but of Troilus and Cressida. K. Stanton points out that critics have been reluctant to afford Cleopatra "full status as tragic hero" because they have inherited a Roman tradition that termed Cleopatra the "prostitute queen" (69). For these critics, Stanton suggests, "'prostitute' easily trumps 'queen'" (69).[2] One example of a recent reading in this vein is Keith Linley's, which praises Octavia's "quiet virtues" and condemns Cleopatra as "one of a long line of demi-courtesan whores, shimmying through Renaissance history and drama, dangerous to morality, a threat to society, and fatal to those who love and serve them" (195).[3] Apart from the fact that even lushes and whores can fall in love, such language merely denigrates certain kinds of people of whom these writers disapprove. Linley's language, his description of sexually promiscuous women as frivolously "shimmying" through history, certainly reveals this kind of denigration. These views reveal an "intensity of revulsion" toward Cleopatra and an adoration of Octavia that the play itself doesn't support (298).[4] In my view, the minimal moral commentary in the play does not produce such a moralistic judgment, and the language and structure are designed to generate a dominantly sympathetic, even if critical, view of the protagonists. Moreover, if we consider that Shakespeare deliberately cultivates the combination of the sympathetic *and* critical view of the title characters, we can allow for Linda Charnes' important point that Shakespeare shows us an experience of love that, like all other emotions, is not separable from the "particular textual material it operates in" (272).[5] This enables us to view their bond as entirely human, powerful because, not in spite of, its earthy origins and trajectory.[6]

It is a mistake to assume that Shakespeare, having created the polarity between Rome and Egypt, expected his audience to assume that Rome was good and Egypt bad —or vice versa. Our own common sense tells us that each symbolic realm is fully adequate by itself, and that we should not assume that Shakespeare's audience would have thought any differently. Antony feels that he must choose between love and ambition or duty, but one might well think, along with Charnes, that these impulses are always entangled and impossible to separate. It could be that the play presupposes that such a polarity exists in the nature of things, but it could also be that Shakespeare shows his protagonist generating and then struggling with this polarity. Indeed, at times it is Antony who seems to embody the excessive sensuality associated with Egypt and Cleopatra the restraint and strategy associated with Rome.[7]

The play's imagery makes the moral value of each realm ambiguous. It contrasts the banks of the serpentine Nile that generate food and life to the monumental but stony Roman pillars. Also, the Roman power structure differs from the power structures that Shakespeare represented in the English history plays. Though those plays may call the ideology of power into question, they nonetheless represent government and authority as having dimensions that transcend personal struggles for rule and standards by which personal power struggles may be judged. In contrast, the Rome of *Antony and Cleopatra* is represented as nothing but the site of a power struggle among individuals, antagonists whose promises are strategic only, who betray each other whenever it suits them, and who show no concern or even awareness of a common good. The play gives us no sense that the lives and well-being of subjects are at stake, or that the contenders for power represent different ideologies of rule. The only appeal to some kind of principle occurs when Octavius justifies his betrayal of Lepidus by accusing him of mistreating the people, but that reference is so perfunctory and Octavius' motivations so obviously self-seeking that the issue is hardly joined. The Rome of *Antony and Cleopatra* is almost totally comprehensible in the Machiavellian terms that Shakespeare has taught us to associate with an Iago or an Edmund.

While we are at first encouraged to see Egyptian values represented by Cleopatra and Roman ones by Antony, such a division doesn't quite work out. For example, Octavius is calculating, single-minded in pursuit of power, and, like Bolingbroke and Hal before him, keeps his motives to himself; and thus is a pure embodiment of Roman values. In contrast, Antony is shown as an Everyman, caught between the conflicting pulls of love and pleasure on the one hand and martial heroism and honor on the other. Cleopatra more fully embodies the substance of Egypt than Antony does Rome. She is the goddess Isis, whose figure represents the enduring and mysterious life of Egypt, and she presides over the river Nile, which will outlast any pillar. But just as the Roman Antony longs for his opposite in Cleopatra, so too does Cleopatra love Antony best when he is most Roman. Both seek in the other the very qualities that they find inimical to their definitions of themselves. The play dramatizes the way in which this inner division leads to a relationship that is compelling because these internal conflicts seem to generate an ever-richer love. At the end of the day, the play may be about the destructiveness of romantic love, or about the difficulty of staying in love when one sees the world as polarized, as made of up of two irreconcilable ways of living and being; it may be about a drunk and a whore, or about a world well lost for love. But whatever its moral, it is about their relationship, a relationship that is depicted in subtle detail. We will consider the vicissitudes of that relationship, and then discuss the various perspectives from which the play invites us to consider what keeps Antony and Cleopatra together.

We first come upon Antony and Cleopatra in playful argument, which is interrupted by an announcement of news from Rome. Antony shows himself divided by the impatience with which he refuses to hear the messenger, which is what Cleopatra implies when she says that his refusal to hear the news is based on his fear of the "shrill-tongued Fulvia" and the "scarce-bearded Caesar." When Cleopatra claims that Antony's blush is "Caesar's homager" (1.1.34, 22, 33), Antony claims to be unconcerned with how he is seen in Roman eyes: "Let Rome in Tiber melt and the wide arch / Of the ranged empire fall! Here is my space" (1.1.35–6). Unimpressed by Antony's rhetoric, she asks, "[w]hy did he marry Fulvia, and not love her?" (1.1.43). Like a person putting a tongue into an aching tooth, she touches on the status of their relationship relative to Roman legitimacy, and on the fact that Antony sees her as well as himself from the Roman point of view.

Cleopatra's suspicions are confirmed when Antony sees the messenger, whom he orders to "[s]peak to me home" (1.2.111) about what is said of him in Rome. He wants to hear the worst in order to excite his shame – and with it his will – to break the "strong Egyptian fetters" that hold him in "dotage" (1.2.122–3). When he determines to "from this enchanting queen break off" (1.2.135), the dangerous magic of Egyptian fetters accompanies the ordinary, complimentary meaning of the adjective. He equates his love of Cleopatra with a dotage that is an emotional equivalent of those waters into which the Roman part of himself might really melt. When a second messenger comes with news that Fulvia has died, instead of even thinking that an impediment to marrying Cleopatra has been removed, he says:

> She's good, being gone;
> The hand could pluck her back that shoved her on.
> I must from this enchanting queen break off
> Ten thousand harms more than the ills I know
> My idleness doth hatch. (1.2.133–7)

He seems to include Fulvia's death with the "ten thousand harms" his idleness has hatched, as though without Fulvia as an impediment to a closer relation with Cleopatra, the latter's enchantments become more dangerous. At the news of Fulvia's death, Enobarbus crows about Antony's impending happiness with Cleopatra, but the triumvir ignores Enobarbus' ribaldry and reflects instead on the political situation in Rome, where "[m]uch is breeding, / Which, like the courser's hair, hath yet but life, / And not a serpent's poison" (1.2.199–201). The image connects the waters into which Rome should melt to waters that breed venom.

By the time Antony prepares to bid farewell to Cleopatra for Rome, we know that he sees her as a threat to his individuality. This fear justifies the bitterness with which Cleopatra asks, "[w]hat, says the married woman you may go?" (1.3.20). She resents not only the Roman powers that control him but also the wife whose legitimacy renders her own position shameful from the Roman, and therefore, in part, from Antony's, perspective. Hypocritically, he tries to soothe her with the news of Fulvia's death, as though he were happy about it.

His duplicity justifies her scorn when she tells him to "turn aside and weep for her; / Then bid adieu to me, and say the tears / Belong to Egypt" (1.3.76–8). Cleopatra's sensual appeal is, once again, balanced by her shrewdness.

Much is made of Cleopatra as the incarnation of feminine wiles,[8] both in criticism and within the play itself. Enobarbus mocks Antony, anticipating the many deaths that Cleopatra will die should Antony leave, and Cleopatra herself rejects Charmian's suggestion about the value of being obedient and tractable. Throughout these scenes, however, we see her expressing genuine anger and resentments, for which she has cause. When her ridicule of his departure, in which she accuses him of faking his sadness at leaving, makes him really angry, she finally puts her anger aside and speaks a moving farewell: "Upon your sword / Sit laurel victory, and smooth success / Be strewed before your feet!" (1.3.100–02). His immediate reaction is to return the tender sentiment, anger seemingly forgotten. He tells her "thou, residing here, goes yet with me, / And I, hence fleeting, here remain with thee" (1.3.104–5). In the wake of their mutual anger, a magnetic attraction reasserts itself. They may posture and preen in front of each other, but noticeably striking feelings always emerge, powerful enough to affect each other and poetic enough to charm audiences; then they reciprocally defer to each other's acknowledged power, Cleopatra to Antony's martial prowess and Antony to Cleopatra's ability to draw Antony to her.

Antony's behavior in Rome justifies Cleopatra's fears. He defends himself against all of Caesar's accusations except for the charge that he failed to provide the military assistance he had promised. He did not deny this aid, he says, but, "[n]eglected, rather; / And then when poisoned hours had bound me up / From mine own knowledge" (2.2.95–7). He blames his "neglect" of duties not on being consumed by passion but on consuming too much alcohol. He therefore trivializes his time with Cleopatra. His use of the term "bound me up" is telling, moreover. The reference to a bind or bond while in Egypt should refer to his emotional bond with Cleopatra. Instead, he admits only to being "bound up" by drunkenness. This implicit treachery sets the stage for more overt faithlessness. Agrippa suggests that the new accord between Antony and Caesar be cemented by a union between Antony and Caesar's sister. With provocative mockery, Caesar rebukes Agrippa, saying, "[i]f Cleopatra heard you, your reproof / Were well deserved of rashness" (2.2.129–30). "I am not married, Caesar" (2.2.131) is Antony's response, and marriage to Octavia is rapidly arranged and consummated. Antony, trying to save face while the Romans tease him, is forced into denying the significance of his attraction to and connection with Cleopatra.

From the point of view of Antony's Roman self, his Egyptian side functions like an unconscious. Being unknown to each other, each side is destructive of the other. Antony here is like a person whose superego, his conscious values, renders normal desires for love and pleasure inimical to his self-definition. Like his dramatic forebear Hamlet, Antony's martial values are in competition with his desires. Antony's not fully acknowledged wish for the pleasures of life, one might say his Falstaff side, makes him an object of ridicule by the Romans. If Antony could accept his natural desires and reconcile them to his martial ambition, he would not need to excuse himself to Caesar, and he would not have to marry Octavia. However, as Freud tells us, being denied, desires grow stronger. The ordinary and innocent desires and angers of childhood, once driven from consciousness, can form the monsters of our nightmares. The more Antony erects barricades to contain them, the more these repressed desires generate guilt and shame that poison the well-springs of his Roman enterprise and generate a deeper and messier connection to Cleopatra.

The consequences of Antony's psychological dilemma shape the rest of the play. Having repudiated his desire, Antony experiences its force as a kind of magic that comes from two directions. Immediately after his marriage and his seeming accord with Caesar, a soothsayer warns Antony against remaining in Rome. Antony's "daemon," says the soothsayer, is "[n]oble, courageous, high unmatchable, / Where Caesar's is not; but near him thy angel / Becomes afeared, as being o'erpowered. Therefore / Make space enough between you" (2.3.20–4). Antony believes that his trivial losses at games with Caesar confirm the Soothsayer's words. This scene resembles the later and more obviously supernatural one in which Antony's soldiers on the eve of battle hear strange music that, they say, signifies Hercules' desertion of Antony. Like the ghost in *Hamlet* or the witches in *Macbeth*, these more-than-natural occurrences exist in the protagonists' external world at the same time as they express their internal psychological states.

After hearing the soothsayer, Antony denies the internal origins, or counterparts, to the external phenomena when, having reflected on the soothsayer's words he concludes, "I will to Egypt; / And though I make this marriage for my peace, / I' th' East my pleasure lies" (2.3.39–41). Even in deciding to return to Cleopatra he betrays her, for he still trivializes the deeper currents of passion that constitute her magic. He ignores the fear roused by the soothsayer's words, and pretends that he freely chooses what we know he cannot help but do. This inner duplicity appears in his illogicality, for he knows, and the sequence of scenes is designed to leave us in no doubt, that his return to Egypt will destroy whatever peace his marriage has secured.

Meanwhile, the vicissitudes of Cleopatra's love have been as complicated as those of Antony, but they are more hidden in the complex imagery by which she expresses her feelings. On the one hand, we have already seen her anger at Antony's poorly disguised ambivalence about their bond; on the other hand, she knows that the exotic charm that makes him ashamed is also the source of her power over him. There is a poignancy and sincerity to this side of her. While Antony denies her significance to him in Rome, she thinks about him. As countless separated lovers have done and will do, she imagines what he is doing at that moment of separation, asking Charmian, "[w]here think'st thou he is now? Stands he, or sits he? / Or does he walk? Or is he on his horse?" (1.5.20–1). This expression of how powerfully she misses him then melts seamlessly into a imaginative reflection on her own power over him. She associates her magnetism with the trans-individual archetype of Egypt and the Nile when she then imagines him thinking of her:

> He's speaking now,
> Or murmuring, "Where's my serpent of old Nile?"
> For so he calls me. Now I feed myself
> With most delicious poison. Think on me,
> That am with Phoebus' amorous pinches black,
> And wrinkled deep in time? (1.5.25–30)

She first imagines that Antony loves her for that which derives from the mystical antiquity of her country, an image that in psychological terms would translate into an archetypical elevation of maternal power. This maternal aspect also appears in the images of the fertile banks of the Nile, and in the many images of food that merge with her erotic powers. Pompey hopes that Antony's lust for Cleopatra's beauty will "[t]ie up the libertine in a field of feasts, / Keep his brain fuming" (2.1.23–4); Enobarbus describes how the first sight of Cleopatra so enchanted Antony that he "goes to the feast, / And for his ordinary pays his heart / For what his eyes eat only" (2.2.234–6); later Enobarbus says that "[o]ther women cloy / The appetites they feed, but she makes hungry / Where most she satisfies" (2.2.246–8), and predicts that Antony "will to his Egyptian dish again" (2.6.128). Her fear of savoring her own power, that "delicious poison," to satisfy her longing for Antony echoes Antony's image of her serpentine power as poison to him. Since it is poison to him, it is to her as well, in that as the serpent of old Nile she merges her individual identity into that of her country. This fusion produces her self-description as tanned by the Egyptian sun and past her smooth-skinned youth, and extends her physical body into that of her country in a way that amplifies the exotic maternal power that works both for and against her.[9]

When Cleopatra learns of Antony's marriage, she rages at the messenger in what is commonly said to be a typically feminine way[10] but is actually another example of the swelling of her love for Antony, an overflow of the limits they set on their relationship. As in the previous tragedies, the comic surface both conceals and intensifies the darker and deeper forces that the images convey. She says, "[m]elt Egypt into Nile, and kindly creatures / Turn all to serpents!" (2.5.79–80). The word "kindly" can mean gentle, but it can also mean natural or of its kind. She is one of those natural creatures, and so the image suggests that she wishes herself turned into one of Nile's serpents. The same image earlier betokened her pleasure in her serpentine power over Antony. The reappearance of the image in Cleopatra's abuse of the messenger suggests that she will now use her serpentine power over Antony to avenge herself for being betrayed. The echo of Antony's image in hers suggests the deep ways in which they are connected, as well as the way that connection becomes dangerous. It is, of course, funny when she frightens the messenger and then interprets his description of Octavia: he describes her as shorter than Cleopatra and "low-voiced" (3.3.14), and she re-imagines Octavia as "[d]ull of tongue, and dwarf-ish" (3.3.16). By marrying Octavia, however, Antony has condemned Cleopatra to "the posture of a whore" (5.2.221), a position that does not do justice her multifaceted power.

Antony returns to Egypt and commits himself irrevocably to Cleopatra, but doing so does not heal his inner division. The succeeding scenes track the slow decline of his martial identity, while neither his followers nor Antony himself can understand the psychological forces that drain his Roman energies. He is self-destructive when he ignores his soldier's wisdom and insists, with Cleopatra, on fighting by sea and on allowing her to join the battle. This stubbornness is an external manifestation of all the internal currents suggested by the previous actions. In the event, Antony's forces do better than predicted, until Cleopatra turns tail and Antony follows her "like a doting mallard" (3.10.20). Neither he nor those around him can understand why in this single action he violates his "[e]xperience, manhood, honor" (3.10.23) and kisses away the kingdoms that made him Caesar's equal. But we have seen how powerfully Cleopatra's archetypal maternal powers work on him. In part, he behaves like a little boy who in fear of his father runs after his mother. Antony is not a coward, but he has little power to resist Cleopatra when he is in her sphere of influence and when confronting the "boy" who represents Roman paternal authority. In running from him, Antony brings his external reality into line with his inner state.

Rome does not melt in Tiber, but Antony's Roman self melts into the Nile, and as it does so he draws closer to Cleopatra and achieves a new kind of strength: the heroism of magnanimity and self-knowledge. In his brief moment of victory after the second battle, we see the generosity with which he praises his soldiers. When Enobarbus can no longer justify serving so irrational a person and defects to Caesar's camp, Antony blames himself and sends his friend's treasures after him. In the aftermath of the disastrous battle of Actium, Antony rages at Cleopatra, but from this anger flourishes Antony's explicit acknowledgment of Cleopatra's power and her reciprocal desire to placate Antony. "Egypt, thou knew'st too well," he says, "[m]y heart was to thy rudder tied by th' strings, / And thou shouldst tow me after" (3.11.55–7). At the same time and in response to this, Cleopatra assumes a submissive role, saying that her sails were "fearful" and asking for Antony's forgiveness and pleading for his "pardon" several times (3.11.54, 59, 67). Her dramatic meekness is yet another demonstration of just how adept she is at pulling on Antony's heartstrings. It also pays tribute to Antony, revealing how little she wishes him to continue to berate himself. It is implied that Cleopatra weeps, then, for Antony shifts from anger to tenderness as he says "[f]all not a tear, I say; one of them rates / All that is won and lost. Give me a kiss. [*They kiss*] / Even this repays me" (3.11.68–70). Although Antony has lost the battle and divided his treasures among his men, Cleopatra's kiss compensates for them.

As Antony's character grows stronger, however, Cleopatra's becomes more equivocal. We are given no reason to doubt Cleopatra's love when she encourages Antony to fight by sea, or to think that it was anything but panic that made her desert him in the battle, but Shakespeare also includes elements of Plutarch's account of Cleopatra's efforts to save herself at Antony's expense. It is as though Shakespeare deliberately shrouds her figure in ambiguity. A second betrayal is suggested when Caesar sends Thidias to promise Cleopatra safety if she will surrender Antony. She talks in a flirtatious way that suggests a readiness to come to terms. Even in the moment of submission before Rome, she calls attention to her magnetism. After she tells Thidias she will kneel at Caesar's feet to save Egypt, but after subjecting herself, she then offers Thidias her hand for him to kiss and says "[y]our Caesar's father oft, / When he hath mused of taking kingdoms in, / Bestowed his lips on that unworthy place, / As it rained kisses" (3.13.83–6). She thereby reasserts her dominance over men, reminding Thidias and the audience that this Caesar will be no different than Julius Caesar in paying homage to Cleopatra's power, in enjoying her charms as much as he enjoys enlarging his own empire.

Enobarbus and Antony think that she will certainly come to terms with Caesar, but we do not know her true intentions. Allan Bloom observes that it is "difficult to choose between the interpretation that she is madly in love with Antony and the alternative interpretation that she simply enjoys her empire over this emperor" (38),[11] Likewise, Charnes describes Cleopatra's character as "an unreadable, impenetrable surface" with a "sphinx-like opacity" (278). Janet Adelman makes the crucial observation that the play "frustrates our ability to judge" (14) the characters *deliberately*, calling this "uncertainty" an "essential feature of the play" (14).[12] The characters are not problems to solve. Instead, through their own struggles to know themselves and love each other fully, they show us the essential mysteriousness or muddiness of human emotion and action. Our uncertainty about Antony and Cleopatra is also important because it allows us to experience the pull of hesitation that accompanies a desire to be fully intimate with someone. As much as we want to give ourselves fully to Cleopatra, to know and trust her, we cannot. As Adelman beautifully says, "[i]f we are finally convinced of Cleopatra's love – and I think we are – we have had to develop a faith nearly as difficult as Antony's, a faith in what we cannot know" (24). The irony is that the more Cleopatra expresses and comments on her immense passion for Antony, the harder it is for us to believe that it is authentic. We are back to *Troilus and Cressida* and *King Lear* then, at the questions that dominated those dark plays: is there a pure form of love, how do we express it without seeming to cheapen it, and how do we ensure it survives time's alterations?[13]

Thus, we are made to experience the uncertainty that is central to Shakespeare's depiction of love in the play. Complete intimacy with Antony, no matter how much she desires it, is always just out of reach for Cleopatra, given that she has cultivated a selfhood based on her ability to subject others to her. Like Antony, Cleopatra is a person divided; he is torn between love and self-esteem, whereas she seeks political survival, even a subtle form of dominance, as well as the fulfillment of her love with Antony. In the lovers' swing between selfishness and selflessness, Shakespeare is able to reveal "the true nature of love" (37),[14] true because it is real rather than pure. Selfishness does not cancel out love, but it certainly muddies it.

Furious at her for seeming to be ready to negotiate with Caesar, Antony now sees her as a Cressida or Helen. The enticing food that enchanted him turns to garbage when he tells her that he found her "as a morsel cold upon / Dead Caesar's trencher" and as a "fragment / Of Gnaeus Pompey's" (3.13.118–20). His anger, and the scene, turns when he asks her how she could "flatter Caesar" (3.13.159) by flirting with his servant and Cleopatra asks simply and enigmatically, "[n]ot know me yet?" (3.13.160). The question could indeed be directed to the audience: her motivations are not clear to Antony or us, but in wondering about them, Antony's rage seems suddenly to melt when he asks, "[c]oldhearted toward me?" (3.13.161). Her answering speech deserves close attention:

>   Ah, dear, if I be so,
> From my cold heart let heaven engender hail,
> And poison it in the source, and the first stone
> Drop in my neck; as it determines, so
> Dissolve my life! The next Caesarian smite,
> Till by degrees the memory of my womb,
> Together with my brave Egyptians all,
> By the discandying of this pelleted storm
> Lie graveless till the flies and gnats of Nile
> Have buried them for prey! (3.13.161–9)

The images of decay, poison, liquefaction, and the river Nile come together, but now in a way that shows us a Cleopatra who struggles to ward off Antony's image of her. Just as Antony saw himself through Roman eyes, so now Cleopatra imagines herself in Antony's eyes as the source of destruction, the destruction even of her own children. She imagines herself as the remnants of the Egyptian earth-mother dissolving into the Nile from which she imagistically emerges. In this image, she becomes in her own eyes a version of what Antony sees when he says that the wise gods should, in order to prevent him from seeing the depth of her perfidy, "[i]n our own filth drop our clear judgments" (3.13.115). Just as Antony asks for more than he wants when he says, "[l]et Rome in Tiber melt," so Cleopatra also when she cries, "[m]elt Egypt into Nile." These interpenetrating images intensify their love for each other and show the inner conflicts that make it embattled but lastingly entangled

Antony maintains his identity even when his followers "do discandy, melt their sweets / On blossoming Caesar; and this pine is barked / That overtopped them all" (4.12.22–24). He is a towering, though stripped figure, while Caesar becomes ephemeral and insignificant vegetation. But once he thinks that Cleopatra has become fatally treacherous, he loses both his rage and identity. His sense of self becomes as shifting clouds – like "black vesper's pageants" (4.14.7). All the world becomes a stage on which the gathering mists of evening represent tragic solemnity. Like the shifting scenes of a stage, the clouds take first one form, then another, and that which seemed solidly real shows itself to have no substance. Finally, he feels his selfhood dissolve fully, "as water is in water" (4.14.11).[15] This loss of self is reflected in the shades of comedy that subvert Antony's last effort at a tragic stance. Wanting to run upon his sword as "to a lover's bed," like a "bridegroom in [his] death" (4.14.101, 100), he bungles his effort at a Roman suicide. He suffers the indignity of being hoisted up to Cleopatra's tower, and turns out to be wrong in his advice about whom to trust of Caesar's followers. His fears that Cleopatra would erode his manhood have themselves done that; but as is her way, she restores to him the stature he had lost and imbues him with power.[16] She renews his dignity – "O sun, / Burn the great sphere thou movs't in; darkling stand / The varying shore o' th' world" (4.15.11–12). The echoes of his words in hers elevate their shared love, the music they make together, despite their ambivalence, mutual betrayals, and inadequacies. However adulterated with self-concern, her love surrounds his decline with grandeur. She weaves a eulogy to his greatness out of the very the words and images that he had used first in empty rhetoric and then in bitter shame, and at the same time she upstages him. Cleopatra says to her women that "[t]he crown o' th' earth doth melt. My lord! / O, withered is the garland of the war; / The soldier's pole is fall'n" (4.15.65–7), but Antony repeats "I am dying, Egypt, dying" (4.15.19, 42) as he struggles to get a proper word in edge-wise; in death they merge, to be recreated from her imagination.

Antony's merger with Cleopatra and his rebirth from her imagination could not be more graphically portrayed than in the fact that the entire last act belongs to her. His dramatic stature finally rests with her as she, in an act of imagination, rescues his image from the silt of the Nile. In imagination she recreates a perfect and undivided Antony:

> His legs bestrid the ocean; his reared arm
> Crested the world; his voice was propertied
> As all the tunèd spheres, and that to friends;
> ....
> His delights
> Were dolphin like; they showed his back above
> The element they lived in. (5.2.81–3, 87–9)

Like Theseus in *A Midsummer Night's Dream,* Cleopatra asserts that her imaginative recreation has a reality beyond that of earthy bodies. When Dolabella disbelieves that there ever was such a person, she retorts that "t' imagine / An Antony were nature's piece 'gainst fancy, / Condemning shadows quite" (5.2.97–9). Compared to the substance of her vision, ordinary reality is as shadowy as Antony's shifting clouds.

Despite some similarities, Antony's and Cleopatra's suicides differ significantly from those of Romeo and Juliet. The action is similar in that the man kills himself thinking the woman dead, and the woman kills herself when the man is really dead. However, unlike their younger counterparts, they have mixed motives. Antony kills himself not only because he thinks her dead, but also because he has lost to Caesar, and Cleopatra doesn't determine finally to kill herself until she has played her last card and knows that she can survive only at the price of being led in Caesar's triumph, where she will see "[s]ome squeaking Cleopatra boy [her] greatness / I' th' posture of a whore" (5.2.220–1).[17] She will become an actor in someone else's drama, and be forced to see herself as Antony saw her when he called her a "[t]riple-turned whore" (4.12.13). She dies for love of Antony and for her own royal dignity, and once the game is up she confronts death grandly, repudiating "earth and water," which together create Nilus' slime. Just as Yorick's skull emerges from the death imagery that pervades *Hamlet,* so the asp seems to emerge from the images of muddy decay. In her final words, she redeems herself in her own eyes by claiming the legitimacy and worth that Antony's betrayal had denied her. She says, "[h]usband, I come! / Now to that name my courage prove my title!" (5.2.287–8).

The central drama of the play consists of a convincing depiction of a relationship between two lovers whose imperfections only draw them closer to each other in a steadfast union. Their story is, however, sandwiched between two other layers. One layer is subterranean, composed of the images that bind the various parts of the play together. We have already seen the ways in which images are shared between the two lovers, but the same images also extend beyond them. The image of melting by which both Antony and Cleopatra describe their experience and others that cluster around it precede Antony to

Rome. There, Caesar, generalizing upon human indecisiveness, reflects that the "common body" that only wants something after it cannot have it is like "a vagabond flag upon the stream, / Goes to and back, lackeying the varying tide, / To rot itself with motion" (1.4.44–7). This image appears in Caesar's description of the popular reaction to Pompey, and it generalizes those used by and about Antony, and the same images will later fuse with others that characterize him. Beneath the apparent opposition, this image links the Roman to the Egyptian world, and this submerged link between the two worlds and the characters who inhabit them grows stronger when Pompey thinks about the ways in which Cleopatra can poison Antony's enterprise. He invokes Cleopatra's charms to "[l]et witchcraft joined with beauty, lust with both" so that "sleep and feeding may prorogue his honor / Even till a Lethe'd dullness" (2.1.22, 26–7). Pompey's image of feeding picks up the various ways in which Cleopatra is referred to as a kind of food, and his image of Lethean forgetfulness transmutes those of the deliciously poisoned waters with which both Antony and Cleopatra have described their love.

On the one hand, these interweaving images form a subterranean drama out of which the human figures emerge and into which they sink. On the other hand, a tide of critique rolls over them. No other Shakespearean play is so full of commentary by secondary characters as is this one, and one would think that this would make clear to us how we are to evaluate the central action, but in fact it doesn't. Philo and Demetrius open the play with their discussion of Antony, but these comments have a double valence. Clearly Philo disapproves of Antony's involvement with Cleopatra, but the very images he uses to condemn Antony also exalt him. When he complains that "this dotage of our general's / O'erflows the measure" (1.1.1–2), the implied image of an overflowing river that will later be linked to the Nile as the source of fertility, attributes to Antony a natural force that competes with the denigration of the word "doting" Antony's "goodly eyes" that "[h]ave glowed like plated Mars, now bend, now turn / The office and devotion of their view / Upon a tawny front" (1.1.2, 4–6). Cleopatra is as much elevated by Antony's more than human-sized gaze as Antony's heroic grandeur is diminished by her. Philo's description of Antony as "the triple pillar of the world transformed / Into a strumpet's fool" (1.1.12–13) endows Cleopatra with enormous power, and his "[b]ehold and see" (1.1.13) enhances the theatricality of their entrance. Later, Pompey's images of Antony as a "libertine in a field of feasts" and of the "ne'er-lust-wearied Antony" in the "lap of Egypt's widow" (2.1.23, 38, 37), despite the intended denigration, imply a powerful sensuality and an inexhaustible response to a magnetic force.

The most influential commentator is Enobarbus. Unlike the others, his characterization as an honest adviser lends his words authority. Though he mocks Cleopatra, he doesn't criticize Antony for being with her; rather, he more than anyone gives the impression that their love is inevitable, and he defends

Cleopatra after Antony follows her out of battle. He also provides the most splendid account of when Antony first saw Cleopatra, as she floated down the river Cydnus on her barge:

> The poop was beaten gold;
> Purple the sails, and so perfumèd that
> The winds were love sick with them. The oars were silver,
> Which to the tune of flutes kept stroke, and made
> The water which they beat to follow faster,
> As amorous of their strokes. (2.2.202–07)

The substance of this description is taken from the play's source in Plutarch, but Enobarbus adds a magical aura by extending the range of Cleopatra's enchantments to the winds and waters themselves.[18]

Enobarbus' personal drama constitutes a comment on Antony's decline. As Antony makes mistakes, plays on his soldier's emotions, and acts less like a Roman, Enobarbus struggles between his loyalty to and love of Antony on the one hand, and, on the other, his Roman martial values and his Roman common sense that teaches him to take his self-interest into account. Like a less than perfect Kent figure, he defects; but the death he suffers in the wake of that defection and Antony's unexpected generosity represents a persuasive tribute to his bereft leader.[19]

These various commentators provide an on-stage audience that reflects both Antony's and Cleopatra's self-dramatization. One thing at least that Antony and Cleopatra have in common is that they like to see themselves seen, and they like the way they appear together. We have witnessed how Philo frames their first entrance. In this scene, too, Antony tries to silence Cleopatra's carping by saying:

> The nobleness of life
> Is to do thus; when such a mutual pair
> And such a twain can do 't, in which I bind,
> On pain of punishment, the world to weet
> We stand up peerless" (1.1.38–42).

Later, in the flush of triumph at his victory, Antony wants to lead Cleopatra by the hand on a "jolly march" through Alexandria, and orders that:

> Trumpeters,
> With brazen din blast you the city's ear;
> Make mingle with our rattling taborins,
> That heaven and earth may strike their sounds together,
> Applauding our approach. (4.8.35–9)

When Antony thinks that Cleopatra is dead, he imagines himself with her in an underworld where they will hand in hand "with our sprightly port make the ghosts gaze. / Dido and her Aeneas shall want troops, / And all the haunt be ours" (4.14.52–4).

Cleopatra's greatest fear is that she will be staged to a mocking audience. She will not come down from the monument for fear of being made part of "th' imperious show / Of the full-fortuned Caesar" (4.15.24–5). In resolving to commit suicide "after the high Roman fashion / And make death proud to take us" (4.15.92–3), she stage-manages her own death, rather than be subject to the "quick comedians" (5.2.216) and "[m]echanic slaves" who will "[u]plift us to the view" (5.2.209, 211) and turn her tragedy into a farce. Unhae Park Langis describes Cleopatra as having an "uncanny ability" of "arcing linear progress into circular eternity: matter and air, mirth and gravity, life and death, comedy and tragedy" (112).[20] We experience the culmination of this ability in her suicide, when, as Langis contends, she "consummately blends Egyptian beauty, carnality, and oneness with nature with Roman firmness of purpose in a heavenward mingle" (118). By this act of will, she overcomes this threat to her dignity by fully staging herself in her robe and her crown. She asserts the meaningfulness of her death as the asp sucks her blood by imagining her audience: "Methinks I hear / Antony call; I see him rouse himself / To praise my noble act" (5.2.283–85). Just as Cleopatra did at the beginning of the play, she here generates her expressive power by imagining Antony admiring it, shaping it through his eyes. At the very last moment, though now in Cleopatra's mind alone, the lovers assert their power by bridging the gap that has always been between them.

Cleopatra's nobility and heroic power depends upon her capacity to overcome the many comic threats to tragic dignity: the exchange between the soothsayer, Charmian, and the others; the comedy of Cleopatra's rage at the messenger; the pervasive jokes about women's wiles; and, most notably, the Clown scene. Like the gravedigger scene in *Hamlet* and the porter scene in *Macbeth,* this episode provides a comic version of the tragic themes in which it is embedded. It gives a grotesque turn to the comic play on women's wiles that preceded it, and to Cleopatra's magnificent death that will follow. The clown tries to warn Cleopatra against the poisonous worm with an anecdote:

> a very honest woman, but something given to lie, as a woman should not do but in the way of honesty – how she died of the biting of it, what pain she felt. Truly, she makes a very good report o' the worm. But he that will believe all that they say shall never be saved by half that they do. But this is most falliable, the worm's an odd worm. (5.2.251–8)

In this passage, the clown unites the humor about feminine wiles with the imagery that associated Cleopatra with food, both tantalizing and rotting, with

Cleopatra's fear of her delight in Antony's image of her as the serpent of the Nile, and with the death toward which she moves. When Cleopatra asks "[w]ill it eat me?" (5.2.271) and he responds that the devil will not eat a woman because she is a dish for the gods, he collects into a Hamlet-like witticism Antony's ambivalence toward Cleopatra that has shaped the entire play. The Clown repeatedly warns that the worm is deadly, even while he wishes Cleopatra the "joy o' the worm" (5.2.279). His grim humor both reminds us of the reality of death, and prepares for the triumphant joy that Cleopatra will indeed get from the worm, which she will imagine as a baby at her breast, "[t]hat sucks the nurse asleep" (5.2.310). In her imagination she begets the "lawful race" (3.13.108) that Antony, when he thought Cleopatra was making up to Thidias, regretted not having bred with Octavia. That double valence is much like that in *Hamlet* when the gravediggers insist on the reality of dead bodies while Hamlet reconciles himself to destiny.[21] The comedy here could threaten the protagonist's tragic stature, but Cleopatra opposes this reductive vision. Dismissing the clown and calling for her robe and crown, she asserts her "[i]mmortal longings" (5.2.281) that lift the air and fire of spirit above the earth and water of the flesh. Garret A. Sullivan Jr. identifies the eroticism of Cleopatra's death, a strain that, like the scene's comic inflection, indicates once again that "multiplicity" is the "fundamental condition of identity" (105).[22] Shakespeare has kept us aware of the fragility of Cleopatra's tragic assertion of "immortal longings" through the comic and erotic undertones of the lovers' suicides – these nuances remind us such longings are often undercut by the fluidity of human emotion and experience. In the moments leading to her death, Cleopatra vows she is "marble-constant" from "head to foot" (5.2.239–40). After she dies, however, in a tender moment, Charmian observes Cleopatra's crown is "awry" and vows to "mend it" (5.2.318–19). The crooked crown highlights Cleopatra's final vulnerability; she no longer has the power to stage herself and, in any case, the props that have contributed to her magnetic power are just that – props. However, Charmian's desire to straighten the crown serves as a tribute to Cleopatra, carrying on the staging that Cleopatra now cannot, protecting her royal appearance. Charmian's concern also testifies to the ongoing affection she has for the dead queen – to straighten or order a loved one's clothes and belongings after death is an extremely intimate, emotional act. The tendrils of the Falstaffian corporeality, the crooked crown on a powerless, mortal body, in this case enhance rather than destroy our sense that she has fulfilled her "immortal longings."

People often say that Antony and Cleopatra's love is not real, but what they usually mean is that it is not ideal. They are, like most people, self-seeking, ambivalent, conflicted. Indeed, their self-dramatizing is often grandiose and even maudlin, overflowing the limits of good sense and proper conduct. Yet for all that they are represented as relating to each other in imperfect and conflicted ways, they are moved by passions that go beyond their consciousness and that continually draw them toward each other. Allan Bloom writes that the love between Antony and Cleopatra is "the perfect example of love for its own sake [...] because it can never be good for Antony as anything other than itself [...] It is literally lawless but undeniably admirable" (36).[23] The tragedy is generous to the imperfect pair despite coming after works of moral extremity like *Macbeth* and *King Lear*. Shakespeare's Egyptian play makes a claim for a bond that is durable because it can never fully extricate itself from the "slime and ooze" of real, and complicated, emotions and investments.

Notes

1 *Suffocating Mothers.*
2 *Shakespeare's Whores: Erotics, Politics, and Poetics.* Houndmills, Basingstoke: Palgrave Macmillan, 2014. For more on critics' views of Antony and Cleopatra, see Sara Munson Deats, "Shakespeare's Anamorphic Drama: A Survey of *Antony and Cleopatra* in Criticism, on Stage, and on Screen." In Antony and Cleopatra: *New Critical Essays* Ed. Sara Munson Deats. New York: Routledge, 2005.
3 *'Antony and Cleopatra' in Context: The Politics of Passion.* London: Anthem, 2015.
4 Linda Fitz (Woodbridge). "Egyptian Queens and Male Reviewers: Sexist Attitudes in *Antony and Cleopatra* Criticism." *Shakespeare Quarterly* 28.3 (1977): 297–316.
5 "What's Love Got to Do with It? Reading the Liberal Humanist Romance in *Antony and Cleopatra*." In *Shakespearean Tragedy and Gender*. Eds. Shirley Nelson Garner and Madelon Sprengnether. Bloomington: Indiana University Press, 1996. 268–286. Maurice Charney writes that Cleopatra has "either been foolishly idealized as a transcendent being or excoriated as a temptress violating all the postulates of Christian doctrine" (*Shakespeare on Love and Lust*. New York: Columbia University Press, 2000. 89). He praises Charnes's correction of these views but believes the lovers are transcendent, writes that they "seem, in their deaths, to be superior to the base, materialistic world they leave behind" (88).
6 In "Shakespeare's Boy Cleopatra, the Decorum of Nature, and the Golden World of Poetry," Phyllis Rackin suggests that those who view Cleopatra negatively will view her dramatic expressions of love as "false" and will condemn them as "merely 'theatrical'." Conversely, she points out that those who are sympathetic to Cleopatra will likely "identify her with her creator as fellow artist" (204). Rackin ultimately advises that we must embrace both responses to Cleopatra if we are going to really "get" the play *PMLA* 87.2 (1972): 201–212. 204.
7 For more on the ways in which Antony and Cleopatra embody or struggle with opposed conceptions of Rome and Egypt, see Harald William Fawkner, *Shakespeare's Hyperontology:* Antony and Cleopatra. Rutherford: Fairleigh Dickinson University Press, 1990. See also Gilberto Sacerdoti, "Antony and Cleopatra and the Overflowing of the Roman Measure." In *Identity, Otherness*

and Empire in Shakespeare's Rome. Ed. Maria Del Sapio Garbero. Farnham, Surrey: Ashgate, 2009; Virginia Mason Vaughan, *Antony and Cleopatra: Language and Writing.* London: Bloomsbury, 2016 (particularly her discussion of the effect of deconstructionist theory on interpretations of Rome and Egypt in the play, p. 117).

8 See Fitz, "Sexist Attitudes," 298–299.

9 For a discussion of Cleopatra's complexion and its relationship to discourses of race in and on the stage, see Ania Loomba, *Shakespeare, Race, and Colonialism.* Oxford: Oxford University Press, 2002. See also, Celia R. Daileader, "The Cleopatra Complex: White Actresses on the Interracial 'Classic' Stage. In *Colorblind Shakespeare: New Perspectives on Race and Performance.* Ed. Ayanna Thompson. New York: Routledge, 2006. 205–220; and Jane Petegree, *Foreign and Native on the English Stage 1588–1611: Metaphor and National Identity.* Houndmills, Basingstoke: Palgrave Macmillan, 2011.

10 Barbara Hodgdon describes reviewers' denigration of a performance of Cleopatra in these stereotypical terms. A reviewer of one performance says that the actress was not "regal" but was just "one particular woman running up and down the scale of feminine vagary" and another reviewer writes that she simply conveyed the "low feminine arts" like "jealous rage" (93, qtd. in *The Shakespeare Trade: Performance and Appropriations.* Philadelphia: University of Pennsylvania Press, 1998). See also "Chapter 3: Maternal Subtexts" in Pilar Hidalgo, *Paradigms Found: Feminist, Gay, and New Historicist Readings of Shakespeare.* Amsterdam: Rodopi, 2001.

11 *Shakespeare on Love and Friendship.*

12 *The Common Liar: An Essay on* Antony and Cleopatra. New Haven: Yale University Press, 1973.

13 Linda Fitz (Woodbridge) comments on the similarities between *Antony and Cleopatra* and *King Lear*, especially each play's interest in whether or not we can know how much we are loved ("Sexist Attitudes," 303).

14 Bloom, *Shakespeare on Love and Friendship.*

15 Richard P. Wheeler writes that "[t]he longing for union is the most powerful need driving Antony: it at once allows him to achieve a richer, more inclusive humanity, and estranges him from the political resources established by Caesar's deflection of all human impulse into a quest for power." "'Since first we were disservered': Trust and Autonomy in Shakespearean Tragedy and Romance" in *Representing Shakespeare: New Psychoanalytic Essays,* ed. Murray Schwartz and Coppélia Kahn (Baltimore, MD: 1980. 158).

16 See Janet Adelman's *Suffocating Mothers* for a description of how Cleopatra becomes "the site of her – and his – imaginative power to restore the heroic male whose loss has haunted Shakespeare's plays at least since *Hamlet*" (191).

17 Cleopatra's distaste for being impersonated by a boy is fascinating because at the time this play was performed, a boy would have played the role. For this

reason, as Carol Cook says, these lines "ring uncannily" ("The Fatal Cleopatra" in *Shakespearean Tragedy and Gender*, 245).

18 John H. Astington discusses a possible source for this description in "Venus on the Thames." *Shakespeare Studies* 39 (2011): 117–132. See also J. Leeds Barroll, "Enobarbus' Description of Cleopatra." *Texas Studies in English* 37 (1958): 61–78.

19 Janet Adelman says that not even Enobarbus' skepticism is a "secure position" in the play because "when he follows his reason, he dies of a broken heart" (*The Common Liar*. New Haven: Yale University Press, 1973. 24). For more on Enorbarbus, see Isamu Tanifuji, "Enobarbus' Minor Tragedy in Antony and Cleopatra." *Essays and Studies in English Language and Literature* 57 (1970): 51–72; Allyson P. Newton, "'At the Very Heart of Loss': Shakespeare's Enobarbus and the Rhetoric of Remembering." *Renaissance Papers* (1995): 81–91; Patricia Parker, "Barbers and Barbary: Early Modern Cultural Semantics." *Renaissance Drama* 33 (2004): 201–244; See also David Read, "Disappearing Act: The Role of Enobarbus in "Antony and Cleopatra" *Studies in Philology* 110.3 (2013): 562–583; In his chapter on *Antony and Cleopatra*, Kent Cartwright says Enobarbus represents the "clown's satiric viewpoint" (243): *Shakespearean Tragedy and Its Double: The Rhythms of Audience Response*. University Park, Pennsylvania: Penn State University Press, 1991.

20 *Passion, Prudence and Virtue.*

21 Adelman quite rightly points out that the play is "a tragic experience embedded in a comic structure" and calls this blending "as treacherous and painful as life itself" (*The Common Liar*, 52).

22 *Memory and Forgetting in English Renaissance Drama: Shakespeare, Marlowe, Webster.* Cambridge: Cambridge University Press, 2005.

23 *Shakespeare on Love and Friendship.*

12

The Tempest

In the four romances Shakespeare wrote near the end of his career, he recapitulates many of the themes and dramatic situations that he explored in both the earlier comedies and the tragedies. These plays, termed Shakespeare's "romances," "tragicomedies" or, simply, "late plays" (*Pericles, Cymbeline, The Winter's Tale*, and *The Tempest*), recast what should be by now familiar material in a new form, similar to that of myth and fairy tale. These plays give greater priority to the symbolism of action rather than to action as mimetic of possible human situations. They focus particularly on the relationship of reality to imagination, the body to the mind, the world to the stage, and the natural to the supernatural. It is through the prism of these questions that Shakespeare gives some of his final turns to the problems of love and authority: these plays participate in the fantasy that broken bonds can be repaired and burdensome bonds can be shaken off even as they subject that illusion to critique.

I think that the tragedies were motivated in part by Shakespeare's belief that if he probed sufficiently deeply, he might resolve the conflicts inherent in the exercise of and submission to power, both in the family and the state, and answer as well the questions having to do with giving and receiving love and preserving a loving connection. However, the more deeply he probed, the more intransigent these problems seemed; the more vividly he portrayed the sources of ambition, aspiration, greed, hatred, and envy, the more inherent they seemed in human nature. It might have been his intention to portray a just universe in which the evil were punished, if not by providence, then by the operation of natural law on their consciences, but, if not his eye for reality, then the sheer force of tragedy prevented him from generating images of a world both just and probable.

Tragedy by definition cannot portray a just world. The impact of tragedy always depends upon a world in which simple judgments are not commensurate with the complexities of life. Furthermore, as we have seen, the moral view detracts from tragic force. For example, *King Lear* shows us the way in which Lear brings his suffering upon himself, but if we end up thinking he got what he deserved, we cancel the tragic impact. The tragic perspective involves

Thinking About Shakespeare, First Edition. Kay Stockholder, revised and updated by Amy Scott.
© 2018 John Wiley & Sons Ltd. Published 2018 by John Wiley & Sons Ltd.

tension between the vision of people in one way or another bringing their sufferings upon themselves, and the vision of a punishment that goes well beyond their deserts. As Edgar says, Gloucester's sexual peccadilloes brought about his blindness, but that is a harsher punishment than we would expect a just universe to mete out; and even if one thinks that Hamlet ought not to have delayed, in most societies delay is not a capital offense. It follows, then, that tragedy in its very nature complicates rather than simplifies our vision of human problems, and writing tragedies, therefore, could not lead Shakespeare to the comforts of sincere love and just rule I have supposed him to be seeking.

In writing the romances, Shakespeare generated dramatic images of such comforts, but he did so at the cost of plausible plots and of the multidimensional characters that make his tragedies so rich. The action in the romances is similar to that of fairy tale or myth in that almost all of the action is largely symbolic. It is designed to show the way in which the universe works more than it is to show the way people act and react. Events and subsidiary characters in these plays primarily represent powers beyond themselves, so that the emphasis is thrown onto the allegorical rather than the literal level, though the plays do contain some powerful representations of human dilemmas and complex character studies. Nevertheless, one's attention tends to be directed to the meaning of events beyond the literal, and relatively less interest falls on complexity of character or verisimilitude. Accordingly, these plays are full of providential, magical, or quasi-magical powers. Like the early comedies, they achieve happy endings, but they are happy in a different way.

Critical attention has been directed to the theme of redemption, restoration, or regeneration that the magical elements of the plays seem to make possible.[1] Robert W. Uphaus suggests that the romances offer "an exit from the seemingly irreversible movement of the tragic experience" by giving characters and audiences a "second chance or fresh start" (5). R.S. White describes the "spell of suspended time," in the romances, in which "decay and death do not immediately exist" (19).[2] The romances translate time and mortality, the agents of an ultimate "end" to human life that are so forbidding and prominent in the tragedies, into the site of regeneration and resolution of conflict.[3] The multiple marriages that conclude the early comedies bring what one might call a naturalistic or creaturely pleasure. That is, emphasis falls on the young marrying and life going on. The romances, which do not use humor to cut into the sense of spreading significance, are more like Dante's *Divine Comedy*, in which the happiness of the ending signifies a transcendent spiritual achievement or cosmic harmony.[4]

Some scholars, however, have rightly charted how certain elements and characters simply cannot be enfolded into theme of regeneration and resolution.[5] Critical inquiry from this perspective often reconsiders the treatment of female characters in the romances – radiantly virtuous daughters (like Marina in *Pericles*, Perdita in *The Winter's Tale*, Imogen in *Cymbeline*, and Miranda in *The Tempest*) and troubled or troubling mothers – the falsely accused and pregnant Hermione in *The Winter's Tale* and Caliban's witch-mother Sycorax in *The Tempest*. Daughters and mothers in these plays can be seen as caught up in what Coppélia Kahn calls "an intense ambivalence toward the family"; this ambivalence, she says, produces "anxiety about – and even disgust at – desire, female sexuality and procreation" (220).[6] Similarly, in writing about *The Tempest*, Janet Adelman argues that Caliban is Shakespeare's "final register" of his "ambivalence toward what it means – from *Hamlet* on – to be a mother's son" (238).[7] The troubled relationships in the tragedies, therefore, might not necessarily be tidied up in the romances if we consider the providential or supernatural forces that magically right past wrongs as having layered and, as both Adelman and Kahn observe, ambiguous effects. Some attention to the plays' ambiguity is vital in ensuring that their seriousness is attended to rather than channeled into the expectations we might have of a so-called "romance genre" (a genre which, in its own various incarnations across time and place, is itself diffuse and heterogeneous).

Whether the plays' messages are read as harmonious or not, whether procreation is redemptive or troubling, the plays' magical elements can evoke a complex response: the audience can embrace the magical aura while still uncertain of whether it is "real" or not. T.G. Bishop describes the experience of simultaneous detachment from and engagement to a work of art as a feeling of "wonder"; it "relies on emotional engagement" to be successful but can also challenge the audience's abandonment to the world of the fiction (11).[8] At moments of magical, supernatural intervention in the play's action, moments Rapheal Lyne calls "tangible and pressing" (6),[9] the audience is likely to be both swept up by and skeptical of what they are seeing – and Shakespeare seems to want his audiences to have this response.[10] Anthony B. Dawson describes this effect as "[d]elight," which is "generated by the doubleness of knowing and seeing, of meta-theatre and theatre, suspension and belief" (107).[11] Generally, supernatural moments in the tragedies comment on or reinforce the action that is already happening, reaffirming aspects already present in the playworld, and manifesting or predicting characters' fears and hopes. In the romances, such moments do not simply comment on the action – they constitute the action itself, and the destabilizing effect they have seems to be one of Shakespeare's aims, part of the message of the overall play. As Lyne describes it, the late plays craft a "constructive mood, open to heightened experience, holding faith in greater things" while still allowing for "sharp doubts" (10).[12]

Though the ambience of these plays, their cultivation of a sense of wonder, differs radically from the others I have discussed, their content does not. The many parallels in characters, situations, and sequences of action make possible a kind of two-way reading of the relations of the plays to each other. The greater ideological clarity of the later plays sheds light on the probable ideological significance of the more complex but similar characters and episodes in the tragedies, while the more fully portrayed passions of the earlier plays illuminate the emotional and psychological implications of the more patterned and abstract later action. *The Tempest* in particular makes a new integration of the motifs and problems upon which I have focused our attention. Within the tightly controlled symbolic and dramatic structure of this play, Shakespeare envisions solutions to the complex problems that he had probed so deeply. We can see him explore the idea of forgiveness, redemption, and regeneration. However, in the process of trying to resolve old problems through such comforting possibilities, *The Tempest* introduces new challenges.[13] With repeated references to and images of confinement – of being held within small spaces (caves, trees), of bodies aging, of bodies plagued by uncomfortable sensations, of bodies being held in servitude – the play complicates the forces of liberation, airiness, and expansiveness that are part of the theme of redemption and regeneration. Prospero's magic, and the play's ability to weave a spell on audiences, makes it possible to believe that liberation can be achieved, but in Prospero's sometimes ambivalent relationship to his own power and those under his sway, it also makes us question what we want to believe.

* * *

In sharp contrast to all his intervening plays, *The Tempest* returns to a tightly controlled dramatic structure that Shakespeare had used only in his first play, *The Comedy of Errors*. The events take place in a single location; its stage time does not exceed by much the chronology of depicted events, and all of its action is tightly interwoven. In part this coherence derives from Shakespeare's having separated the play's present from its past in a sharper way than he had done before, so that the story of the events that led to the present on the island becomes a kind of flashback. This dramatizes the role of prolonged time in human affairs, as had been done in the earlier romances, without sacrificing the precision and force of narrowly focused action.

Crucial to his crafting of this play is Prospero, upon whom Shakespeare conferred more creative power than he did on any other character. Prospero is a magus, a man learned in occult lore, who joins earlier dramatic examples of the figure, like Greene's practitioner of white magic, Friar Bacon in *Friar Bacon and Friar Bungay* (c. 1589), who eventually renounces his powers; the dark anti-hero of Marlowe's *Dr. Faustus* (first played in 1594), who makes a deal with the devil; and the scam artist Subtle in Jonson's satiric take on the magical arts in *The Alchemist* (1610). Prospero is not associated with the dark arts, but the powers with which Shakespeare endowed Prospero do make him a problematic figure. W.H. Auden once said that "[o]ne must admire Prospero because of his talents and his strength; one cannot possibly like him," a feeling Auden attributes to his "coldness" (57).[14] Similarly, G. Wilson Knight says that "as a person, he is, no doubt, less warm, less richly human" than the tragic heroes in Shakespeare's canon who were faced with circumstances similar to his (197).[15] That both men view Prospero as cold, "less warm" than tragic characters and view this coldness as a obstacle to our connection with him and his humanity indicates a certain challenge the character poses to interpreters.

There are therefore a variety of critical attitudes toward Prospero and his powers, and the play can be performed to either emphasize or minimize these aspects of his character. Though Prospero tells Miranda that he withdrew from political life in Milan, his control over the island begins to look like a form of rule, one that Dustin A. Gish calls "despotic" (237).[16] So too, Stephen Greenblatt, writes that Prospero's magic, directed toward spying, listening, monitoring, blocking, and tormenting others, is the "romance equivalent of martial law" (130).[17] Prospero can also be conceived, rather narrowly, as an irascible old man, as a kind of comic *senex,* a conventional character type in Roman comedy.[18] Today, some see Prospero as representing the evils of nascent colonialism, and the play does in part derive from pamphlet accounts of journeys to the new world. In this interpretation, Caliban becomes a symbol for an indigenous people imposed upon, enslaved, and exploited by a colonial force.[19] This perspective has led to fictional re-imaginings of the play from the perspective of the indigenous people.[20] Other critics read the play as a critique of the cruelty with which King James maintained his authority by instigating, and then viciously punishing, traitorous plots in order to demonstrate his power.[21] Prospero's authority over the island is never simply tyrannical or straightforward, however. We will see that Caliban's fate in the hands of other characters – his humiliation – would be a greater punishment than those that Prospero threatens. Moreover, though Prospero and Miranda certainly abuse him verbally, the text itself doesn't dictate that Caliban be physically punished on stage, and the play does make clear we cannot consider Caliban as an innocent victim.

Some critics and audiences have been tempted to see in Prospero a mirror of Shakespeare himself; they see Shakespeare, through his character, contemplating his own mortality and retirement from playwriting. Thus, in Act 5, when Prospero decides to break his staff and drown his book, Shakespeare was imagined to be signaling a farewell to his own career.[22] Yet this view willfully ignores the fact that Shakespeare did not stop writing plays after *The Tempest*: he went on to write, with John Fletcher, *Henry VIII* and *The Two Noble Kinsmen.* Gordon McMullan explains that deeply rooted assumptions about "late" writing itself contribute to a sense that art is more authentic and more personal the closer it is to death.[23]

While it is not possible to make of Prospero and Shakespeare a perfect correspondence, Prospero's magic *is* a dramatization of creative power – its scope, its effects, and its permanence – in ways that encompass but are not limited to the creative power of the poet or playwright. I will argue that Shakespeare created Prospero as a magus in order to probe the relationship between body and mind and reality and art as he began to do in the comic vein in *A Midsummer Night's Dream*. Through this more intense exploration in *The Tempest*, Shakespeare is able to suggest that while always confined by the body, the mind can accomplish a certain kind of "magic." Prospero uses his more than ordinary human powers to redesign his world, repair broken bonds, and create new bonds between people by combining Machiavellian astuteness with a spiritual conception of power. While Prospero, as his relationships to Ariel and Caliban show us, is never above his body; his art is associated with a liberating force.

Geographically there is only one world in this play, and it is the pastoral world of the early comedies writ large. The real world has dropped into the past on one end and been projected into an imagined future on the other. In a sense, the whole play is a moment out of time. However, this single world appears in two very different ways to different characters. From Prospero's point of view, all is known and meaningful; there are no accidents, for everything occurs under his surveillance or with his permission. For those under his power, however, the island is a world full of accidental, puzzling, and strange events that leave them helpless and vulnerable.

The most important of Prospero's projects concerns getting Miranda married to a suitable man. To this end Prospero has caused Alonso, the King of Naples, to suffer an apparent shipwreck and to believe that his son, Ferdinand, has been drowned. When Miranda complains to Prospero about the terrible storm she witnessed, he tells her that "I have done nothing but in care of thee, / Of thee, my dear one, thee, my daughter" (1.2.16–17). Miranda, her name deriving from the Latin to admire or gaze at, is characterized almost exclusively by compassion and wonder, and there is little doubt that she, like Cordelia in *King Lear*, represents an ideal manifestation of pure love between father and daughter and husband and wife. Having been banished along with Prospero from Milan, she has been brought up away from the corrupting vanities of court life that we see in the portraits of Ophelia, Cressida, Goneril, and Regan.

Miranda's compassionate heart appears in her first words: "If by your art, my dearest father, you have / Put the wild waters in the roar, allay them" (1.2.1–2), for, she says, the cries of the sailors "knock / Against my very heart" (1.2.8–9). While Miranda expresses the depth of her feeling, that the shipwreck has impacted her "very heart," Prospero associates this heartfelt compassion with an elevated strength of spirit. He urges her to dry her tears and remarks that the shipwreck has "touched / The very virtue of compassion" in her (1.2.26–7). Her "very heart," that is, the truest part of her physical self, manifests a "very virtue," an equally pure but more elevated version of her physical experience of emotion.

She further manifests the native correctness of her instincts by falling in love with Ferdinand as soon as she sees him, and Shakespeare shows her connection to him is both reciprocal and persistent. That their love is reciprocal is clear when Miranda offers to help Ferdinand as he carries logs as part of

Prospero's plan to test his constancy. Ferdinand makes it clear that the task of moving logs, a fruitless endeavor in reality since he is simply moving them from one place to another, is difficult physically. He calls it a "mean" and "heavy" task (3.1.4–5). Miranda is prepared to share the burden with him and her offer further amplifies the perfection of their connection. "If you'll sit down" she says, "I'll bear your logs the while. Pray, give me that" (3.1.24–5). She frames her offer, a gift to him, as *his* gift to her, indicating the perfect reciprocity of their union.

We later see Miranda consciously acknowledge that her love for him goes beyond worldly concerns when they play chess together. At first Miranda teases him that he is cheating, presumably because he is winning, and when Ferdinand says he would not cheat "for the world" (5.1.175), she says that "for a score of kingdoms you should wrangle, / And I would call it fair play" (5.1.176–7). Miranda's response here touches on the world of political ambition, the "wrangling" so often dramatized in the histories and tragedies, and transforms its evils into something just, something "fair." Her complete love for Ferdinand enables her to see the world from this perspective. She also reveals she is content to allow him to "win," in some sense accepting submission to him without the fear and risk we have seen in other plays. The struggle for power between lovers has been shifted into the context of a harmless game where the stakes are low. Miranda is happy to lose because their love has made a game of competition.

Ferdinand manifests a complementary suitability by falling in love with her, for in doing so he not only physically desires her, but he also recognizes her virtues and her rarity. He tells her honestly that he has "liked" many women for their "several virtues" but says that only Miranda is "[s]o perfect and so peerless" (3.1.42–3, 47) to earn his love. In taking her to be the goddess of the island and in believing her perfect, he shows both the exaggeration of romantic love and his apprehension of an underlying truth that will sustain their connection beyond the initial period of infatuation. Furthermore, just as Miranda is by nature submissive to her husband, so Ferdinand is amenable to Prospero's correct authority, though, interestingly, only after a properly manly struggle. Ferdinand is as ideal a man as can come from a corrupted world, but the stain of that world appears when, believing his father dead, he is, like Prince Hal, a little too eager to call himself "Naples." Prospero's administers a kind of prophylactic measure by forcing Ferdinand to carry logs, the same punishment that Caliban endures for having tried to rape Miranda. Ferdinand here suffers a taming of the flesh, so that he will have the humility to submit to and recognize correct authority as a precondition to exercising the rule he will inherit, to ensure his worthiness as husband to the divine Miranda. Prospero's task for Ferdinand is not done strictly as the punishment it seems, though, but also as a means of proving and then enhancing the couple's connection, for as Prospero astutely comments when he sees they have fallen in love immediately, "this swift business / I must uneasy make lest too light winning / Make the prize light" (1.2.454–6). Prospero here self-consciously decides to play at parental disapproval, an echo of the disapproval that throws Romeo and Juliet together and forces their initial attraction to each other to transform initial desire to eternal commitment.[24] In an interesting contrast to Oberon in *Midsummer Night's Dream,* Prospero does not use his magic directly to alter peoples' feelings, but only to arrange propitious circumstances that cement a steady bond from already sincere emotions. He rejoices that Miranda and Ferdinand love each other, but their love is not enforced by witchcraft, such as that Brabantio accuses Othello of using; it is rather the free gift of their hearts. Once Ferdinand and Miranda declare their love, Prospero marvels at the "[f]air encounter / Of two most rare affections!" (3.1.74–5). The unique quality of Ferdinand and Miranda's virtues draw them together even though Prospero creates the ideal conditions for their attraction. The result is a truly peerless union in Prospero's estimation.

The ideology in terms of which this marriage is judged appears in the wedding masque, in which the union is blessed by images of a benign fruitfulness and fertility, from which Venus and her unruly son Cupid are excluded, because they represent the unruliness of lust, against which Prospero repeatedly warns Ferdinand. In order to remain benign, sexuality within marriage must be contained within the purifying confines of "sanctimonious ceremonies," without which "[s]our-eyed disdain, and discord shall bestrew / The union of your bed with weeds so loathly / That you shall hate it both" (4.1.16, 20–2). The imagery, which reminds one of *Hamlet,* emphasizes the corrupting power of illicit sexuality. In *Hamlet* it pollutes the kingdom, and here it threatens to pollute the psyche and spirit, but the pollution of illicit sex would not end at the borders of a hateful marriage, for this marriage is not only a private matter. In the early comedies as well as in *Romeo and Juliet* and *Othello,* we have seen how romantic love conflicts with social institutions, but in the world managed by Prospero's magic there is no such conflict. This perfectly loving couple will return to the ordinary world to rule over Naples as the radiant center of as perfectly harmonious a polity as is possible in a real world.

However, Ferdinand and Miranda cannot be sent to rule in Naples until it has been prepared for them. That process constitutes the story of the court party, a story that is, like those in the earlier romances, one of redemption and restoration. Whereas in the earlier romances it was for the most part left to fate or fortune to provide the therapeutically punitive circumstances, here that task falls to Prospero. The first stage of Alonso's punishment consists in making him believe that his son, Ferdinand, is dead, for a ruler who conspired against Prospero and Miranda does not deserve to have an heir. The second stage is to provide Antonio the opportunity to re-enact the crime he initially committed against Prospero, only this time against Alonso. When Ariel puts Alonso and the others to sleep, Antonio suggests to Sebastian, Alonso's brother, that he murder Alonso so that, like Antonio and other younger sons in earlier plays, he can usurp his older brother's place. Sebastian declares himself ready for temptation – "I am standing water" (2.1.222), he says. Throughout this play, such images signify corruption and foul growth in contrast to images of moving waters in which things suffer only a "sea change / Into something rich and strange" (1.2.404–5). Like more consequential villains before him, Antonio conceives of status and power in terms of clothing when he tells Sebastian to note "how well my garments sit upon me, / Much feater than before" (2.1.274–5). Ariel awakens the court party. The third stage begins when Ariel throws all the participants, as they are about to kill the sleeping Alonso, into a period of suffering, loss, and loneliness, and they wander confusedly amidst the mud and briars that represent their own inner states of being, looking for another opportunity to murder Alonso.

The fourth stage of punishment consists of the illusory banquet prepared by Ariel and his ministers. This banquet gives the wrongdoers the illusion that their sins will gain them the luxury, honor, and power for which they had committed crimes in the real world. At the very peak of their anticipation, but while they still suffer hunger and thirst, they are confronted with an object lesson on the illusory nature of these worldly pleasures in contrast to spiritual truths when Ariel whisks the banquet away and appears as an avenging harpy.

Traditionally, harpies are earth spirits whose task it is to avenge any violation of kin ties. Vengeance involves bringing the past into the present, which is what Ariel does as he reminds the court party of their past sins. Prospero becomes equated with the Fate of the previous plays, when Ariel says that he and his fellows "are ministers of Fate" (3.3.61). Fate here becomes an agency that works through human conscience, as a law of nature. As Gonzalo puts it, the guilt for past sins is like poison, the effects of which begin to "bite the spirits" (3.3.107) long afterward. Violating natural law weakens those who do it, as it did for Macbeth, and it ensures that the sins of the past will have consequences for the present. Thus Ariel says, "[t]he powers, delaying, not forgetting, have / Incensed the seas and shores, yea, all the creatures, / Against your peace" (3.3.73–5), but we know that the seas and shores were incensed by Prospero, who, like Fate, oversees the scene. It is only Alonso and Gonzalo who get the point. Alonso says:

> O, it is monstrous, monstrous!
> Methought the billows spoke and told me of it;
> The winds did sing it to me, and the thunder,
> That deep and dreadful organ pipe, pronounced
> The name of Prosper; it did bass my trespass.
> Therefor my son i' th' ooze is bedded; and
> I'll seek him deeper than e'er plummet sounded,
> And with him there lie mudded. (3.3.95–102)

It is as though Alonso has not heard what we have, and we have heard in Ariel's words an allegorical representation of Alonso's vaguer and more generalized experience of nature itself turning against him. Alonso realizes that his past crime now causes him to hear the name of Prosper echo in the dark music of the winds and seas, and he accepts that he has lost his son as a consequence of his crime. His realization shows his readiness for redemption, while the evil brothers' refusal to understand reveals them as irredeemable. The last stage begins when the court party is sent off for a final period of "heart's sorrow," the condition for escaping the forces that threaten them (3.3.81).

The third story line has to do with Caliban and Stephano and Trinculo, the drunken clowns who come upon him. This subplot, in part, clearly burlesques the story of the court party, but we have seen in other plays that humor, particularly burlesque-like humor such as that of the gravediggers or of the clown who brings the asp, often carries the deepest level of significance. On one level this comic plot concerns the punishment of and reformation of Caliban, whose sin was to indulge his desire for Miranda. He was not wrong in recognizing her beauty, and he shows a kind of natural wisdom when he says of Miranda that she "as far surpasseth Sycorax / As great'st does least" (3.2.102–03). This natural appreciation of the good on a simple level also appears when Caliban promises to show Stephano and Trinculo "clustering filberts" (2.2.169) and other good things of the island, as well as when he describes the "[s]ounds, and sweet airs" of the island that "give delight and hurt not" (3.2.138). However, Caliban fails to control his sexual desires, desires that are inappropriate because they are not reciprocated and therefore turn to force for their satisfaction. These sins are equated with drunkenness when Caliban drinks Stephano's liquor and takes the drunken butler for a god. Though the drunken scenes are the source of great comedy, it is a mistake to overlook the significance that is established by the relation of these scenes to the rest of the play.

As we have seen in other plays, a scene can amuse us at the same time as it threatens the tragic dignity of a character or the meaningfulness of the tragic action. Caliban's choice of Stephano for his god contrasts to Ferdinand's and Miranda's vision of each other as gods, each person's choice of deity expressing their inner state of being. There is no escaping the degree of emphasis Shakespeare places on the consequences of illicit sex, or the rigor with which he condemns drunkenness, which here represents the befuddled brains that allow the unruly passions to overcome reason. Funny as these characters are, their comic antics come as close to success as does the serious business of the court party, and the consequences of their success would be even more devastating. The controlling reason that Caliban would destroy resides in Prospero's brains, and the knowledge that empowers reason is in Prospero's books, which Caliban wants Stephano to destroy. Prospero's brain is equated with his reason and with the books that contain the knowledge that permits him to exercise it. Therefore, when Caliban proposes to his companions that they drive a nail into

Prospero's brains, he expresses precisely the danger that drunkenness and licentious indulgence in the body's pleasure represent to the controlling mind. The link between disordered passions and political disorder that we have seen in *Hamlet* is made here when Trinculo says that if the other people on the island are "brained like us, the state totters" (3.2.6). Ariel punishes them for their drunken pact when, speaking in Trinculo's voice, he enrages Stephana. Just as Puck's love juice represented the mutability of human passions, so the quarreling that follows from Ariel's provocations represents the discord intrinsic to their fellowship. The pinches that Prospero orders to be inflicted on them represent the pinches of conscience which they are too blind to recognize as such.

Just as Ariel arranges for the court party to be confronted by an illusory banquet representative of their own falsity, so he quells Caliban's revolutionary band with a display of gorgeous apparel. The costumes hanging before Prospero's cell are the outward signs of status and honor; they give visual form to the verbal images of clothing woven into the play's poetry. The scene asserts that these material signs can be lost or stolen, but the real power that resides in Prospero's brains, or in genuine reason, cannot be taken in this way. Caliban's education occurs when he realizes that his companions can be distracted from the true source of power to "dote thus on such luggage" (4.1.232). Caliban has a good sense of certain aspects of both reality and abstract ideals. The costumes are "but trash" (4.1.225) to him, he recognizes Miranda's transcendent beauty, and he appreciates the islands' beneficence and hears its lovely sounds. He functions as an allegorically heightened version of Falstaff on the one hand, his earthiness representing the body. On the other hand, he seems to have the potential or desire to rise above this earthiness. The body knows its own pleasures and has its own wisdom, but it has no restraining principle, which can come only from the mind. Caliban's drunkenness and worship of Stephano signify the body's desire to be free of the mind, but when Caliban realizes how fallible is his god, Prospero emerges as a true authority figure. The body has come to recognize its own nature and to pursue true good when, to Prospero's offer of pardon, Caliban says:

> I'll be wise hereafter
> And seek for grace. What a thrice-double ass
> Was I to take this drunkard for a god
> And worship this dull fool! (5.1.298–301)

Many people are bothered by the cruelty with which Caliban is treated, and there is good reason for audiences to be troubled, both by the cruelty with which Prospero speaks to Caliban and by the fact that Caliban is punished more severely than are Sebastian and Antonio. When Caliban chafes against serving Prospero earlier in the play, Prospero and Miranda call attention to his base status, terming him a "lying slave," "[f]ilth," an "[a]bhorrèd slave," "savage," and "[h]ag-seed" (1.2.347, 349, 354, 358, 368). Prospero promises that if Caliban does not follow his command, he will punish Caliban physically: "I'll rack thee with old cramps, / Fill all thy bones with aches, make thee roar / That beasts shall tremble at thy din" (1.2.372–4). It is a strange sort of punishment, as is the punishment of being "pinched to death" that Caliban fears when he realizes his plot to overthrow Prospero has been discovered (5.1.279). Prospero threatens Caliban with the kind of pain associated with the vulnerability of an aging physical body, a vulnerability that no one, not even Prospero, can escape. The punishment, almost comic in its blending of violence and triviality, enfolds Caliban in the humanity Prospero's degrading name-calling seeks to deny. In turn, in the context of Caliban's humanity, Prospero's insults can only sound all the more offensive.

Caliban is a fascinating and vital character in the play, a necessary figure against whom we are compelled to question Prospero's authority. As Marco Mincoff observes, Caliban "appears as little better than a brute beast" but paradoxically seems "dignified" and "intelligent" compared to Stephano and Trinculo (100-1).[25] Moreover, Caliban's "delight" in and knowledge of the island strikes Mincoff as "beautiful and touching" (100). Because we cannot simply dismiss Caliban as a "brute beast," we cannot take for granted that Prospero is just in his dealings with him.

The play insists that the elevation of the mind occurs not outside of but in tandem with the body's experience of pain and discomfort deeply embedded within the human experience – whether emotional or physical or both. The mind is encouraged to seek higher truths and purpose when it chafes against its imprisonment in the fallible, mortal body. Freedom from the incessant grind of time on the body can be obtained negatively and temporarily by the oblivion that drunkenness affords or positively and lastingly in the pursuit of elevated virtues and in the reach of the imagination. Because we measure Caliban and Prospero against each other and because they both chafe against something inescapable, neither one is fully enslaved or fully free. They are implicated in each other's pursuit of freedom and enlightenment, both seeming to make it possible and threatening it.

That Shakespeare expects his audience to ultimately accept Prospero's treatment of Caliban also appears in the contrast made between the direct physical suffering that Caliban fears he will experience at Prospero's hands and the humiliation Caliban would suffer were he at the mercy of Stephano and Trinculo. The treatment of Caliban is conceived of in terms of "profit," and it moves in two directions – toward and away from Caliban. When it comes to Caliban's past relationship with Prospero, the idea of profit is directed to Prospero *and* Caliban. Prospero intended to benefit Caliban by teaching him and caring for him. Thus, Caliban remembers "[w]hen thou cam'st first, / Thou strok'st me and made much of me, wouldst [...] teach me how / To name the bigger light, and how the less" (1.2.335–8). Caliban responds to Prospero's tender treatment, with a return of it, reminding Prospero "then I loved thee" (339). Caliban's attempted rape of Miranda proves a violent rupture of this bond, of this exchange of emotional and intellectual profit. In the wake of it, Caliban says his only "profit" from Prospero's teaching is that he has learned "how to curse" (366–7), a kind of negative return on love.

On the other hand, Trinculo's first thought on seeing Caliban is that he can make money *from* Caliban him by staging him as a grotesque spectacle:

> Were I in England now, as once I was, and had but this fish painted, not a holiday fool there but would give me a piece of silver. There would this monster make a man. Any strange beast there makes a man. When they will not give a doit to relieve a lame beggar, they will lay out ten to see a dead Indian. (2.2.28–33)

The mention of England could not fail to drive home the social criticism to the audience, but it also argues that a Caliban's fate in a real world with Trinculo would be worse than it is on Prospero's island. The point is enforced when Stephano indulges his pretensions to royal status by having Caliban lick his shoe (3.2.23), and when Antonio's first thought on seeing Caliban is about the possibility of selling him into slavery. The profit here is entirely financial and is in no way offered to Caliban. He is to be pressed into an unequal relationship defined by exploitation and subjugation.

Caliban's reformation leaves some loose ends, for the play makes no mention of what is to happen to him once Prospero leaves, and insofar as he represents body, body cannot be left. If we let our minds travel further than the play itself, then we might imagine Caliban finally reigning on his island – ironically enough, as a king with no subjects. While we may quail at the terms by which Prospero berates Caliban, the idea of profit can tell us how much we are to differentiate between Prospero's treatment of Caliban on one hand and Stephano and Trinculo's treatment on the other. Prospero's cruelty to Caliban reflects not an innate desire to exploit but an emotional reaction to a trust that has been breached, a love that has been betrayed. The implication is that Prospero would not react so angrily toward Caliban now had he not loved him as he did then, invested emotionally and intellectually in him. At the end of the play, Prospero reveals that he is indeed still invested in Caliban when he says "[t]his thing of darkness I / Acknowledge mine" (5.1.278–9). While it can certainly be interpreted negatively as Prospero still believing he *owns* Caliban, who is no more than a "thing," it can also signify that Prospero's sense of self depends on Caliban, that Prospero's emotions have been, and still are, engaged.[26]

Caliban, Trinculo, and Stephano can be hilariously funny, but the humor does not cancel the serious implication of their actions, which represent the kind of disorder on a physical level that the court party represents in the political world. As we have seen in *Hamlet* and in *King Lear,* Shakespeare sees each as an aspect of the other, and both as in principle equally dangerous to the commonwealth over which Miranda and Ferdinand are to rule. As we have seen in *Henry IV,* the body's impulses and needs, as represented by Falstaff, threaten to undermine the validity of the political ideals and aims in the name of which the major action is undertaken, and, as we have seen in *King Lear,* comedy threatens to undermine the meaningfulness of human experience. Because the fairy-tale frame of this play ensures that Prospero will prevail, we are free to laugh easily at actions that in a tragedy like *King Lear* would destroy the foundations of life.

This returns us to the questions with which we started: what are we to make of Prospero, how are we to understand his entitlement to manipulate and control the lives of others, and what is his story? Some aspects of the answer have already been suggested. Prospero is presented as a magus, and in the Renaissance conception a magus is one whose studies of the secret correspondences that link the multiple levels of the cosmos have transformed his spirit and given him a glimpse of a reality that is higher than the political and personal dimensions of experience.

The story of how Prospero became a Magus emerges when he tells Miranda the story of their past. That story is a Lear story in miniature; by withdrawing from the responsibilities of rule, he releases the evil forces in those beneath him, and Antonio becomes the last in the line of Shakespeare's usurping younger brothers. The evil spreads, so that others become corrupted as well, and Milan as a whole suffers as it loses its autonomy to Naples. Like Lear, Prospero suffers the consequences, and is set out to sea (rather than banished to a stormy heath). Their purposes, however, were different. Lear speaks of a "darker purpose" (1.1.36) behind his abdication. There has been much critical controversy over what that might mean, but there is certainly no indication that Lear is inclined toward intellectual pursuits.[27] Prospero's purpose was to advance his studies in those "liberal arts" that had already made Milan the first of all the signories and made Prospero "the prime duke, being so reputed / In dignity" (1.2.72–3). Though Prospero was at fault for abandoning his responsibilities, he chose between two good purposes, both of which cannot in the nature of things be accomplished at the same time, for the books he values "above" his "dukedom" (1.2.168) were those from which he derives the extraordinary powers that make him master over the island. Prospero completes the education that Hamlet broke off. Because of his advanced spiritual state, Prospero was able to keep with him the virtuous daughter whom Lear disowned. The compassionate Miranda merges with the piteous winds and seas; she becomes a human incarnation of the benevolent aspects of nature over which his secret studies gave him power. He reassures her that in her infancy she was no burden to him, but was rather

> O, a cherubin
> Thou wast that did preserve me. Thou didst smile,
> Infusèd with a fortitude from heaven,
> When I have decked the sea with drops full salt. (1.2.152–5)

Prospero's powers, then, are based on intelligence used in the service of loving purposes. His purposes are contrasted to those of Sycorax, who, as the antithesis of Miranda, is the last in the line of evil women that stretches back as far as Joan of Arc and Queen Margaret in the *Henry VI* plays. The sexual side of her evil magic spawns the would-be rapist Caliban, and the cruel side of it appears in her imprisonment of Ariel, so that for twelve years he did "vent [his] groans / As fast as mill wheels strike" (1.2.282–3). She dies before Prospero comes to the island, but she is in a sense defeated by Prospero, the superiority of whose powers is shown when he cancels the spell that keeps Ariel in the cloven pine, performing an act of liberation literally beyond her power.

This brings us to the question of who or what is Ariel, in line with the principle that supernatural beings can be understood only as an extension of some human conception. Though Ariel's function is similar to that of Puck in *A Midsummer Night's Dream*, Ariel is more benign. Although Puck does no harm, as an image of the randomness of nature, he expresses indifference to human foibles and suffering. In contrast, the delicate Ariel will not perform Sycorax's evil commands, and he expresses something like compassion when he tells Prospero that were he human he would be moved by the sufferings of the court party. The imagery contrasts Ariel to the earthy Caliban in associating him with the other three of the four elements that comprise nature. He moves like fire and air during the illusory storm, and he flies on the winds and goes through the clear and moving waters. He drinks the air, and after his release he will be found "[w]here the bee sucks" and "[u]nder the blossom that hangs on the bough" (5.1.88, 94). He is, then, a nature spirit, like the fairies of *Dream.* That is why the court party hears only the winds and waters, while we hear Ariel speaking to them. This is consistent with his androgynous quality, which is testified to by his being played equally well by both men and women.

However, unlike the earlier figures, Ariel represents only the beneficent aspects of nature. Therefore Prospero, in defeating the cruelty and sexual corruption represented by Sycorax by means of the powers given him by his studies, achieves the ultimate power to control and shape to his conscious purposes the forces of nature that are benign, but that in ordinary life are only randomly available. In one important way, Ariel's nature defines Prospero's, for as a nature spirit he gives assurance that Prospero's magic involves neither demons nor angels. In the controversies of the time, demonic magic was condemned, angelic magic was sometimes justified; while some people argued that the distinction between black and white magic rested only in the intentions of the magician, most people thought that the difference lay in the kinds of powers that were called upon. In associating Ariel so firmly with nature, Shakespeare reassures his audience that Prospero is a kindly Magus who abstains from invoking forbidden powers.

But if so, why is Prospero so harsh to Ariel at the play's beginning? The relationship between Ariel and Prospero tells us about the difficulty that ordinary humans encounter when they try to exercise the kinds of powers that are attributed to Prospero. As we have seen, he arranges the circumstances that constitute the world for all the other characters, and he functions for them as a kind of spiritual therapist. If he were an allegorical figure, there would be no difficulty here, but he is portrayed as a human being with responsibilities. David Young points out that Prospero's magic "exists at the expense of similar abilities in others" (167), for even Ariel, a symbol of liberation in the ability to "be everywhere and to continually change shape and character," seeks "complete freedom" and is threatened with punishment by Prospero (167).[28] This leads Young to argue that in the play, "confinement and freedom, mastery and servitude, are not so much unalterable opposites as they are mutually complementary, aspects of the same thing" (170). While this view detracts somewhat from our sense that Prospero's powers are absolute, it does allow us to absolve him of the charge of being primarily despotic, as the play itself is rather unsatisfying if simply interpreted as an allegory about tyranny. Young brings the theme of magic into the argument, suggesting that a magus who does not realize the mutuality of mastery and servitude will become a Faustus, "clinging to the illusion of mastery which is in fact his bondage to greater powers" (170). That Prospero's moods and profits depend on Caliban and Ariel speaks to this truth. Prospero's ultimate deferral of control to the audience at the end of the play further consolidates this message.

If we naturalize the entire situation, leaving magic out of the picture altogether, then Prospero is like a person who has taken on the power to cause other people pain for their own good. He justifies doing so on the grounds of his belief in his own wisdom, and in the name of an ideal of correct rule, but the situation he has set out to rectify is one upon which his own welfare and that of his beloved daughter also depends. He has reasons to hate and to seek vengeance, not unlike the characters in the tragedies, and he is certainly not as impartial as an allegorical representative of Providence should be. His power to control others for their own good must involve an equal self-control. Prospero must act as though he were impartial, and to keep his actions unsullied by the least tinge of self-interest in a circumstance that fully engages his deepest needs and passions.

Success at remaining impartial is all but impossible, but the play assumes the existence of magical powers, and through Prospero Shakespeare dramatizes the psychology of beneficent superpower. Prospero's irritability with Ariel suggests both the difficulty of restraining this force and of retaining the self-control necessary to use his powers rightly, and the otherwise loving relationship between Ariel and Prospero expresses the virtue of Prospero's endeavors. This view of Prospero accords with his distress at the wedding masque, for a person in Prospero's position would feel some pain at seeing his daughter marry, even though that was what he most wanted. The sequence of the action suggests that when Prospero is reminded that Caliban is stalking toward his cell, he recalls Caliban's earlier rape attempt, and that image coalesces with his anticipation of Miranda's marriage to Ferdinand. The strain of this constant need for self-control, the hint that Prospero is subject to forces his magic cannot fully contain, also accounts for what otherwise appears as a contradiction in Prospero's motives.

Early in the play Prospero reassures Miranda that he does not intend harm to Alonso and the others, and Ariel also implicitly promises them that all will be well. When Prospero assembles them, he cannot help but feel the desire for revenge, and he says, "with their high wrongs I am struck to the quick" (5.1.25), but he still perseveres in his original resolve: "[t]hey being penitent, / The sole drift of my purpose doth extend / Not a frown further" (5.1.28–30). As a man, he can desire revenge as strongly as anyone else, but as a Magus his higher knowledge gives him the power to hold himself apart from such motives. It would seem that Shakespeare conceives the Magus in analogy to the doctrine of the king's two bodies: Prospero's art is infallible, but his ordinary person is not. Of course, such strict self-control for so demanding a task cannot be borne forever, and keeping constant primacy of mind over matter leads to a kind of physical suffering of its own. Ariel's services have a fixed term; Prospero must renounce his "rough magic" (5.1.50), and the enormous demands on Prospero's energies are manifested in the weariness with which he contemplates the return to Milan.

This conception of the magus differs somewhat from the conventional one of his time. In alchemical and other magical literature, the ideal practitioner is so transformed by his practice that his base passions are transmuted. Such a person would no longer need self-control, for all of his self would be entirely radiant. One may not believe in magic, but if one did believe in forms of power that cannot be fully explained, then Shakespeare's version of the magician would seem convincing.

This brings us to the final question about the reality of Prospero's magic and the play he stage-manages. The beginning of *The Tempest* is deliberately confusing, since Shakespeare could have introduced us to Prospero before showing us the storm. The storm that terrifies the men on the king's ship seems as real as the one that torments Lear. The entrance of Prospero here transforms the seemingly real storm and the world it represents into illusions, especially in contrast to the superior reality of the fairy-tale island.

This transposition of levels of reality, where the stage illusion claims a higher reality than the real world, appears in other ways. Common sense would tell both Shakespeare's audience and us that the world is more real than the stage. Shakespeare challenges this view when the feast that signifies the illusory goods of the real world · fades before the greater reality of Ariel's sermon. The transposition culminates in the gathering of all the characters outside Prospero's cell. The court party is "spell-stopped" (5.1.61) after having wandered for hours in the mazes that represent their erring ways in the real world. The real world becomes the illusion from which they awaken to a vision of Prospero, and he expresses this transposition of reality in two passages that are highly significant, not only for this play, but also for the concept of reason that has been at work in many of the plays we have discussed:

> The charm dissolves apace,
> And as the morning steals upon the night,
> Melting the darkness, so their rising senses
> Begin to chase the ignorant fumes that mantle
> Their clearer reason [...]
>   Their understanding
> Begins to swell, and the approaching tide
> Will shortly fill the reasonable shore
> Than now lies foul and muddy. (5.1.64–8, 79–82)

In the first section of the passage, the charm that dissolves is compared to the darkness of night and to ignorant fumes. These fumes rise from the standing water of wrongdoing. Prospero's charm allows people to experience external versions of their internal states. It dissolves here because they are now ready to recognize their internal states, and therefore their reason can emerge from the clouds of desire that previously obscured it. By opening their eyes to reason and putting aside what had seemed real but was in fact illusory, they begin to awaken to a higher reality.

In the second section of the passage, their understanding is likened to moving waters, to a swelling wave that moves on the tides. These tides are beyond ordinary understanding, but are the basis of Prospero's powers, and thus he can now bring their understanding to the shores of reason. He represents the understanding that can fill with moving waters the otherwise foul and muddy standing waters of the mind. In the real world, those shores have been befouled by Alonso's and Antonio's crimes. Without an understanding of spiritual reality, reason becomes merely instrumental and therefore can be put in the service of the illusory goods sought by ambition and lust. However, under Prospero's tutelage, human reason will be informed by right understanding of true value and become an instrument of virtue. When the courtiers open their eyes on the banished Duke of Milan, they also awaken to a reality higher than that of the ordinary world; by implication, we in the audience witness on the stage a reality higher than that in which our bodies sit.

Prospero had already expressed the ideology behind this attempted seduction of one's sense of reality when he told Ferdinand that, like the actor-spirits who have just melted into thin air:

> The cloud-capped towers, the gorgeous palaces,
> The solemn temples, the great globe itself,
> Yea, all that it inherit, shall dissolve,
> And, like this insubstantial pageant faded,
> Leave not a rack behind. We are such stuff
> As dreams are made on, and our little life
> Is rounded with a sleep. (4.1.152–8)

The "great globe" cannot fail to evoke the image of the macrocosm to which the Globe theater stands as microcosm. The "baseless fabric" of the stage illusion that represents the real world will fade away. In doing so, it will represent the truth that the real world and all its grandeur will also fade away. The stage world can thus express a higher reality, because its very transience reveals a truth about reality that is obscured from us by our immersion in it.

This uncertain and shifting relationship between real and imaginary worlds continues into the Epilogue, the imagery of which erodes the distinction between the island world and the stage upon which it was enacted in ways that recall both the mechanicals' play and the epilogue of *A Midsummer Night's Dream*. Prospero's secret studies by which he achieved a vision of a higher reality have empowered him to set the real world right by restoring justice. It is ironic that the powers by which Prospero rights the wrongs of the past are of the kind that cannot be conferred by the "real world." They are, rather, those that are the fruit of imagination, like Shakespeare's own.

Notes

1 Howard Felperin describes the work of interpreting literature within the romance genre as challenging because it transcends "considerations of time and place" (*Shakespearean Romance*. Princeton: Princeton University Press, 1972. 8). For a discussion of the structure of prose romance, see Northrop Frye, *The Secular Scripture: A Study of the Structure of Romance*. Cambridge: Harvard University Press, 1976.

2 *Let Wonder Seem Familiar: Endings in Shakespeare's Romance Vision.* New Jersey: Humanities Press, 1985.

3 Some see the theme of regeneration as decidedly Christian. For example, E.J. Devereaux says the play is about the "forgiving of sin and the restoration of faith in the bond between and each other and God" ("Sacramental Imagery in *The Tempest."* In *Shakespeare's Christian Dimension: An Anthology of Commentary.* Ed. Roy Battenhouse. Bloomington: Indiana Press, 1994. 254). See also Roger A. Stritmatter and Lynne Kositsky. *On the Date, Sources and Design of Shakespeare's* The Tempest. Jefferson, North Carolina: McFarland & Company Inc., 2013.

4 G. Wilson Knight describes the difference between Shakespeare's comedies and romances, suggesting that the romances "find themselves often reversing the logic of life as we know it, redeveloping the discoveries and recognitions of old comedy into more purposeful conclusions, impregnated with a far higher order of dramatic belief" (*The Crown of Life: Essays in the Interpretation of Shakespeare's Final Plays.* London: Oxford University Press, 1947. 194).

5 For a useful summary of arguments for and against the romances' themes as harmony and redemption, see Kiernan Ryan, "Introduction." *Shakespeare: The Last Plays.* Ed. Kiernan Ryan. London: Routledge, 1999.

6 "The Providential Tempest and the Shakespearean Family." In *Representing Shakespeare: New Psychoanalytic Essays.* Eds. Murray M. Schwartz and Coppélia Kahn. Baltimore: Johns Hopkins Press, 1980.

7 Ruth Nevo views Shakespeare's romance characters as being engaged, in one form or another, in an Oedipal struggle – for instance, she interprets fathers who wish to regulate their daughters' sexuality as acting on an unconscious incestuous desire for their daughters, which itself is rooted in a failure of the son to fully break away from the mother (*Shakespeare's Other Language* London: Methuen, 1987). See also Diane Purkiss, "'As like Hermione as is her picture': The Shadow of Incest in *The Winter's Tale."* In *Maternity and Romance Narratives in Early Modern England.* Eds. Karen Bamford, Naomi J. Miller. Farnham, Surrey: Ashgate, 2015.

8 *Shakespeare and the Theatre of Wonder.* Cambridge: Cambridge University Press, 1996. Holger Schott Syme notes that Shakespeare's romances depend on producing a "wondrous presence" that offers "unmediated access to the marvelous" (*Theatre and Testimony in Shakespeare's England: A Culture of Mediation.* Cambridge: Cambridge University Press, 2012. 205).

9 *Shakespeare's Late Work.* Oxford: Oxford University Press, 2007.

10 For a discussion of wonder in Shakespeare and *The Tempest's* "ambiguous attitude toward wonder," see Peter G. Platt, *Reason Diminished: Shakespeare and the Marvelous.* Lincoln: University of Nebraska Press, 1997. In *The Winter's Tale,* Leontes reacts with wonder that the long-dead Hermione's statue comes back to life – his response is likely to be similar to ours. For a useful caution against reading the plays as cultivating an illuminating experience of wonder, see Paul Yachnin's chapter "Magical Properties" in

The Culture of Playgoing in Shakespeare's England: A Collaborative Debate by Anthony B. Dawson and Paul Yachnin. Cambridge: Cambridge University Press, 2001. Here Yachnin points out that the experience of wonder might be a result of Shakespeare's plays becoming literary objects.

11 *Culture of Playgoing.*

12 *Shaksepeare's Late Work.*

13 For further discussion of the perspective of Shakespeare's romances on the darker themes of the tragedies, see Simon Palfrey, *Late Shakespeare: A New World of Words.* Oxford: Clarendon Press, 1997; and R.A. Foakes' chapter on the late plays in *Shakespeare and Violence.* Cambridge: Cambridge University Press, 2003.

14 "Excerpt from 'Balaam and the Ass.'" In *The Sea and the Mirror.* Ed. Arthur Kirsch. Princeton: Princeton University Press, 2003.

15 *The Crown of Life: Essays in Interpretation of Shakespeare's Final Plays.* G. Wilson Knight Collected Works. Vol. III. London: Routledge, 2002. 208.

16 "Taming *The Tempest*: Prospero's love of Wisdom and the Turn From Tyranny." In *Souls with Longing: Representations of Honor and Love in Shakespeare.* Eds. Bernard J. Dobski and Dustin A. Gish. Lanham: Lexington Books, 2011. 231–260.

17 "Martial Law in the Land of Cockaigne." In *Materialist Shakespeare: A History.* Ed. Ivo Kamps. London: Verso, 1995.

18 Diane Elizabeth Dreher describes the characteristics of the *senex* figure in *Domination and Defiance: Father's and Daughters in Shakespeare.* Lexington: University Press of Kentucky, 1986. For a short bibliography of Shakespeare's use of roman comedy, see Stuart Gillespie, *Shakespeare's Books: A Dictionary of Shakespeare Sources.* London: Continuum, 2001. 419–420. See also Bruce Louden "The Tempest, Plautus, and the Rudens." *Comparative Drama* 33.2 (1999): 199–223.

19 For work on *The Tempest* and colonialism, see Paul Brown. "'This thing of darkness I acknowledge mine': *The Tempest* and the Discourse of Colonialism" in Jonathan Dollimore and Alan Sinfield. Eds. *Political Shakespeare: New essays in Cultural Materialism.* Ithaca and London: Cornell U.P., 1985. 48–71; John Kunat. "'Play me false': Rape, Race and Conquest in *The Tempest.*" *Shakespeare Quarterly.* 65.3 (2014): 307–366; Frantz Fanon. *Black Skin White Masks.* Richard Philcox. Trans. New York: Grove Press, 2008. Mannoni, Octave. *Prospero and Caliban: The Psychology of Colonization.* Pamela Powesland. Trans. Ann Arbor: University of Michigan Press, 1990; Pesta, Duke. "Acknowledging Things of Darkness: Postcolonial Criticism of *The Tempest.*" *Academic Questions.* 27.3 (2014): 273–285; Patrick M. Murphy. Ed. The Tempest: *Critical Essays.* New York: Routledge, 2010; Rob Nixon. "Caribbean and African Appropriation of *The Tempest.*" *Critical Inquiry* 13 (1987); 557–577. Duke Pesta. "'Thou dost here usurp the name thou

ow'st not': *The Tempest* and Intercultural Exchange." *Essays on Values in Literature.* 67.2 (2015): 127–146; Melissa E. Sanchez. "Seduction and Service in *The Tempest.*" *Studies in Philology* 105.1 (2008): 50–82; G.A. Wilkes. "*The Tempest* and the Discourse of Colonialism." *Sydney Studies in English.* 21 (1995/1996): 42–55; Deborah Willis. "Shakespeare's Tempest and the Discourse of Colonialism." Studies in English Literature, 1500–1900 29.2 (1989): 277–289.

20 For instance, see Aimé Césaire's play *Une Tempête*, Marina Warner's novel *Indigo*, and George Lamming's novel *Water with Berries*.

21 See Gary Schidgall, *Shakespeare and the Courtly Aesthetic*. Berkeley: University of California Press, 1981; Curt Breight, "'Treason doth never Prosper': 'The Tempest' and the Discourse of Treason." *Shakespeare Quarterly* 41.1(1990): 1–28. Stephen Orgel, "Prospero's Wife." In The Tempest: *Critical Essays*. New York: Routledge, 2001. 231–244; Paul Raffield, *The Art of Law in Shakespeare*. Oxford: Hart Publishing, 2017.

22 For a brief example of this perspective and arguments against it, see E. Klett, *Cross Gender Shakespeare and English National Identity: Wearing the Codpiece*. New York: Routledge, 2009. In a compelling variation on the perspective, René Girard says "[n]ot Prospero alone but everything and everyone in *The Tempest* allude to Shakespeare's creative process" (*Theater of Envy*, 343). Girard interprets Caliban as a representation of Shakespeare's early plays and Ariel as a representation of the "more refined, ethical and noble literary mode that the later Shakespeare wants to substitute for Caliban" (347). The entire play, then, is a work of "self-parody" (352).

23 *Shakespeare and the Idea of Late Writing: Authorship in the Proximity of Death*. Cambridge: Cambridge University Press, 2007.

24 Girard cites this moment when arguing that the play is about Shakespeare's own playwriting career (*Theater of Envy*, 350).

25 *Things Supernatural and Causeless: Shakespearean Romance*. Newark: University of Delaware Press, 1992.

26 R.A. Foakes describes how this engagement is reflected at the level of language: "Caliban's curses against Prospero are as rich and inventive as Prospero's invective and threats against him [...] and his poetry is every bit as good as that of his master" (153) *Shakespeare, The Dark Comedies to the Last Plays: From Satire to Celebration*. London: Routledge & Kegan Paul, 1971.

27 Roy Batthenhouse surmises that Lear's darker purpose "has been to buy by his 'giving' a private preserve for self-indulgent living" and a "superworldy status – essentially for the freedom of a demigod, accountable to no one but himself." *Bloom's Reviews: William Shakespeare's* King Lear. Ed. Harold Bloom. Broomall, PA: Chelsea House Publishers, 56–57.

28 *The Heart's Forest: A Study of Shakespeare's Pastoral Plays*. New Haven: Yale University Press, 1972.

Epilogue

Prospero and Shakespeare

Throughout his writing career Shakespeare rang constant changes on the relation of the stage to life, and he endowed Prospero with a large measure of his own capacity to control the lives of his fictive characters. It is therefore not unreasonable to see Prospero's magic as related to the creative powers of his author. In this very speculative epilogue, I use the analogy between Prospero the magician and Shakespeare the playwright to reflect on Shakespeare's ideas about art and the relationship in particular, of the stage to the world.

In order to do so, I must discuss an aspect of Prospero's powers that I only touched upon in the previous chapter. To wield power over the minds of others, as Prospero does, is to shoulder an extraordinary responsibility. Indeed, Prospero begins to show signs of extreme fatigue: he is by turns impatient and affectionate with Ariel, he breaks off the wedding masque in agitation and he suffers from great world-weariness toward the end of the play. When Miranda wonders at all the "goodly creatures" suddenly assembled outside of Prospero's cell, he responds with a kind of tired cynicism: "'Tis new to thee" (5.1.184, 187). Even his homecoming doesn't cheer him: he will return to Milan where he says "[e]very third thought shall be my grave" (5.1.315). Prospero feels anxiety while he has his powers and depleted after he renounces them. This feeling of emptiness resembles what Macbeth felt when he said that his "way of life / Is fall'n into the sere, the yellow leaf" (5.3.22–3). Prospero's lassitude raises a question: why plan to renounce his powers just before he assembles his enemies before his cell?

He does so for several reasons. On a symbolic level, Prospero must renounce his powers because they are powers of the imagination, and imagination can control reality only in a fairy-tale world. In the real world, imagination can give a glimpse of something beyond, and in *The Tempest* Shakespeare gives a glimpse of a world in which ordinary reality yields to the mind's powers. However, mind or imagination cannot directly transform the intransigent

Thinking About Shakespeare, First Edition. Kay Stockholder, revised and updated by Amy Scott.
© 2018 John Wiley & Sons Ltd. Published 2018 by John Wiley & Sons Ltd.

materials of the real world. By working on the minds of his subjects, Prospero has improved the chances for Naples and Milan to become better under the benign reign of Ferdinand and Miranda, but he knows that he cannot wield such control in those actual cities, that it cannot be perfect, and must be left to the vagaries of chance and fortune. Ariel must go free, his staff must be broken and buried, and his book must be drowned.[1]

On the naturalistic and personal level, Prospero must renounce his powers both because they drain his energies and because he likes them too much. Just as a therapist, doctor, or politician is not supposed to get carried away with her own importance, so Prospero must resist the ego gratifications of power if his justification for wielding it is his moral superiority to the Claudiuses, Macbeths, and Lears of this world. His affection for his magic appears in a harmless way when he lays down his magic cloak saying, "[l]ie there, my art" (1.2.25), but Prospero allows himself to revel in his power only in the process of renouncing it:

> I have bedimmed
> The noontide sun, called forth the mutinous winds,
> And twixt the green sea and the azured vault
> Set roaring war; to the dread rattling thunder
> Have I given fire, and rifted Jove's stout oak
> With his own bolt; the strong-based promontory
> Have I made shake, and by the spurs plucked up
> The pine and cedar; graves at my command
> Have waked their sleepers, oped, and let 'em forth
> By my so potent art. (5.1.41–50)

We see Prospero perform the first part of what he describes when he creates the illusory storm, but he goes beyond what we have seen when he boasts of having taken Jove's own powers, and beyond even that when he claims to have awakened the dead. We haven't seen Prospero rouse the dead, but we have seen Shakespeare do so, especially in the history plays, and as Prospero here exalts and revels in his powers, he merges with his creator. This merger suggests that Shakespeare thought about his own art as a kind of magic, and thought of himself as responsible for using it in the service of an exalted vision. If Shakespeare as artist-magician thinks of the relation between himself and the powerful of his world as analogous to Prospero's relation to Alonso, then Shakespeare implicitly claims for his art the morally transforming power and wisdom, free of self-interest, that he attributes to Prospero. If Shakespeare did in this way identify with his character, he would also have to restrain any tendency he found in himself to revel in his creative powers, and he would not want to see his motivations as in any way sullied by self-interest.

However, Prospero benefits more than it might seem from his use of magic. After Prospero reveals to the court party that Ferdinand is alive and about to be

Miranda's husband, Gonzalo exclaims, "[w]as Milan thrust from Milan, that his issue / Should become kings of Naples?" (5.1.207–208). We know from the beginning that Prospero prides himself on being the prime duke. While in the Elizabethan world, dukes are lower than kings, Prospero has exercised power beyond that of any king, and the upshot of the whole story is that his progeny will be kings. This is a somewhat ironic conclusion to a story that begins with the contrast between Prospero, who was "rapt in secret studies" (1.2.77) in his study, which was "dukedom large enough" (1.2.110), and Antonio who grew power-hungry. Macbeth got only a barren scepter from his crime, but Prospero, like the virtuous Banquo, has triumphed in the end.

Shakespeare too benefited from his art. He presumably enjoyed some status from having his plays more frequently performed at court than those of any other dramatist; he acquired the coat of arms that his father failed to acquire; and he became one of the wealthiest men in Stratford. If Shakespeare did in his heart of hearts think of himself, as playwright, as more exalted than the court he served, such satisfaction in his individual achievement would violate the ideology of self-forgetful service that we have seen in the plays. It may be that dealing in subliminal ways with such mixed motivation made him weary, and perhaps in the process of writing *The Tempest* he realized the consequences of indulging in one's creative powers.

A careful look at Prospero's Epilogue, his final reflection on how the world is like a stage, lends weight to such an hypothesis:

> Now my charms are all o'erthrown,
> And what strength I have 's mine own,
> Which is most faint. Now, 'tis true,
> I must be here confined by you
> Or sent to Naples. Let me not,
> Since I have my dukedom got
> And pardoned the deceiver, dwell
> In this bare island by your spell,
> But release me from my bands
> With the help of your good hands.
> Gentle breath of yours my sails
> Must fill, or else my project fails,
> Which was to please. Now I want
> Spirits to enforce, art to enchant,
> And my ending is despair,
> Unless I be relieved by prayer,
> Which pierces so that it assaults
> Mercy itself, and frees all faults.
> As you from crimes would pardoned be,
> Let your indulgence set me free.

Prospero defines his power in terms of an ideal of beneficent magic, but only at considerable cost has he revealed and pardoned the deceiver. In this spirit of weary success, the island is transformed into and overlaps with the stage, and the actor who plays Prospero is superimposed on the island Magus. When the merged figure says "I must be here confined by you, / Or sent to Naples," the "here" equates the bare stage on which the actor stands to the bare island on which Prospero has exercised his power. As well, the actor's power, and by implication the dramatist's whose words the actor speaks, merges with Prospero's magical power to control the denizens of the island. The speaker feels confined to the barren island unless he can enter into the marriage celebration in Naples, and confined to the stage unless swept into a celebration of the performance. Since nothing on the bare island can release him from his isolation, he wishes instead for the ritual of audience applause to release him from the bare stage. There being no corresponding term to complete the analogy with the island, the speaker, now in Prospero's voice, equates the audience's applause with his power to send the others to Naples. By implication Shakespeare now gives the audience the powers that belonged to Prospero on the island, and subtly identifies himself with the sinners whose reformation or containment he, as Prospero, effected.

Unless released by applause, his ending will be despair, like that from which he saved the court party when he confronted them with images to illustrate the illusory nature of worldly power and pleasure. By equating himself with the island sinners, he empowers the audience to approve of Prospero's magic and, at the same time, Shakespeare's creative powers to bring the island to life, to release him from the despair of the barren island stage. However, the desire for applause and consequent fame hovers dangerously close to the worldly goals criminally pursued by Antonio and Sebastian. He converts the magical power he has attributed to the audience's applause to its prayers, for which he begs instead. The combined figure of actor, playwright, and Prospero who speaks the Epilogue makes it seem that Shakespeare felt his project was not complete unless gifts of equal effort are exchanged – to give pleasure to an audience and to give approval to a playwright. Shakespeare may have shrunk from fully realizing the implications that could be drawn from his having identified his theatrical art with Prospero's magic, but perhaps he came to feel, or to suspect, that the meeting of true – that is, equally invested – bodies and minds was the real secret of his "art to enchant."

Note

1 According to Alvin B. Kernan, we can see Prospero channeling Shakespeare's own "mixed attitude toward theater." He has "partly a proud insistence on its ability to get at the truth of things and partly a feeling of shame about the crudities and deceits of its methods" (*Shakespeare, The King's Playwright: Theater in the Stuart Court, 1603–1613*. New Haven: Yale University Press, 1995. 166).

Index

References to Notes contain the letter 'n', followed by the number of the note.